BEINSA DOUNO

THE WELLSPRING OF GOOD

Love the perfect way of Truth and Life. Make Good the foundation of your home, Justice your measure of things, Love as an adornment, Wisdom your shield, and Truth your light. Only then you will come to know Me, and I shall reveal Myself to you.

Beinsa Douno

THE WELLSPRING OF GOOD

The Last Words of the Master

Evera Books

Walnut Creek, 2015

First published in Bulgarian in 1992 by Royal, Varna, Bulgaria
First published in English in 1999 by Sila i Jivot, Burgas, Bulgaria
Second edition in English in 2002 by Kibea, Sofia, Bulgaria
2013 edition in English by Bialo Bratstvo Publishers, Sofia, Bulgaria
2015 edition in English by Evera Books, Walnut Creek, CA, USA

Compilation and translation into English by Antoaneta Krushevska
Editor: Sean Vernon
Cover and graphic design by Steve Eagle
Cover art by Veneta Docheva

Acknowledgments

We would like to thank Boyan Boev and Boris Nikolov for their preservation of the words of the Master for future generations.

Copyright © 2013 by Bialo Bratstvo Publishers
Published by Evera Books, 2015
All rights reserved.

ISBN 978-151-434-875-8

For more information about Beinsa Douno and available materials:
http://www.beinsadouno.org
http://www.everabooks.com

CONTENTS

Explanatory Notes 10
Introduction 12
Preface by Harrie Salman 14
Prologue: the Home of Temelko 16
The Great Omniscient Cause 17
The Meaning of Life 18
Life is the Musical Manifestation of God 20
Be Perfect 21
The Love of the One 22
Pure and Impure Food 27
The Wellspring 28
Unity in Love 30
The Border between Two Epochs 32
Music—the Path of Attainment 35
The War 41
The Divine Sculptor 43
The Meaning of Suffering 45
Mindful Suffering 46
The Uppermost Limit 48
Trials in Life 49
The Roots 50
Suffering with Love 51
Freedom 54
Pedagogical Questions 55
The Qualities of the Disciple 62
The Path of the Disciple 65
The Disciple 66
Health 68
Faith and Knowledge 69
Divine Providence 71
Visitation by God 75
Paneurhythmy 78
The First Violinist 79
The Inner Work of the Disciple 81
Communion with Nature 89
The Great Substance 92
The Two Laws 93
The Psychic Causes of Disease 94
The Disciple—He Who Is Tested in Life 97

Perfection of the Human Soul	103
Right Breathing	104
The Music of the Future Culture	106
The Sacred Name	109
Sleep as a Process for Renewal	110
The Mystical Circle	112
The Qualities of Divine Love	115
From a Letter by the Master	118
He Is Coming	118
The Second Law	120
Laws of the Material Life and the Spiritual Life	122
The Gifts of Love	126
The Still Small Voice	130
The Unknown Love	132
The Conditions for Attaining Real Knowledge	133
Divine Poetry	134
Receiving and Giving	137
Trials in Love	138
Divine Justice	139
Humility	144
Happiness and Eternal Bliss	146
The Law of Love	147
The First Impulse	150
Divine Love	151
The Universal Language	154
Guidelines for Earthly Existence	154
Cosmic Consciousness	158
Divine Science	160
Realization of Human Aspirations	163
The Senses	165
The Law of the Whole and the Parts	169
The Path toward Love	171
A Letter to the Master	172
Love Will Be the Organizing Principle of the New Culture	172
The Future Order	176
Unity in Love	180
The Two Paths	181
The All-embracing Love	185
Steadfastness	187
The Future Perspective	189
Relative and Absolute Reality	190
In the Mountains	192
The Divine Teaching	195

Bulgarian Folk Songs	198
Entering into the Great World	200
The New Relationships	201
The True Human Being	203
The Eternal Home	205
The Invisible World	207
The Two Fundamental Laws	212
The Great Universal Brotherhood	213
The Master	218
The Truth	221
The Laws of Thought	223
Property	226
The New Human Being	228
Guidelines for the Spiritual Student	228
The Beloved of the Human Soul	229
Coming to Know God	234
Eradication of the Old	236
The New Epoch	241
Daybreak	245
The Intelligence of Nature	246
The Law of Divine Justice	249
Regarding Intuition	253
The Culture of the Angels	254
The Songs of the Master	264
The Colors	268
Joy	270
Acquaintance	271
The Path of Attainment	272
The Music of Nature	275
Beauty	279
Selflessness	281
Torment, Labor, and Work	282
The Social Problem	289
The Master about Bulgaria	290
Rejuvenation	299
Selfless Service	300
The Little Brothers	302
The New, Sixth Generation—One of Love	305
The Human Being of the New Epoch	307
The Slavic Nation	311
The New Order	314
The Path of the Strong Ones	315
The New Agriculture	318

A Letter from the Master	320
Love without an External Stimulus	320
Measures within Nature	323
Ideas about Music	329
The Good	333
Co-Workers with God	336
The Service to God	338
The Sky	342
The Laws of Human Development	342
Gratitude	346
The Three Stages of the New Culture	348
EPILOGUE	350
Biographical Information about the Master Beinsa Douno-Dates and Events	351
APPENDIX	355

Explanatory Notes

In previous publications the following sentence: "Man, a term used to denote individual humans (male or female)," was included to explain the use of this word throughout this book. However, some recent comments on the sexist language connotations led to the decision to elaborate much more on the subject how to use the generic, "man," "he," and "his," in this book.

In the Bulgarian language, there are different words for a human being. C*hovek* is used for *Homo sapiens* regardless of gender, *mazh* for a male, and *zhena* for a female. When the Spiritual Teacher Beinsa Douno spoke the Word of Wisdom, he often used *chovek* to address any human being; and because this word is in the masculine form, it led to the use of gender specific words like *toy* (he) and *negov* (his) throughout his lectures, in case of substitutions. However, in English the word "man" is used with both meanings: as a generic term for *Homo sapiens* and as a term denoting an adult male. This has led to many controversial discussions regarding how to avoid the use of a word that could be considered sexist by some readers. Our purpose is to keep the language as close as possible to the original, but at the same time to make clear what is the exact meaning, in order to avoid confusion.

In *Garner's Modern American Usage*, University Press, Oxford, 2003, Bryan A. Garner writes on page 717, "But does avoiding sexism mean resorting to awkward devices such as he/she? Surely not, because that too would distract many readers. What you should strive for instead, if you want readers to focus on your ideas and not on the political subtext, is a style that does not even hint at the issue." And further on: "The traditional approach has been to use the masculine pronouns *he* and *him* to cover all people, male and female alike."

In a similar line of thinking, we decided to include this note as an explanation in the hope that the readers will focus on the meaning and depth of the Message brought by the Master

Beinsa Douno, rather than being distracted by the form of some words. We replaced where it was appropriate, "man" with "one," "someone," "person," or "individual." But this was not always possible to do without changing the meaning of the Word spoken by the Master. Therefore, except where we specifically describe a female person, the generic masculine pronoun is mainly used throughout the book to include both sexes. In a similar manner, "Brothers of Light" refers to Beings of sublime consciousness, and "Brotherhood" to a Fellowship of brothers and sisters in a spiritual community, or to people living in a fraternal way, in love and harmony.

Another sensitive issue which may lead to misunderstandings of the word of Beinsa Douno is related to the word "race" mentioned in different contexts. This word was widely used at the time as a classification system that categorizes humans in large and distinct populations or groups. Although the term is still used today, it is often replaced by other words that are less questionable.

According to the Master so far there have been five stages (or races) in human civilization. The Master explained that at any of those stages each distinct group of people was characterized by certain qualities. He believed that the "sixth stage," which he called the "new epoch of Love," was approaching and that it will include advanced people from all nations, races, ethnical, and social groups. He called the people of that new epoch of Love the "sixth race."

We replaced, when possible, the word "race" by another word. However, in some passages this was difficult without changing the meaning of the Master's message, which always focuses on uniting all human beings in Love.

Introduction

*"The Light shines in the darkness,
and the darkness did not overcome it."*[1]

John 1:5

Petar Konstantinov Danov (also Peter Deunov)[2] was born on July 11, 1864 in the village of Nikolaevka, Bulgaria, to the family of an Orthodox priest. When he was 24, he traveled to the United States for graduate studies, receiving degrees in medicine and theology. Two years after his return to Bulgaria, at the age of 33, Peter Deunov was called by Christ to impart His Teaching and took the spiritual name Beinsa Douno.

The Master, Beinsa Douno began his mission by offering lectures to a small group of followers. He preached the Divine Teaching of that Love which brings Life, that Wisdom which brings Light, and that Truth which brings Freedom.

Eventually, his followers grew to include many thousands in Bulgaria and abroad, and in 1927 a settlement was created for his community of followers near the Bulgarian capital of Sofia. The Master called the settlement "Izgrev," which means "Sunrise." There he lived among his disciples and established an esoteric school for young people. Esoteric classes were provided for adults as well. He gave daily talks to his disciples and Sunday sermons open to the public.

Music held a special place in the life of the community. The Master was a great musician and composer who created

---

1. All citations follow the NKJV or the NRSV of the Holy Bible. For the sake of consistency capitalization is preserved even when it does not correspond with the cited edition.
2. According to generally accepted transliteration norms, the secular name of the Master should be Petar Danov and his spiritual name Beinsa Duno. However, the name Peter Deunov and Beinsa Douno has already gained considerable popularity through its French transliteration. We decided to keep these versions in this book as well as in our various English publications for the sake of consistency.

many spiritual songs and melodies that he would play on his violin. Playing musical instruments and singing was an integral part of the community's daily activities. He introduced Paneurhythmy as a method for spiritual development and continued evolution of humankind. Paneurhythmy is a system of meditative movements set to music and performed during the spring and summer months in the open air. The Master encouraged his followers to perform Paneurhythmy and to exercise in the mountains, where the cosmic forces could be received in their purest state.

The Master never failed to address the ordinary things in life. In his lectures, a special place was devoted to nutrition, the causes of disease, the function of marriage and parenthood, and the education of the coming generation. As he lived during the time of the First and Second World Wars, the Master would explain the causes of those events and offer methods for avoiding further destruction.

After the bombing of Sofia in January of 1944, the Master moved with a group of his followers to the village of Marchaevo, near Sofia. Here he gave his last directions and guidance, summarizing his previous lectures and outlining the future of humankind. These last words were taken down in shorthand and presented by his closest disciples, Boyan Boev and Boris Nikolov, in the book "The Wellspring of Good."

The life of the Master Beinsa Douno perfectly exemplified how to live rightly and, more importantly, how to perfectly abide in the two Great Laws: love for God and love for one's neighbor.

The Master ended his earthly life in Sofia on December 27, 1944, with the words, "A small task has been accomplished for God."

Preface
by Harrie Salman[3]

This book is an extraordinary compilation of modern spiritual discourse. It is a vivid testimony to the mission of the Bulgarian Spiritual Teacher Peter Deunov, known also as the Master Beinsa Douno, during the last year of his life. We see him living as an evacuee in a small house for nine months at the end of the Second World War with a number of disciples and presenting to them a synthesis of his vision of a coming New Culture of Brotherhood and Love. He took them on daily walks in nature and answered their questions while, at the same time, instructing them in plain words on the essential elements of the Teaching he brought to the world.

Very significantly, Peter Deunov discovered two small wellsprings on the slope in front of the house where he was staying. One of them he named, "The Wellspring of Good," and the other, "The Wellspring of Health." Together with his disciples, he built basins for the water and made paths to them. These sacred acts of making the "living water" available to human beings had a deep symbolic meaning as well. The Teaching that he brought from the School of the Great Universal Brotherhood is a Wellspring of the new spiritual Life.

Before humankind can receive the New Culture, it should first go through a process of cleansing. The Master explained that this is the reason for the tribulations of the 20th century. This purification process is the eradication of old karma. Through suffering, we pay off our old debt. He also pointed out the positive ways of receiving the New Life through Love.

During the last phase of the Second World War, Peter Deunov gave new hope to humankind. The problems we have to

---

3. Harrie Salman is a Dutch professor of philosophy, cultural studies, and sociology, lecturing in universities in the Netherlands, Russia, and the Czech Republic. He is the author of nine books on European culture, including *The Healing of Europe: The Awakening of European Self-Consciousness*, *Searching for the Invisible City: A Spiritual Biography of Russia*, and *Rising of the Inner Sun: Rudolf Steiner and Modern Spirituality*.

overcome are temporary and part of the initial stage of the Second Coming of Christ that, according to him, began in 1914. The return of Christ is, in fact, the central theme of modern spirituality, which calls humankind to awaken and abandon the old way of life.

The words of Peter Deunov introduce the reader of this book to a way of modern spirituality. It includes new care for our health, what we can learn from Nature, a new experience of music and sacred dance (Paneurhythmy), insights into the basic laws of human life, a new vision of educating children, an awareness of the gifts of Love, and the way to work for a new social order that is based upon this Love.

Among the teachers of modern spirituality, Peter Deunov occupies a special place. He is speaking from a long spiritual tradition of a country that has brought forth two other mystical Schools in the past: the Schools of Orpheus and of the Bogomils.[4] In doing so, he gives voice to the longing for a real human community and the spiritual unification of humankind. The Teaching aims to prepare people for the new global Culture of harmony and unity that is to be established in the future.

During the horrors of the Second World War, Peter Deunov vehemently spoke out against the bombing of unprotected cities and the tendency to justify wars ideologically. He expressed disapproval of the weapons manufacturers who declare new wars in order to remain in business. This remains true for our times. People need to work for a New Culture of Love and turn to the Wellspring of Good, heeding the words of Peter Deunov: "The good that you do is like sowing a field. Sow that you may reap. In this world, God does not allow the least good to go unblessed."

---

4. *Bogomils* refers to an ascetic spiritual movement that arose in tenth-century Bulgaria. The Bogomils were persecuted as heretics by both the Eastern Orthodox and Byzantine Churches. Bogomil means "dear to God."

Prologue: the Home of Temelko

Then came the Day of Unleavened Bread,
when the Passover lamb must be killed.
And He sent Peter and John, saying,
"Go and prepare the Passover for us, that we may eat."
So they said to Him,
"Where do You want us to prepare?"
And He said to them,
"Behold, when you have entered the city,
a man will meet you carrying a pitcher of water;
follow him into the house which he enters.
Then you shall say to the master of the house,
'The Teacher says to you,
"Where is the guest room where I may eat
the Passover with My disciples?"'
Then he will show you a large,
furnished upper room; there make ready."
So they went and found it just as He had said to them,
and they prepared the Passover.

Luke 22:7–13

When the air raids over the city of Sofia started in November 1943, the Master went every day with a group of followers to the Mount Vitosha.[5] He was deep in thought. He hardly spoke and would spend the entire day there. Whatever the weather, he climbed the mountain with steady, rhythmic steps. In deep silence, he accomplished a work of great importance. Forty-two times did the Master walk to the mountain. When infused with the Spirit, movements on the material plane can have wondrous power.

When destruction struck the city and people were overwhelmed by fear, panic, and terror, the Master said, "The conditions for people to maintain their communion with God no longer exist in this place. Let us leave."

---

5. Vitosha is a mountain of volcanic origin situated near Sofia, Bulgaria.

He said this with sadness and distress, as if he wanted to say, "There is no longer air and sunshine here. Let us leave."

After a massive bombing on January 10, 1944, Beinsa Douno and a group of followers retreated to a nearby village called Marchaevo, to the home of a follower named Temelko. The Master created a small world in which the sky above was clear, the Sun was shining, and one could breathe freely. The stormy waves crashed upon its firm shores and were powerless to interfere with the radiant peace that reigned there.

In those days of fear and hardship, many people found refuge, support, consolation, and encouragement there. They renewed their strength to endure the tribulations. All of this is passed on in the talks presented in "The Wellspring of Good."

The Great Omniscient Cause

Reveal Yourself to me in Your Way
—and as is Your Will.

A prayer of the disciple

It had been snowing for a few days. Everything had disappeared under the white cover. The houses of the village had almost disappeared as well.

When the paths were shoveled, the disciples returned to the house for lunch. In spite of the snow, there were again many guests. After lunch, we sang some songs and then went outside. The air was cold, clean, and revitalizing.

The Master took a deep breath of refreshing air, looked around, and then gazed toward the blue sky. He rested his gaze on the careworn faces of the people and said:

Everything comes from God. People ask, "Where is God?" God is in the air. Through the air that enters you, God gives you Life. God—the Great Omniscient Cause—is in the water, is in the light, is in the bread. You abide in God. With the light, He loves and caresses you. God reveals Himself through the Sun, through the fruit—but we do not comprehend Him. Whenever we are weak, God is within that weakness. Sometimes we think that we are very independent, when in reality, we have entered into God, and it is His Strength that we are feeling. Whenever we think that we are strong, God puts us at the opposite polarity: weakness. Yet when we become humble, He uplifts us. What kind of Mind is this that provides for every sun in the Universe?

There exists a silent caressing breeze that we call "the Breath of God." As for me, the day is meaningful only in so far as I can see God Who is hidden within Nature.

The Meaning of Life

This morning we climbed the high conical peak above the village with our beloved Master. The snow was soft and powdery; it was the first snow of the winter. When we reached the summit, the Sun was just peeking out from behind the mountain ridge. It warmed and softened the air that was still chilly from the night before. On the mountain, bright calmness reigned. It was one of those moments when the unity and harmony of the wondrous mysteries of life become evident. When the Great Life touches human souls, it reconciles and erases all differences. The radiance of the One Life envelops and permeates everything. After we had spread out whatever we had upon the snow, we sat around our beloved Master. The winter Sun was shining warmly. It caressed us like the gentle hand of a mother.

The Master said:

People ask me if I have been to the World beyond. I do not visit the World beyond; I live in it. They ask, "Have you been to see God?" I have not been to see God; I abide in God, and I study God within everything: within the stones, the plants, the animals, the water, the air, and the light. God is present within everything that lives. Within the least as well as within the greatest, I can see God. I am glad and rejoice when I hear God's still small Voice.

You expect to see God when you die. If you live in worldliness, after you die, you will remain on Earth. Some people say that they want to see God. Are you not seeing the manifested Light of God? It is the manifestation of the Angels, of God. From now on, work continuously at feeling God's Presence at all times and within all things. When you arrive at a summit of a mountain in the morning, see God there.

Everything that is outside of us, everything that is inside of us, everything that surrounds us, represents a form through which the Great Intelligent Cause manifests. Behind me, above me, around me, is God. As long as you think about God, God is before you. As soon as you stop thinking about God, God is behind you. It is better when God is before you. In times of one's greatest trials, suffering, and hardship, God is made manifest to that person in one form or another and will provide help. To commune with the rocks, the plants, the animals, the wind, the whole of Nature; this is a privilege for you. Why? It is because all things originate from God. When people live within the Divine Sphere they see God everywhere and within everything. Once they depart from this Sphere, they become confused.

When I speak about God, I refer to the Sacred, the One Reality, that can be experienced everywhere. If you search for Him, you will experience Him within all people as well as within the animals, the plants, the air, and the water. Let everyone understand that the God of whom you speak has not been inherited from your grandmother or your grandfather; let everyone know that you have had a great experience, and that your internal Light is a result of this experience.

To live for God and to see His Life in all beings, even to enter into the consciousness of an ant, is truly great. While on Earth, you cannot understand or relate to this, but when you are in the Sublime World, the World of Consciousness, you will understand.

To see God means to strive toward that Supreme Eternal Law that rejuvenates man and gives him new life and that brings light and warmth to him. If people consider it to be a privilege to meet and converse with a great poet or philosopher, how much greater a privilege it is to have the opportunity to see God. Do you know what it means to see God? This is the meaning of Life. It is a great thing to connect with this Supreme Intelligence.

You will first find God in the least of things—in crystals, in wellsprings, in flowers—and only then in the greatest of things.

There are people who do not like it when one speaks to them about God. And yet, when you meet people like this, you will see that they are in need of God. Tell them, "You never expose yourself to the light and as a result you are frail and anemic." Do not speak to them about God. After that tell them, "You need fresh air. Breathe deeply; otherwise you will become ill." On another occasion tell them, "Your blood is impure. You need to improve the food you eat; otherwise, you will become ill."

People perceive God as an abstraction. And yet, God is the One Reality. The air and the light are the means through which you can have immediate and unlimited access to God.

Life is the Musical Manifestation of God

The luncheons with the Master were held in common, and usually ended in song. We sang in unison. The harmony came from differences in the tone of the voices. Music gives to man the opportunity to concentrate and focus, to feel the great harmony and unity of life.

The Master said:

It is said that God created man in His image and likeness. In this case, man represents a Divine book. Through the study of the human being, one can come to understand Nature.

You cannot love anything that is not Divine. What you do not understand still brings joy; but what you do understand is merely the outer wrapping of the Unknown.

The one who does not understand the Unknown is not ignorant, but the one who does not investigate it is. Even when you investigate the Unknown, it will remain a mystery to you.

The Great Omniscient Cause emerges and manifests through multiplicity. Why did God desire to create the world? To manifest Himself.

You need not search for God in the World beyond. He exists in this world too. All beings are included within Him.

When you think about God, you should feel the Sublime and experience Life in its wholeness. To be in harmony with God is to understand the wholeness of Life. When you are disposed in this way, can you say that the world is not good?

Everything that God has created has value, but human beings do not appreciate what surrounds them. The Essence of Life is what creates the forms. The Unknown is what creates. The known is the vehicle of the Unknown.

Only One Master exists in the world. This is God, the One Reality to Whom man can pray, and from Whom everything is received.

God is invested in every human being. This investment is found in our minds, our thoughts, yet its fulfillment is implanted in our hearts.

Someone owes you something, but insists that he does not. Yet within himself, he knows that he is indebted to you, no matter what he has said to deny it. The same is true for those who deny the existence of God; within their hearts, they know that God exists.

People say that no one has ever seen God. This is true for the physical world. You say that you have not seen God, nor have you seen the Angels. You have seen God and the Angels, but you have been blind. This is all. The day will come when all the people in the world will see the manifestations of God.

There is a hell, but God has not created this hell. There is a Paradise as well, but God has not created this Paradise. God has created something much greater.

Be Perfect

Someone asked the Master, "What is the new way of doing God's Work?"
The Master explained:

We need to participate in God's Work; that is, we need to think, feel, and act as God does. We need to work with Nature in a new way, as God works. He works in an all-perfect way.

God is long-suffering; we should be patient. God is all-knowing; we should be wise. God is all-loving; we should be loving. God is all-powerful; we should be strong.

It is God who gives us the impulse to think and to work. You feel low; God uplifts you. You feel despair and wish to die; God gives you the impulse to live. You do not want to work; from within you, God says, "Go and work."

I aspire that my thoughts and intentions be in accordance with God's intentions. I do not wish the weather to change because of me, but I subject myself to the weather that the Great Omniscient Cause has ordained.

What is your task? Continuous self-development and self-perfection. God is the continuous manifestation of Perfection and man is the continuous self-improvement on the path to Perfection. This is the meaning of the Scripture, "Therefore you shall be perfect, just as your Father in Heaven is perfect."[6] Man needs to continuously correct his imperfections on the path to Perfection.

The Love of the One

There were days when the home of brother Temelko was filled with guests. People came from the city as well as from all parts of the countryside. Everyone wished to see the Master, to speak with him, to receive instructions as well as encouragement and advice. The Master received guests privately or in groups in his small room where he listened to them and spoke with them. The luncheons were held in common, as with a family. The small dining-room was overfilled with guests, and the sisters served them. After lunch, we usually sang a few songs and then the Master would speak.

One brother asked, "During these unsettled times, what should the brothers and sisters do?"

To this, the Master replied:

Study the lectures and sermons. One needs to start from the very beginning and apply them. Every Word is given under a particular conjunction of the planets and the Sun. We are

---

6. See Matthew 5:48.

influenced by the celestial bodies: the Earth, the Sun, and the central Sun as well. And in every position of these three celestial bodies, and the remaining ones as well, the Idea and the Word of God is made manifest in a specific way.

Then the Master explained:

God has given to all beings what is essential. However, cases exist in which the human soul passes from one state into another. During these transient phases, gloom and darkness can penetrate human consciousness until the individual again enters into the Divine Consciousness—into Love—in which Light and Joy abide. It is necessary for a person to pass through these transient states as a condition for evolution. During these intermediate conditions, the person again dwells within the realm of Love, but his clouded consciousness prevents him from seeing the Light. Therefore, when you are sad, you should realize that you are passing from one state of your consciousness into another. This passing from the human consciousness to the Divine always brings something new. Someone says, "I experience much suffering." The greater and longer lasting our suffering, the greater and more powerful our Joy and Love afterward. This can be verified. It is not an abstraction but Science.

You need to see God's Love within the smallest things. When God created the world, He held us in His Mind, Heart, Soul, and Spirit. Because of this, we need to look at the Creation of the world as a sacred act of Love and be ready to make every sacrifice for our Creator.

When all abandon you and you remain alone, you need to understand that there is One who is with you. God will tell you, "You are not alone. Be still: I am with you always." Not one of you has had this experience of terrible loneliness.

The only Being Who thinks of us in every moment, without ever forgetting us, not even for a single instant, is God, the Great One, toward whom everyone should strive.

The only purpose of suffering—the misery of life—is for us to come to experience God's Great Love and to know that

Providence will deliver us from all the suffering and misery of life. This we will come to understand at the end of all times.

All trials through which you pass at present are for the sole purpose of coming to know God, the Primordial Cause. And when you come to know Him, Joy will appear.

Someone thinks that he has been forgotten. This is a misunderstanding. No one can remove you from the Divine Consciousness. The minute that someone thinks that he is a separate being, he creates his own adversity.

Those who are one with the Divine have a distinctive quality: they have no fear. They do not consider what might happen to them, or what people might think of them. One's strength lies in one's faith in Divine Order. Externally, God withdraws from us that He may not disturb us; and yet, internally, He enters into us that He may encourage us. Much turmoil might happen in the world. Downfalls and advances alike might happen to people. And yet, no matter what situation they might find themselves in, God continues to keep the same relationship with them. You die, God gives you a blessing. You do something wrong, still God gives you a blessing.

All suffering and joy ensue from God's Love. Why? You do not understand His Love; and in not understanding it, you pass through suffering. There is no greater joy than to realize that you are alive, that there is One who loves you. From within He tells you, "Fear not: I will arrange everything for you. The day will come when you will receive My blessing."

If you could go to one of the Higher Worlds, you would find there many who love you and who are sending their good thoughts and feelings to you.

Those who come to understand God's Love will never ask who God is.

If you were to amass the love of all of humankind—of all the saintly, good, and righteous people, of all the Angels and the heavenly Deities—their love would represent but a minute part of God's Love.

I say, "Blessed are the people because God loves them." In this lies your misfortune: you are not aware of God's Love for you. One thing is expected of you: that you realize that He Who loves you does everything for your good.

God's Love lies in His constant giving. This is called "influx." When the opposite process takes place, life becomes meaningless. As long as this influx from His Life to ours occurs, we are enlivened and joyful.

Why did God create you? So that there would be someone to love. Why are we on the Earth? So that we may come to know how to love God. As long as man is not connected with God, he resembles one who is stranded on a desert island.

Only the Infinite is able to close the door to negative forces, the door to the bad conditions.

God's greatness does not lie in the Creation of the suns and the galaxies. This He can accomplish in a single instant. And yet, you are sad: everyone is pushing you around. You need a little help. Everyone who passes by you says, "Nothing will come of this person." And yet, God—the Creator of the Universe—stops His Work, descends without being noticed, and whispers to you, "Fear not. Do not be discouraged. I will help you. Even today, I will settle your affairs." And you will have a great flash of joy. These are the great things that God does. This is the great Truth.

I speak of the God who visits people in their broken and sorrowful hearts. He lifts the downcast to the summit of Divine Consciousness that they may do as all do: breathe pure air and absorb Divine Light.

Every being is a unique form through which the Divine Consciousness manifests. Therefore, God watches over each form as He would over a delicate flower that the Divine may manifest through it.

What is "Eternal Bliss"? Eternal Bliss is the sum of countless small blessings that flow continuously like a wellspring composed of countless small droplets that come one after another without interruption.

The Great One has a particular quality: those who hate Him—He draws to Himself the most.

The evil in the world is due to our lack of understanding of the conditions in which we find ourselves. God is not angry with us because of our errors. It offers Him the opportunity to manifest His Mercy toward us and correct them. After five or six years have passed, you will come to understand the consequences of your errors and will make amends.

For example, consider a person who builds a nice home and rents it to some tenants who manage to ruin it within a year. I interpret this as follows: God has created the world very sensibly, but we ruin it and search for the cause outside of ourselves instead of within.

The Law states: God loves all beings equally. But not all benefit from His Love. Some are aware of this, and yet others are not. God loves human beings as much as the Angels, but there is a difference: Angels are aware of God's Love and are open to receiving it, but human beings are not always aware of it.

Consider those foolish people who build a house, but put only one small window in it. Others build a house with large windows through which abundant light passes. You might say, "Look how this person is showered with abundance." This is so because his windows are larger. Depending upon the size of the window that you open, that much light and that much air will enter. God's blessings—the light and the air—will enter of their own accord as soon as you open up. And yet, they will enter only as much as your window permits. In this same way, you will receive the power and blessings of the Divine World according to how open the windows of your consciousness and your soul are.

God's blessings infuse all beings. Inferior beings cannot contain them, as all would flow out. We need to become still as the motionless surface of the water that God's image may be reflected in us. If He is reflected in us, we will progress. If the image of God is not reflected within, we will remain as we are. We need to be pure so that God's image may be reflected in us. Peace and purity are the two conditions for God's image to be reflected in us. As long as we do not believe in God, we are not able to receive His Love.

God never lets blind people spread His Light. God withdraws His gifts from the foolish person so that others will withdraw their trust in him and not be deceived. God will place the foolish one in bed so that he cannot lie and abuse another's confidence.

Sometimes people think that God is angry with us. We think that God is angry with us, while in reality, we are the angry ones. We see our image in God and say that He is angry with us. Set aside this delusion. God is not a god of anger. God is the God of Love. It is because we become angry, we think that God, too, is angry. This is our mistake. When God punishes you, this punishment is His lesson to help us revert to the right course.

I will tell you a great Truth: to every being, God manifests His Love in a specific way. God's Love for every being is specific.

Pure and Impure Food

Some of the brothers raised a question about food. The Master responded:

The danger exists that we might stumble in our development if we do not know how to eat, how to drink water, how to breathe, and how to assimilate food. Man possesses an inner sense that advises him regarding the kind of food he should take; and if he permits this sense to guide him, he will choose his food properly. One can re-establish this sense when one lives a life of purity.

Why should one not overeat? Because a great portion of brain energy goes to the stomach and this means that the brain cannot complete its work. When one overeats, one squanders a lot of brain energy on the work of the stomach. There needs to be a certain amount of reserve energy for the brain.

By consuming vegetarian food, one becomes more purified. Meat contains more toxins and makes a person coarse and primitive. When animals are slaughtered, the fear that they experience forms terrible toxins in their organisms. The people who eat this meat assimilate these toxins into their system, and as a result, disease states appear, especially neurasthenia. One of the reasons for the existence of disease is the indiscriminate slaughter of animals.

Whoever wants to join the mew epoch of Love needs to, through inner persuasion, give up eating meat. Man needs to recreate his organism. Should he not be able to do so, he will continue to live with animal instincts for a long time.

When water comes to a boil, an expansion occurs within it. As a result, prana—electromagnetism—is released, and then the water can be more easily assimilated by man.

It is very interesting to observe how Intelligent Nature purifies water. When it evaporates and rises to the higher strata of the atmosphere, the water breaks down into hydrogen and oxygen. In this way, it is completely revitalized. After that, the hydrogen and oxygen re-unite through electricity. The water dies and is reborn (as man does) so that it may be renewed.

When we hold a piece of bread in our hands, we should be filled with gratitude for the sacrifice that it has made. Go deep within yourself, contemplate, and say, "I desire to sacrifice myself as the bread does."

When you eat an apple, put your love into it, empathize with the tree on which it grew, and your soul will contact the Advanced Beings who have worked on its development. If you come to love the apple and receive it into yourself, you will improve your energy more than you would have, had you worked upon yourself for an entire year.

The Wellspring

Not far from the village there was a wellspring of mineral water. Its plentiful water meandered away. The water was warm, soft, and flavorful. The Master drank from it, and finding it excellent, recommended it to everyone. There were some nice meadows on the sapling-covered slopes surrounding the wellspring. We often went there with the Master. The countryside was unpretentious and pleasant. The grass was growing; the leaves on the trees were unfurling; and the flowers were blooming, each in its time. The birds sang, and life pulsated with its measured and steady rhythm.

The Master's thoughts were a translation of the Great Book of Nature. Within it, the One Eternal Rhythm of the One Life was made known.
The Master said:

What causes one to rejoice the most is God. Everything that inspires you is God. What gives you vitality, encouragement, and strength in every moment is God. God is present in all of this.

A Great, Sublime Idea can only be born out of the bond between two Intelligent Beings. This is the Law. We need to have a connection with God for a Sublime Idea to arise within us. All thoughts that flow through the mind, all feelings and desires that flow through the heart come from a great wellspring. This wellspring is the soul. The wellspring of the soul is fed by an even greater Wellspring. This is the Divine Spirit. The Wellspring of the Divine Spirit is fed by a still greater Wellspring that is the Absolute Unknown, the Spirit of Creation.

Every Thought that brings the Essence of Love to the human soul comes from God. Every Thought that brings the Light of Wisdom comes from God. Every Thought that brings the Freedom of Truth to the human soul comes from God.

Everything that does not come from God carries within itself poison and death. This is because everyone who does not receive Divine Thought experiences suffering and death. Through all the Angels, through all Advanced Beings, God's Love is manifested, but to a different degree. Love, therefore, comes from one Source, from One Center.

If you desire to go where Love is, you need to go to the Eternal Wellspring: to God. We cannot come to know Love apart from God.

You are a door through which God enters to teach you how to love. He is the only One who can show you how to love. Allow yourself to be taught by the One alone. It is said in the Scriptures, "God is our Teacher."[7] He who permits God to teach him will be dressed in the most beautiful of clothes.

---

7. See also John 3:2, "This man came to Jesus by night and said to Him, 'Rabbi, we know that You are a Teacher come from God; for no one can do these signs that You do unless God is with him.'"

The life of the person who is in accord with Divine Law is pure poetry, music, and song. That person is brave, resolute, and filled with noble and sublime feelings. Should one part with this Law, one will become mistrustful, with concerns about everything: fear for one's life, fearful that old age is coming and that there are not sufficient resources, and so on.

Pay attention to the least impulse. The small thoughts and feelings that manifest through you—these come from God.

Where is God? God is in all those places where Love, Wisdom, Truth, Life, Knowledge, and Freedom are present. His Presence gives us the most beautiful experience of the Spirit. It refreshes us and uplifts us.

Some people say, "Let God set the world right." God has inscribed His Word within people's hearts, and in doing so, He has already set it right. It now remains for what He has written within man to be made manifest.

Unity in Love

The Master spoke to his disciples:

Show gratitude and appreciation toward everyone who helps you. Love comes from God. Those who love you are transmitters of God's Love. Someone might brag that he has done you a favor, that he has done some good for you. He is not telling the truth.

Christ tells us, "For I have come down from Heaven, not to do My own will, but the will of Him who sent Me."[8] Within you dwells a misunderstanding, a lack of contentment. This is due to your not understanding that Love is unified, undivided.

It is naive to think that two or more people love you. One alone exists in the world Who can love you—no one else. Some think that many people love them: their father, mother, brothers, sisters, and friends. In reality, this is not so. If you think that

---

8. See John 6:38.

many people love you—this is only because it appears to be so. You are loved by only One: God. As soon as God comes to love you, all people will love you.

This is a true story about two young people who loved each other. After they had been living together for ten years, the man noticed that his partner was beginning to see his weaknesses and was starting to criticize him. So he disguised himself as a young man and began to flirt with her, writing her love letters. The woman said to her husband, "I know men who are refined and have a noble character." He agreed with her and admitted that he was not so refined. Sometimes the man, while in his disguise, would say to his wife, "Your husband is a very good man. Love him."

Through all who love you, it is One Being alone who is loving you. This is God. Since Love is indivisible, when someone tries to divide Love, suffering is born.

As human beings we think, feel, and act, but we need to realize that it is God Who is working from within. If, for a second, we allow ourselves to think that it is us doing everything, then we are on the wrong path.

Someone accomplishes something and imagines that he is the author. However, out of affected piety, that person says, "God did this." No, one needs to be honest with oneself and admit that it is God working within. A person can be compared to a letter carrier who opens the mailbag, takes out a letter, and hands it to you. When he arrives at another place, again he opens the mailbag and delivers another letter. This is how one serves people. You might think that by carrying letters and handing them out you will become poor. No, you will become wealthy. You fill the mailbag with letters, and you are wealthy. When you deliver the letters, you become poor in order to fill the mailbag again. By delivering a letter to the people whom you love, you befriend them. You have not written the letters; you only deliver them.

So often we say, "my love." It is important to return to the unifying Love—that is, to the Love of God—to let this Love manifest through us. We need to come into contact with the "clean air," not the "unclean." By "clean air," I mean the all-embracing, Divine Love. By "unclean air," I mean love with admixtures.

God wants something of us now. He does not demand it by Law. We need to discover what it is that God is asking of us.

When you love someone, do you not want to know what they are like?

God, Who has come to love us, makes accommodations to do things on our terms. For thousands and millions of years until now, it has been God Who has been making the accommodations. As He accommodates us, we also need to accommodate Him.

Here is how this will come to pass: one needs to have an excellent mind through which God is able to manifest, an excellent heart through which God is able to manifest, and an excellent soul through which God is able to manifest.

You love a person for his enlightened mind. This is one-third of the truth. You love someone for his heart. This is also one-third of the truth. When you come to Divine Love, it embraces all things. In this case, you love the Divine, God, within the human being.

The Border between Two Epochs

The Master would go for a walk almost every morning, accompanied by friends. No matter the weather, he would not miss going out. He loved to be in the open, walking in the Sun. He moved quickly and with ease. His attention was vigilant for each wonder of the beauty surrounding us. Sometimes, during such morning outings, the Master would shed light on questions that would arise. On one such outing, the question about evolution and involution was raised.

The Master answered:

Involution is turning away from God, and evolution is returning to God. Involution is leaving home and going to work. Evolution is returning home from work with the experience that one has acquired. Moving down means moving into darkness; climbing up is rising toward the Light.

The story of the fall of man into error is one of the great mysteries of Life. This story has a symbolic bearing upon the issue of involution. It concerns the time when man was with God and dwelled among the Angels. The human being alone wanted to come down to Earth to learn. People descended to Earth to study, and when they had come to the unfavorable constraining conditions, they began to think about their Father, about God.

God understands human nature, and for this reason, He did not give humans immortality, allowing all who do not fulfill His Will to age. When He sent man to Earth, God began to take away from him what he possessed. This is a consequence of the involutionary process.

For as long as you were outside the material world, you were idealists: you strived toward God and desired to sacrifice, to share everything. Nevertheless, when you descended into the material world, you forgot everything. In the process of descending, you lost something. You need to return to that state in which you were at the Beginning. Since ancient times, many beings have lost their primordial, sublime Life. The infinite Love of God strives to permeate them so that He may restore the Life and Light they have lost. Love wants to awaken all those who have fallen asleep, bringing back to life all of the "dead." History keeps silent regarding the cause of these beings having lost their sublime Life. They have experienced a great catastrophe. Their life is a great tragedy. Many legends exist regarding the reasons for this tragedy. The whole of humankind has lived through this tragedy.

A new epoch is now coming for humankind in which the Intelligent World will show people the way that they can return to their primordial Life and come to stand on good, solid ground. At present, most people live amid life's illusions.

During the involutionary process—that is, during the process of descending into the material world—materialized souls descended through great resistance into the densest matter of the Earth. In the process of descending, considerable energy is generated. This is the most difficult path, the path of Wisdom. Although the Teaching of Love—that is to say, the path of ascent or evolution—has been taught to people, they still walk on the most difficult path.

The Devas, the Angels, move along the easiest path: the path of the least resistance. That is to say, the Angels move along the path of Love, and people along the path of Wisdom. Until recently, humankind was descending. As human beings begin to ascend, they will meet the Angels and will come to know them.

At present, we are in the transient time between involution and evolution. Because descent is followed by ascent, at the border between the two epochs—that is, in the transient period—the greatest resistance, the greatest suffering, exists. This is why there are so many delays and obstacles at present. Nevertheless, once the evolutionary process begins, the forces will be directed upward. Then there will be no obstacles.

The methods for development of the Eastern nations were good at one time, but now they cannot be applied as they were in the past because we are at the beginning of the evolutionary process and no longer in that of the involutionary when these methods have been given. The methods that the Hindu philosophy has used before are involutionary. Now new evolutionary methods need to be given to the Western nations.

At the boundary between the involutionary and evolutionary epochs is Christ. His Appearance heralds the beginning of the evolutionary epoch. However, the majority of people today continue to descend; that is, they are still on the involutionary path. In this way, they will not solve their problems. In such a case, another impulse upward toward the Sun needs to come.

Three categories of souls exist. Those who are descending are in their involutionary period, those who are ascending are in their evolutionary period, and a third category of souls has stopped in one place. These souls are at the lowest point in their development, having not yet begun to ascend.

While ascending, should you encounter beings who have stopped, and you connect with these beings, they will draw power from you, causing you to lose momentum. Beings also exist with whom you walk in a parallel manner. Here we come to the question of related souls. You should help the others, but without becoming intimately involved.

Why is it necessary for one to descend and sink into matter? That one may clothe in layer after layer, each layer denser than the others in order to gain experience. After that, man begins his ascent by clothing himself in increasingly sublime forms. The final movement will be upward.

Those who do not want to connect with God will be tossed by the waves out of the predominant current on the Day of the Lord, where they will need to wait for another period of ascent. That is, they will need to wait for another Wave.

All those who are ascending toward God will enter into Heaven, but those from the other period will remain descended, outside of God. The door will be closed to them for a while.

Because Christ was mentioned in relation to the beginning of evolution at the beginning of this discourse, one of the brothers asked the Master to say something about Christ.
The Master explained:

Christ is the Transformer of the Energy that comes to us from God. Without Christ, we could not ascend to God. Why? It has been said that God is an all-consuming Fire.

To explain this concept, we can use the following analogy. The Sun's energy has such powerful vibrations that should it come directly down to Earth, we would not be able to bear it. This is why several transformers exist between the Sun and the Earth through which the Sun's energy passes. This alone makes solar energy bearable for us.

Music—the Path of Attainment

Music was an integral part of the Master's life. It was his natural environment. The Master worked in accordance with the Laws of Music. For him, it was not only about the aesthetic of sound, but of Life itself. "The good Life is music," he would say. He played the violin and also sang. As a part of his Teaching, he introduced many songs that were a model for the new music. Sometimes he showed us how to sing the songs with his deep, pleasant voice, expressing all of the nuances. Not only his voice, but also his expression, posture, deep feelings, and unity of thought and emotion gave an unusual power to each song. Sometimes he accompanied his singing with gestures, which revealed, in a deeper way, the content of the song.

In his lectures and sermons, the Master spoke extensively about music, revealing its deep meaning and many-sided applications. The Master once said:

Make use of music for your spiritual development, as do the Advanced Beings in the Sublime World above. The new epoch of Love that is coming will give a new impulse to music. If someone wants to do something bad, play some music, and this person will relent. Awaken the Divine within people, and they will listen to its Voice.

There is always the desire within you to be heard by someone when you sing. Be assured that you have the best audience. The whole of Heaven listens when you begin to sing. From Above, you receive the best evaluation. Do not be afraid that there is no one Above to listen to you. There is an audience there that appreciates your singing.

It might happen at times when you cannot reconcile with your neighbor. But once you begin to sing, the song within you will awaken the readiness to reconcile. This is the power of music.

Why does one need to sing? So that one may not lose what one has. You are near the point of attaining something beautiful. Sing, that you may not lose it. Those who sing are strong, and those who do not sing are weak. Sing, because this is what Love requires of you. You need to sing so that you may live. Music is the transmitter of Life. No culture can exist without music.

You need to visit a meeting of the Initiates in order to see what kind of music is there. You need be in the presence of these Initiates when they are singing, to perceive their deep understanding of music, and to comprehend the real meaning of music. For one to become a student of one of these Initiates, one first needs to be knowledgeable of contemporary music. You need to be a very good singer so that when you go to them, you will be able to comprehend their music.

Once true music permeates the world, there will be no more disease. Disease will exist, but one will experience a pleasant feeling while the ailment lasts and will overcome it easily.

When you sing, the Divine World opens to you, and you receive Divine Life. You lose if you do not sing. No matter what happens to you—sing!

It is beneficial for you to paint well, to sing well, and to play an instrument well so that you may know how to accomplish any task.

Those vibrations that are curative are included within the process of singing. When an ill person sings or listens to singing, he will recover.

Through music, you can bring about a certain degree of realization to what you desire. Through music, things can be brought to fulfillment. What one is singing about can be realized, but what one does not sing about cannot be realized. You cannot go before God if you do not sing. You cannot be a poet if you lack musical sensibility. You cannot go before people and have them love you if you do not sing.

On another occasion, the Master said:

The true image of Love is musical. Those who do not sing—even if they talk about Love, or whatever else—in reality, sleep.

Uplift and development cannot be accomplished without singing. The person who does not know how to sing cannot be a disciple. For the disciple of the Divine School, music is one of the important elements that serves as a shield to protect the disciple from internal and external unfavorable conditions. A correlation exists between musical sensibility and the capability for reason. The greater appreciation for music a person has, the greater that person's ability for reasoning.

Singing needs to have three elements: it should be activated by unconditional Love, it should be permeated with faith, and it should also be permeated with hope. That is to say, we need to sing with the idea that what we sing about can become realized.

Singing needs to be an uninterrupted impulse of Life. Without singing, life, as it is at present, would obliterate everything noble within us.

Music heralds the application of the Divine Virtues. I have in mind music as a method for applying Love. If you do not have a musical ear, you cannot love people. Love is a great blessing for all. The first thing that it gives to a person is music.

What is Love? The Science of music. In and of itself, Love is elusive. Only the one who is musically sensible can understand it. When someone is a bearer of Divine Love, he speaks musically. When you are attuned, you enter into the experience of each tone. You can come to perceive music as speech, as language.

All people whose feelings have hardened lack music within themselves, while those with gentle feelings have music. They can sing or play an instrument, and thus their consciousness is higher than the consciousness of those who do not sing or play music.

When one sings, there should always be an object for the song. If someone sings for God, he will be eternally young and will attain immortality. After passing through the transition, he will continue to sing in the Invisible World. If, however, one sings for the world, he will be forgotten.

You need to have an enlightened mind, heart, and soul for the appreciation of music. Having two standards is not acceptable. You need to have only one ideal: to serve God. What will people say about you? Let them say whatever they would like.

While singing, think about your internal audience. At the present, people lack the right idea of what music is.

The musical genius is a channel of Divine Energy, and those who listen will receive this energy. The good musician needs to be a good transmitter of the Divine: he should give.

One needs to sing with inspiration. By singing beautifully, one also perceives beautiful thoughts and feelings. When you listen to talented singers and musicians, you make a connection with Advanced Beings who manifest themselves through them. The vibrations of these Beings penetrate far into space through the voices of these singers and are uplifting to human souls. Few are the songs that are carried through space. Seldom is when an ancient Egyptian or Hindu song can be received. A song or musical piece that does not remain in space is not true music.

The subconsciousness, the consciousness, the ego consciousness, and the Higher consciousness should all participate in the singing. Those who want to sing well need to be calm within. If you sustain negative thoughts and feelings within yourselves, you cannot sing or play an instrument. Technically, you can play and sing, but not with your soul.

Wisdom makes use of music. From now on, the world of music belongs to Wisdom. Performance, which is the external aspect of music, cannot be manifested without Wisdom.

Music is a great art. Through it, the character, thoughts, and feelings of a person can be expressed. How can you give musical expression to the vibrations of the mind and of the heart? The heart vibrates rapidly, while the mind vibrates sublimely.

Sublime Beings apply music readily, whereas it is much harder for ordinary people to apply music. Let an ordinary musician try to correct one of his errors through music.

According to a person's musical sensibility, one can discern his character. The more advanced a person's musical sensibility, the more stable his character.

You are sad. If you are a violinist, play, and your state will change. Even if you play only one note, your state can change. Today there are many more musical instruments available than there were in the past. Through them, you can help yourselves change your state. There was never a time when so many musical instruments were available as there are now. Good musicians are those who have the knowledge to change positive energy into negative and negative into positive. Have you tried to play or sing in order to change your bitter feelings into sweet ones? You can try, in this way, to use the power of music. It is good for one to apply music in order to transform one's state. When one is tired or sad, one needs to sing.

On another occasion, the Master said:

Music influences the digestion. When your stomach does not function well, sing, and you will see the influence that music has on the digestion of food. The disciple needs to set aside time for singing every day—10, 15, or 20 minutes—before starting his work.

The development of a person's capabilities and talents depends upon singing. When you sing, you give your potential a chance to develop.

Every song can be sung either loudly or softly. If you sing loudly, you will attract inferior beings. If you sing softly, you will attract more advanced beings.

Whoever who is not musically sensible—in whom the sense of rhythm is not developed—is not patient or punctual and lacks a sense of order. Whereas, the person who is musically sensible, is patient, punctual, and has a sense of order. One can seldom find musicians among murderers or criminals.

Because people are not well-attuned, they are in different states; and for this reason, not all songs appeal to them equally.

Those nations that have had good music have advanced.

Some people are opposed to contemporary music being played and sung in pubs and coffeehouses. But the singing and playing of music in pubs and coffeehouses has contributed a great deal to human development.

One needs to sing because musical dust collects within him that he needs to shake off.

When we try to sing and play Divine music, we will always make mistakes. This is not because there exists a mistake in Divine music, but because we need time to learn how not to make mistakes. You need to learn to attune yourselves.

If you do not feel like singing, you may be in a diseased state. If you have the desire to sing, you are healthy.

It is possible to sense the music that emanates from a person.

Someone thinks that it is easy to become a genius. A person needs to serve a singer of genius for thousands of years to observe how he works, what he does. Only then can that person become a singer of genius as well.

Remember: without music, you can go nowhere. Either you should play an instrument or you should sing. Your misfortunes are due precisely to the fact that you neither sing nor play an instrument. You expect someone to come from outside to sing and play for you.

All mistakes can be corrected through music.

There exist places in Nature whose gateways can be opened only by those who hold the power of music.

The War

Today during the afternoon conversation, a question about war arose. Several brothers and sisters expressed their opinions.
The Master said:

What is war? It is God's anger with the sons of disobedience. In other words, when people commit many crimes, Mars is given the power to unleash war. That is to say, the created karma is paid off through the suffering of humankind.

Some people consider it impossible to renounce their father and mother as well as themselves, that they may serve God as Christ commanded. Are people not currently ordered by law to renounce their families—father, mother, wife, children—to go into battle?

If people refuse to make sacrifices voluntarily, they will be forced to do so from without. Everyone can see the impending catastrophe, but not everyone knows how to avoid it. For centuries, unconscious mechanical forces have been accumulating like floodwaters in front of a dam. The strain is so great that catastrophe is inevitable. Soon the dam will give way. The energy that has accumulated within people hides great danger. Until now, this energy has remained yet to be utilized. In the past as well as in the present, people have continued to demonstrate great cruelty. At present, millions of people are becoming the victims of human madness. Afterward, justification is found in external causes.

Enormous amounts of gas, oil, and other resources are wasted due to the modern technical means of air, ground, water-based, and submarine warfare. Nature has strictly defined how much of these goods can be utilized. She severely punishes those who go too far with wastefulness. Humankind will bear the consequences for squandering these fuels.

Unprotected cities are being bombed! These wars are unprecedented. This terror is unprecedented—attacking a city with two thousand airplanes with high-caliber bombs. Nobody has the right to deprive a human being of what God has given him. If you have a window through which you see God's Light, no one has the right to deprive you of that Light.

When two blood brothers fight and pull each other's hair, it is not the desire of their father and mother. When nations today fight, this is not in accordance with the Will of God.

There exists the tendency to justify the war ideologically by saying that it is for the good of the nation. Yet what did those who fought for their nations accomplish in the past? Egypt, Syria, Babylon, and Rome were great nations. They fought, but what did they achieve? Nothing.

There exists a small group of arms manufacturers who declare wars. As soon as the weaponry has been used, peace comes. After that, the production of arms resumes, no matter that millions of people will become cannon-fodder.

People say, "Let there be no more war!" Yet wars are the result of people's actions. We say, "For there to be no more war, people must overcome greed." As long as people do not obey Divine Law, war will continue to exist. If they obey Divine Law, they will never engage in combat.

The Divine Sculptor

During numerous conversations the Master gave explanations for the reasons behind suffering.
He said:

As it is difficult for one to climb high mountain peaks, so it is difficult to climb the high reaches of spiritual life. Life is climbing a high mountain peak. Someone tells me, "I moan. I am tormented." Naturally, you go to the heights, and for this reason, you find it difficult.

One suffers because one has strayed from God and does not know how to return. Moving away from God leads to deprivation, suffering, misfortune, hardship, disease, and death. The greater the suffering, the greater the turning away. Therefore, in order for this deviation to be set right, you need to return to the primordial Life.

The reason for human suffering and hardship lies in the unfulfillment of God's Will. The trials of life come in order to distinguish that which is pure gold from that which is only gilded. What is gold is put to work, whereas whatever is gold-plated is put aside.

One should not bring suffering and conflict upon oneself. Sometimes the Spirit comes and tells someone to do something, but that person refuses with the excuses that there are no favorable conditions or proper disposition. Then come the great difficulties in one's life.

The suffering that you have in your life is due to your being without Love. Remember that the misconceptions, conflicts, and suffering in your life do not come from God. The suffering and misfortunes in your life are due to a lack of understanding of the great Principles and Laws that Nature is using.

What do you understand of the concept "the Wrath of God"? It indicates that much human error has accumulated and that Intelligent Nature is using Fire to consume all this error. In this way people are liberated.

Suffering indicates that one has come into conflict with the Laws of Intelligent Nature. The one who does not attain Divine Wisdom, suffers.

The lack of understanding of the wholeness of Life is the source of suffering. Those who would like to free themselves of suffering, need to change the direction of their movement. In order to achieve this, one needs to be courageous and resolute. When someone commits a crime, suffering knocks at the door and forces that person to begin thinking.

God has created a harmonious world, and the existing suffering in this world is the result of human actions. At first, Nature tries to teach us with gentleness, and if we do not understand, the storm comes. Nature manifests herself to be like us. She conforms to us, and then we understand her language.

One brother asked, "Why do good people suffer and not bad ones?" The Master said:

The good gardener prunes the cultivated trees, leaving the wild ones to grow untouched. For how long? Until their turn comes to be pruned. When a sheep is slaughtered, the other sheep stand by and watch, but the same thing will happen to them. Their turn has not yet come. To the one who has not suffered, suffering is yet to come. To the one who has endured suffering to the end, suffering will come no more.

When people suffer, it is because they have missed certain opportunities. They have been delayed for one minute, and the train has left the station.

When a weak person thinks he has been punished by a strong one, he should not blame the strong person, but say, "I am not smart enough." A strong person never punishes a smart one. The weak person has been punished not because of his weakness, but because he is not smart. The weak should not think of himself as being strong. The moment you stop thinking of yourself as being strong, punishment will cease.

All those who crucify Christ within themselves will burn like wood. This is the suffering through which they will pass.

You complain that someone has beaten you. The reason for this is that you are standing too close to him.

He who knows why he has been punished attains true initiation. It is necessary for the person who desires to liberate himself of all suffering to be virtuous and possess right thought.

When the Real Life comes, there will be no more tears. After every sadness something new, something great, is born within the human soul. All great ideas are born after great sorrow. Until the new is born within the human soul, man will continue to know suffering. As soon as it is born, he will be filled with Joy. People see God in times of sorrow.

The Meaning of Suffering

In many of his sermons, as well as in his talks, the Master spoke about sorrow, shedding light upon its deep inner meaning. In those days, it was especially important to enlighten people on this subject. When suffering is understood, it is easier for people to bear it and receive the benefits it brings.
The Master said:

Suffering is not punishment. It is given as a lesson. We give a completely different connotation to the word "punishment." Punishment means there is a lesson to be learned. If suffering comes to you, do not become disturbed. A specific blessing is hidden within it that will come after you have endured the suffering. Do not force the given conditions. Remember: the blessing for which your heart and mind are longing will come in time. Be watchful not to let this blessing pass you by.

Do not avoid suffering, but profit by it. The apostle Paul said, "For I consider that the sufferings of this present time are not worthy to be compared with the glory which shall be revealed in us."[9] The psalmist said, "I feel good that I am saddened." Through suffering Love prepares the conditions for new joy to come. The suffering of today is a condition for future joy.

Suffering and sorrows are Divine Plows that prepare the ground, so that the seeds of future virtues will be able to sprout.

---

9. See Romans 8:18.

When someone suffers, he becomes a better person and more sensitive.

The awakening of the consciousness does not occur mechanically, but comes through the impulses that come from suffering. The more difficulties a person encounters, the greater the possibilities are for personal growth. The great people had to endure great ordeals. This does not mean that these great people knew only suffering. They also had joys so great that they are not known to the ordinary people.

Mindful Suffering

The city of Sofia was desolate and destroyed, burned to the ground. Life withdrew from it, as the city had been abandoned by its people. It was wintertime, and the sky was hanging over it, dark and heavy. No light could penetrate through it; one could not see a solution. In those days when people were coming to see the Master for consolation, they could grasp the meaning of his words more readily and understood that they needed to endure to the end.

The Master told them:

Whoever suffers and endures to the end is a hero. One who suffers is a hero. Such an individual will become a true human being. Nothing will become of a person who does not suffer.

Be thankful to God when a trial comes. All tribulations are a blessing for a person. After each trial, one attains something good.

In order to polish a stone, one needs to chip and grind it. The same is true for a human being. Polishing, suffering, is necessary so that one may awaken.

It is difficult for people to become aware. They need to be boxed into a corner in order to awaken. Every time the consciousness falls asleep, suffering comes to awaken it. After that comes rejuvenation and uplift. Suffering will uplift you. Be joyful that you suffer so that you may bear fruit.

God will transform the suffering of people into precious stones that will be placed as a wreath upon their heads. In the future, people's suffering will adorn their heads.

When Nature puts someone in restraints, she has his best interests in mind and has, as her goal, the awakening of the hidden forces within. All suffering, constraints, and trials in one's life aim to awaken the higher consciousness within. When Nature imposes sorrow, we feel wrongly toward it. When a mother puts her child in the tub to bathe him or her, the baby cries and thinks that this is bad. The child does not understand that the mother means to do well for her baby.

An army general was tried, convicted, stripped of all his rights, and sent to jail. After ten years he was released. He then said, "I now understand life. It has become clear to me that my position as a general and all other things are nonsense." A person whose skull has been broken several times grows wiser.

As a result of suffering one's way of thinking is gradually set right. When the thinking is set right, the consciousness awakens. Through suffering, a new consciousness arises in the human being. This is the meaning of suffering.

The gifts that Living Nature gives to man are meaningful tribulations. Within them are hidden the experiences that enable human beings to develop. The fruit of these tribulations are the impulses that help them to grow.

People are given as many trials as necessary for the development of their souls. These trials are not arbitrary. When I speak about them, I am referring to mindful suffering. People have come to their present development because of these hardships and trials. These prepare humankind for the Coming of Love.

The Uppermost Limit

The Master told us:

The ordinary person is unable to suffer in the way that the great ones do. Suffering comes according to the degree of development. When you come to pass through the trials of Job and of Christ, you will attain a new idea of Life. If you do not pass through these trials, you will never come to comprehend the secrets of Creation.

People have not yet reached the uppermost limits of suffering in order to leave their human nature and become like Angels. You need to pass through two conditions: the greatest sorrow and the greatest joy. After that, you will come to understand the real inner meaning of Life. Finally, you will come to that Bliss in which all things are harmonious. This cannot be explained in the human language.

Within Nature, one great Law predominates: Human souls develop through suffering, and through it, they learn the great mysteries of Life. Every suffering is an open door through which one comes to know God. Without suffering, people could not come close to God. This is the path on Earth. The Angels come close to God through joy.

Suffering is the path on which you walk so that you may develop the Divine within. Through suffering and trials, you become humble so that you may see God. Only then can you comprehend His greatness. You will come to realize that you are a wanderer on this Earth who has come here to learn.

Servants need to first serve a bad master so that they will be able to appreciate the good one afterward. Storms are needed to clear away the fog within you, then the Sun will shine.

When suffering comes, transform it into a virtue. One who has suffered greatly will become gentle and virtuous. Without suffering, you cannot attain gentleness or virtue. Through suffering, one gradually changes and finally makes the choice to lead a pure and holy life.

Trials in Life

Once the Master explained about the trials in life:

Each hardship is a trial that one needs to endure. When a trial comes into your life, tell yourself, "This trial has come so that I may correct one of my faults." When one attains self-control, the hardships and suffering will vanish.

The suffering of the present times heralds a New Life for which refined matter needs to be prepared. As a result of the suffering, the matter of the brain will become more and more refined. To suffer means to send down roots deep into the ground and to work. Through suffering, conflicts, and contradictions you acquire experience with the great Laws that direct Life. The contradictions that exist in the present life will not be repeated in the future one.

What represents the end of suffering? Awareness. If you become more aware after you have suffered, you will give thanks because this suffering has been meaningful. If, after having suffered, you have not attained awareness, the suffering was not meaningful.

When the ground has been cultivated—this represents suffering, a cataclysm for the worms and ants. On the other hand, the New Culture is sown in the soil through this cultivation. Human suffering is similar to this cultivation through which the New Culture is sown in human souls.

In order to cleanse your body, you use a washcloth. Through suffering, the human body is cleansed from within. If the human body is not cleansed from within, Divine Thought cannot be correctly transmitted. Through hardship, the nervous system is purified. When every nerve is purified, then one can properly receive all Divine Light and Thought. Why does suffering come? For the sole purpose of eliminating the impurities in the brain.

The Angels understand the profound meaning of the suffering of humankind. They know that the blessing for humankind is hidden within it.

The great people of genius did not have the best conditions of life; whereas those who have had good conditions have achieved very little. The working conditions of Beethoven were very poor. Suffering impels man to work. It is very hard to overcome difficulties and suffering, but it needs to be done! Christ overcame them and ascended.

One day when you complete your development, you will thank God for all the misfortunes in your life. These are where the greatest blessings have come from. Through suffering, people are tested and become tempered.

The Roots

The Master once told us:

It has been predetermined that some people can only learn from their own mistakes. If one would talk to them, they would not understand. People like this learn on the path of suffering.

When there is something in your life that causes you to suffer, know that God is preventing you from taking a wrong turn. Knowing about the great misfortune that could befall you, Providence sends trials. To prevent this misfortune, Providence sends a smaller suffering.

Each failure is a future success. This means that there is something to work toward.

Suffering represents a great Divine Science; without it, one cannot learn. Suffering brings Knowledge.

When trees are planted close together, they grow thin and tall. When they are planted at a greater distance apart, they grow strong and full. The same is true with people. Under difficult conditions, they become idealistic; under normal conditions, they become materialistic.

In Nature, there exists a Law: As long as you have not cried, you cannot grow. Either you need to cry, or someone else needs to cry for you. If you cry for someone, you are helping that person. People consider weeping a weakness, but it is not. Not a single being exists who has never wept.

Suffering is the roots. Be glad for the roots. The branches are the joys. Be glad for the branches. No tree exists without roots. In this way, suffering and joy complement each other. Consequently, the fruit of the tree corresponds to the Divine World.

It is not that we want suffering, but it is a necessity. Suffering represents plowing; joy represents sowing. Suffering needs to be transformed into joy. What has been sown needs to sprout. Ordinary people suffer as well as great people, but with this difference: ordinary people suffer and become embittered, whereas great ones suffer and progress. In all of life's trials, we need to serve God alone, the One Idea alone. And if we do not give in to the temptation and trials, we will come to know ourselves.

Suffering with Love

The Master said:

If, in spite of difficulties, one continues to walk on the path of life without stumbling, that person is strong. Those who are strong endure all trials. Suffering is a heavy burden that we drag upward. It is fortunate that there are Enlightened Beings who help us. God says, "Call upon Me in the day of trouble; I will deliver you, and you shall glorify Me."[10]

Through your trials and suffering, you can determine the degree of your development. If your spirit is strong, you endure. If you suffer and bear your suffering with joy, you have Love. The more you progress, the greater are the suffering, trials, and tribulations that you encounter in life. Be thankful that you have difficulties so that you may come to know your character and the

---

10. See Psalm 50:15.

strength of your belief. You need to be ready to renounce everything for Love, Wisdom, and Truth.

It is utterly disagreeable to me when I see that someone suffers without Love. It is something else if you have the consciousness, the courage, to suffer for Truth. This, however, is only possible with Love.

What would I gain if I subjected you to trials, persecutions, and hunger for my own sake? If, in your souls, the profound desire arises to come to know God and the whole of Life, your suffering will be mindful: this is suffering with Love. When I meet such people, I am ready to embrace and congratulate them. If you do not suffer with Love, I will tell you, "Brother, you cause me great sorrow." Why? Because you suffer without Love.

Why is it that God, who is Perfect and all-Knowing, has allowed these contradictions? So that He may test your Love. God asks, "Can you love Me after all the suffering? If you can love Me, your Love is true. But if you love Me only after I have given you the greatest bounties, this is to be expected."

God has put people under these conditions now in order to separate out as if by putting them through "sieves." After He has tested them, He will accept them into His Kingdom; He will give them Power, Knowledge, and Wisdom with which to reign the world.

When a certain trial is given to someone, that person can endure it. No trial given to someone exceeds that person's endurance. When suffering comes to you, put on your new clothes. And when you have endured it, take off your new clothes, put on your usual clothes, and become like all others.

When you are sad, rise above your sadness. Many of your troubles are illusory. In the earthly life, there will always be disappointments. Someone is a great actor and is accustomed to being applauded. When that person becomes old, people will applaud someone else. He says, "How beautiful it was at one time." In the future, this person will again have good conditions. Life does not consist of one day alone.

Suffering is only for a moment. It lasts for a short time. The Wrath of God lasts only for a moment, yet His Mercy endures forever.

Two extremes exist: too much suffering is superfluous, but to be without any suffering is the other extreme. You need to have at least a few pennies worth of suffering.

We lack compassion for people who suffer. We also lack compassion for the animals to which we cause suffering.

When one suffers, one needs to wait for the Sun to rise. As soon as the Sun rises, the suffering disappears. When you pass through a trial, think of all the beings who suffer and say, "Many people suffer with me." People with awareness stand above suffering. The human spirit is above everything. There is no power that can crush it. Therefore, you need to overcome suffering.

You have endured so many things in the past, but you have forgotten. There was a time when there were many volcanic eruptions and lava flows, during which people have been buried in the ashes and in the lava. So much have humans endured on Earth!

A New Culture is coming. Everything that has happened will be forgotten. As long as one is ill, he thinks he will never forget about his illness; but as soon as the illness goes away, he forgets about it, as if it were only a dream.

Freedom

This morning we went with the Master to the wellspring. It had snowed during the night. The sky was clear, but some snowflakes were still falling. They sparkled like diamonds and made the air even more refreshing. A gentle breeze was blowing. When we reached the small peak above the wellspring, we gathered around the Master. One of the brothers said, "Master, tell us something about freedom."

The Master looked for a long time at the vista in front of us. The bright sunlight made him glad. He was breathing in the fresh air as if he was tasting Life itself. Then he looked at us and said:

Freedom can exist only where God is. If you think in the way that God thinks, you are free. Only the one who is perfect is free. The only perfect Being is God. In the absolute meaning of the word, "free" only means God. Therefore, without God, you cannot be free. Without God, there is no Life. Free are those who serve God. If you search for freedom, serve God!

Those who serve people are not free. Neither is the one who is served by people. To discover the Law of Love is to discover your freedom. Freedom does not come before Love. This is where all are in error. We desire to be free before we begin to love. Freedom comes as a result of Love. That which does not set one free is not Love.

If you desire to be strong, allow God's Love to manifest through you. Love makes you your own master. You are influenced sometimes by dark forces; you do things that you do not wish to do. This indicates that you are influenced. The Invisible World comes now to set you free from this influence. You need to become masters of these circumstances. Do not permit beings who stand beneath you to command you. In order for one to liberate oneself from those lower beings, one needs to have Love. The moment one comes to know Love, every crime, every transgression, will vanish. Therefore, until people come to know Love, transgressions and crimes will exist.

Those who do not cope with their karma, and subject themselves to it, are not free. Only the Love of God dissolves karma. Karma is a heavy, sticky mud that is difficult to wash away. Only Love can eliminate it. Human karma can be eliminated only through Love, the Love of God. Your conditions in life will improve when you lay down Love as the foundation of your life. In the Life of Love, there is no karma.

Two Laws exist: the Law of Karma and the Law of Dharma. One enters the Law of Dharma through Love. Everyone can try this: If you have Love in your heart, even the biggest snake that comes across your path will yield to your way and will not harm you.

The son receives his share in his inheritance when he comes of age. As the relationship of the father is to his sons, so it is of Nature to humankind. At present, human beings are in their age of infancy and live according to the Law of necessity. When we reach adulthood, we will live according to the Law of Freedom.

Pedagogical Questions

Many of the brothers and sisters were teachers. They used the methods of education given by the Master, and when they went to visit him, they shared their experiences. The Master listened to them with great attention, developed the methods further and added to what he had already given. He introduced them to the methods of Living Nature showing them how they could be applied in the schools. In this way, he laid the foundation for a new educational system. Once during a hike in the mountain, questions concerning child education arose.
The Master said:

The educational system needs to be changed. Something new needs to be introduced. The human spirit strives for new ways and methods through which the Divine Life can be manifested on Earth. All of you need to contribute something to the New Culture. Something new needs to be introduced in the human education to completely change people's concept of Life.

Some of the educational methods that are used today are little more than training. You educate a person under certain circumstances, but when placed under different conditions, that person slips back into the old ways. Children are knowledgeable, but the window through which they are looking is too small. As the child becomes older, the window becomes larger. The abilities of children are within them. God has implanted the new in the human being, and it comes from within. The educators need only to create conditions for the development and growth of what is implanted in the soul by God and not try to introduce their own ideas. In contemporary education, we want to make the child like us. This is wrong. Instead, we should give the children the impulse to develop what is already implanted within them.

If some students are nervous, let them be nervous. Those who are quiet, let them be quiet. You can make them jump, but this is unnatural for them.

You can divide the human life into periods of seven years. However, from another point of view, you can divide it into periods of 33 years. In his 33rd year, every human being—consciously or unconsciously—enters the spiritual life. Something within that person finds a balance. In one's 66th year, one enters into Wisdom. After this age, one is already living in the Divine World: the soul and spirit manifest within that person. This needs to be applied in education because in the first 10 years, an impulse is given that will bear fruit during the corresponding period.

There is a Law, according to which you cannot give to others what you do not have. You cannot convince people of something if you yourself do not believe in it. You cannot awaken the good in man if you do not possess it within yourself. The same applies to Knowledge and Love. This Law should be applied to education.

The education of a child is in the mother's hands. What the mother brings to the child during pregnancy is important. After that—after the children are born—it is more difficult to educate them. Therefore, I say that mothers will put the world in order. During pregnancy, the mother can inspire her child toward wisdom and intelligence; she can influence feelings and also strengthen the will of her child.

After the birth, the connection between mother and child continues, but in a different way. A child who is not held in the mother's arms loses something valuable. There is a connection between the physical bodies of the mother and the child.

Therefore, the child should not live far away from the mother until at least the age of 14 or 15.

What the mother can give her child in one year, the relatives and the environment cannot provide in 20 years. Statistics show that children who have grown up until the age of 20 with the love of their parents possess nobler characters than those who have been deprived of their parents' love. The Law states: If the parents' love toward their child is weak, the child is more likely to become ill. In order for you to be healthy, the love of your mother needs to permeate your soul fully.

If the father and the mother have thought of committing a crime, then the child to whom they have given birth could think of this as well. Therefore, people need to be pure; that is to say, they need to have pure thoughts and feelings. When a person has a negative thought, it can incarnate with the child.

When you, as a mother, caress your child's head, say, "May Divine Thoughts enter you. May you carry Light to humankind. May you help your weaker brethren. May noble thoughts permeate you."

Whoever treats plants and animals well will be kind to people as well. This is the morality of the New Culture. The mother needs to teach the child that Divine Life permeates the whole of Nature: the flowers, the trees, the little flies, and the birds—everything.

As long as the children believe that the teacher does not lie, the teacher has authority. However, if the children notice that the teacher is not telling the truth, the teacher no longer has any authority over them. The same is true for parents.

Never speak in a negative way, "Do not do this! Do not do harm!" But instead say, "Do good." Instead of the words, "Do not lie!" say, "Speak the truth!" The less you speak about negative things the better. We should speak about the positive.

Sometimes when gifted children pass to the World beyond, they help from there and uplift less gifted children on Earth.

One brother asked the Master, "Is the relationship between family members maintained in future reincarnations?"
The Master answered:

It is retained according to the love existing between them.

There are three kinds of students, and you need to take these three types into consideration. First, there are students of the objective mind; their learning is based on facts, on observation. Second, there are students of the literary mind. These are students who can go from the facts to the laws. And third, there are students of the philosophical mind who go from the facts to the laws and from the laws to the principles. When you work with students, you need to consider these differences and know how to work with each group of students.

One woman, a teacher, said, "Because I cannot know who is from which group, and because I need to work with all students, I will provide food in my lectures for all three kinds of students: of facts, of laws, and of principles. In this way, everyone will perceive and comprehend that which is necessary for them."

The Master continued:

It is impossible to educate two people in the same manner. There exist as many different educational methods as there are people on Earth. In their education, the same principle can be applied, but never the same method. The failure of contemporary culture is due to the teacher using the same method of education for every child. This is a mechanical understanding.

If a child makes a face, do not pay attention. Before the teacher enters the classroom, the whole room is in a cloud of dust. When the teacher enters, he should not show discontent, but tell the students to open the window for a while. The primary thing is to not pay attention when children are not keeping quiet. For example, if one child has stolen a piece of fruit, the teacher should call him over and give him a whole bag of fruit. When working with children, one needs to be very patient.

One female teacher told me that when she asked a student to go to the blackboard to present the lesson, the child did not want to, and so the teacher became angry. However, if I were in her place, I would leave that student who was not willing to speak and would ask another one instead. If that child also does not want to, I would ask another one. On another occasion, I would ask that student who does not want to stand up now. And if that child does not want to participate again, I would let him or her be once more. After a few attempts, that student will be ready to get up and talk.

One sister asked, "If a student is noisy and disruptive, what should I do?"
The Master replied:

Go to this child and start a conversation. Ask, "What is the name of your father and of your mother? What does your father do? Do you have any brothers and sisters? What are their names? How old are they?" and so on. Then this child will become closer to you and will become well-behaved.

You need to possess those methods that cultivate good thoughts and feelings. The educational method of today is mechanical. It is only concerned with the sorting of facts.

Another sister asked, "The students ask me many questions and once a month I discuss them in class. How should I handle these questions?"
The Master responded:

First, let the students try to answer these questions by themselves. For those students who cannot answer, you will explain. The teacher needs to build on whatever the students already have within themselves. They carry within themselves great treasures. The teacher needs only to help these treasures be discovered. The teacher should tell this to the students and help them realize that they carry these treasures.

Speak to the students about the Love that brings health, about the Wisdom that liberates from contradictions, and about the Truth that liberates from limitations. The young generation can be set right only in the following three ways: through the Law of Love, through the Law of Wisdom, and through the Law of Truth. If you rely on the Law of Love, right Life will manifest. If you rely on the Law of Wisdom, right ideas and true knowledge will manifest. If you rely on the Law of Truth, Freedom will be brought forth. These three Laws need to be united into one.

For Love, you should begin with eating. What do I mean by this? For example, those who are eating need to share their food with others. This is the way the manifestation of Love begins. Love needs to begin with material things. Education should begin first with eating food, drinking water, breathing air, and absorbing light.

In the primary school, the children need to learn to create through their hearts and imaginations; and in the secondary school, through their hearts and minds.

If a teacher wants to put the students on the right path, but appeals only to their minds or their hearts, there will be no results. But if the teacher speaks to their souls as well, there will be good results.

When some students are not quiet and are naughty, it is because they know that the teacher does not love them. In such a case, the teacher needs to find one good aspect of their characters and begin to love them, and they will be transformed. When they are naughty, they are saying, "See, we are just as you think of us. We behave according to your opinion. You think that we are not good, do you not? And so, we are not."

In teaching, as well as in child-rearing, the child needs to learn from nature. Growing flowers should be used as a method in the new system of education. The children should study the flowers. They need to learn to love them. In every schoolyard, there should be a garden. It is necessary to have something that can serve as a channel for the Divine energies: cherries, apples, plums, pears, quinces, walnuts, and others. Yellow flowers transmit intelligence, red ones, vitality and health. When you encourage children to plant flowers—yellow, red, white—the flowers will educate them through their colors.

In every school, it is necessary to have a garden where children can work. We also need to know the right proportion—how many apple, plum, pear, and other fruit trees to plant—and what influence each tree will have. Each tree that the children grow influences them. In such a way, everything in nature acts educationally. Fruit trees teach children generosity, love, the service of giving and helping others. It is necessary to explain to the children that these trees give their fruit without asking for anything except that we sow their seeds.

Tell the children: "Be hard workers like the bees; be persistent like the plant; be strong and firm like the oak. Nobody should cause you to deviate from your ideas." Nature needs to be studied in such a manner. If you had given such explanations to the children, you would have obtained quite different results. All of these children would have given a new impulse to humankind.

The first subject with which to begin the new education is music. One thing that I would like is for Bulgarians to be musical. Music should work in their minds and in their hearts. In schools, special attention should be paid to music as an important educational factor.

Paneurhythmy[11] should be introduced into the schools. The one-hour-a-day used for Paneurhythmy will prepare a new generation.

You can create an organic geometry that would be very interesting for the students. This means: You should study the forms and lines that are encountered in Living Nature. In child education, every form has some influence in a specific way. A pear and a bunch of grapes are Angelic creations. Angels are the true artists. In the future, we will not talk to children about good and bad, about straight and curved lines, about singing in tune. There will be no moralizing. Geometry and music will be used to speak to them with drawings and lines about life. The figures and forms of Nature will be studied and interpreted.

If I were a teacher, I would write many children's stories—stories that would be accessible to them—to emphasize to the children, through these fairy tales, that when one does good, there is a gain, and that when one does wrong, that person loses strength, wealth, or beauty, and so on. I would tell them stories about stones, flowers, trees, and animals.

With children of genius, the soil in which they are sown is very rich. Their internal and external conditions are very good. In such conditions, it is very easy to work. With talented children, the soil is not quite as good; and still less so with the ordinary

---

11. "Paneurhythmy" or the "Cosmic Rhythm of Life" consists of movements with music and lyrics. It is performed outdoors.

children. And yet, from the ordinary children the talented can be brought forth; and from the talented, those of genius.

For every ten ordinary children, one who is talented is necessary; and for every ten talented children, one of genius is required. If there are no children of genius among the students, the last ones cannot develop correctly. The children of genius and the talented ones will be an inspiration to the ordinary ones.

I would place one dishonest child between two honest and conscientious ones. They will influence and educate such a child. I would place a child who is too generous between two selfish children, in order to distribute the goodness. In such a way, everyone will benefit.

One should not study only in order to earn one's living. Knowledge is necessary for human development and not for earning a living. One should love knowledge and not look at it as a profession. If a person thinks of knowledge as a condition for earning a living, that person will gradually become decadent. If one receives it with love, one will be uplifted. This needs to be applied in education.

The New Teaching that the Universal Brotherhood of Light—the Cosmic Council of Light—is bringing should first be applied in the schools. The right conditions in which to grow to maturity need to be given to the young people who are coming now. They come with great potential.

The Qualities of the Disciple

In the morning, a minor incident occurred. The world of personal feelings sometimes needs to express itself. In the afternoon, the disciples stood slightly embarrassed in front of the Master, feeling uneasy. The Master was silent for a while, then said:

When you enroll in the Divine School, the first two requirements are humility and obedience. If you desire to become disciples of the Brotherhood of Light, you need to have humility.

In addition to humility, four more qualities are necessary. The first of them is absolute honesty. Whatever one promises, one should fulfill. The second quality is goodness. This virtue makes a person steadfast. The third quality is intelligence. A disciple's mind needs to be flexible in order to immediately grasp all the subtleties. The fourth quality of the disciple is noble character.

Honesty, goodness, awareness, and noble character—these are the four qualities intrinsic to the disciple.

Pursue those great ideals that you have possessed since your childhood. The disciple should have a high ideal and pursue it steadfastly. This ideal leads to Knowledge, Freedom, and Love.

For one to make life meaningful, that person needs to be imbued with the Great Ideas of the Spirit. The greater the Ideas that one has received, the more meaningful one's life will be.

The disciples need to possess one essential idea. This does not mean that they need to think about it from dawn to dusk. It is sufficient to take a few minutes each day to think about it for them to bring it to realization in their lives.

The disciples need to develop their faith and hope. They need to be prepared for every kind of suffering. They need to develop sublime thoughts and feelings within themselves and endure all trials without hesitation.

If you follow the ways of the world, you will attain nothing, even if you were to walk the Earth for thousands of years. God gives blessings to the humble; that is, He gives them a right understanding of life.

I speak to those of you who are ready to be disciples, who are standing in front of the door of discipleship. You say, "We are disciples." Of course you are disciples. The grade you are in is significant. There are people in the elementary school, in the middle school, and in the secondary school. In addition, there are also differences from one student to another.

Work without letting external conditions disturb you. When one feels discouraged, it is because of those souls who have fallen behind and whose state of mind one has perceived.

Work and perseverance are required of all disciples.

It is difficult for an ill child to learn in school. As long as unhealthy issues exist within you, you are not in the Divine School. To be accepted into the School, you need to rid yourself of malice. The moment that people have freed themselves from it, they will be able to properly understand all things. You all need to progress, to be strong, to be able to bear insults and contempt.

When one does not express one's feelings, when one suppresses them, they ferment. To avoid this fermenting, it is necessary to transform and ennoble one's feelings. If one does not make a conscious effort, one will remain stagnant.

Human salvation lies in nothing less than the incineration of the residues that one carries within from the past. When people renounce the transitory desires of the flesh and surrender to the strivings of the spirit, only then can they evolve. Real attainment lies in diligent work on Earth, so that the Invisible World becomes interested in you and helps you.

There is a fairy tale about a certain hero who was digging a tunnel between two kingdoms. If, while he was digging, someone would come and engage him in a conversation, he would turn his head to look back, and the entire section that he had already dug would collapse, and he would need to start all over again. Therefore, dig and never turn back until you have dug the tunnel between the two kingdoms.

The disciple needs to depart from the sphere of temperament and enter the sphere of positive thought that brings inspiration. For this purpose, the spiritual student needs to contemplate. To contemplate means to connect with the consciousness of the Sublime Beings. People of the New Teaching need not be exalted, but they should be inspired.

Once you have entered the School, you need to be aware that you will undergo trials—be they large or small.

What is the situation of the disciples who have knowledge of the Laws? Each day they know all that is awaiting them for resolution. As disciples, you have much knowledge, but some of it you still need to apply. I will give you an example. A certain disciple went to see his Master. The latter said to him, "The first and most important task is to love God; the second is to love your neighbor." The disciple said to himself, "Now I have what I need to work on." He left, and for several years, he studied these Commandments. After that, he returned for new instructions.

All of you have plenty of assignments, but you go here and there to find someone else to resolve them for you. There are assignments that you might not be able to resolve by yourselves, but the assignments that you can resolve, you should do by yourselves.

Do not hasten. Do not eat cherries that are not yet ripe: leave them to ripen. Until things are ripe, work on them. Pick the cherries only when they are ripe. Until the grapes are ripe, take up the hoe and cultivate.

Could you be accepted as a member of a choir if you do not sing? Could you be admitted to an orchestra if you do not play an instrument? In the same way, you cannot be accepted into the World beyond if you are not ready. Otherwise, you will come to its gate and be sent away.

The Path of the Disciple

We were in the mountain with our beloved Master, sitting around a fire. The weather was foggy, damp, and cold. The flames of the fire rose high and strong, spreading warmth all around. These were the only things that interrupted the stillness of nature. During such moments, the small life melts into the Great One. Our last conversation was about the path of the disciple. For a while, there was silence. Everyone was listening within. There were many questions waiting to be answered.

Then the Master spoke:

The disciple of the Universal Brotherhood of Light walks simultaneously on the Path of Love, Wisdom, and Truth.

The first thing in the world that you need to understand is Love. You need to make a great experiment of it. If you do not meet your obligations with Love, you are neither friends nor disciples. If the disciples have no Love within their heart, they are not accepted into the School of the Universal Brotherhood of Light.

If, in Love, you cannot sprout like little seeds—if you are not prepared to sacrifice everything for Love—you will remain ordinary people. You can become everything else, but never a disciple of the Brothers Initiate—never the sons and daughters of the Kingdom of God. If one small act of your friend can tempt you to stray from the Path, you are not ready to be disciples.

Your first task for this entire year is to learn to love. The second task is to find a way to manifest this Love. Your third task is to learn under which conditions your Love should be made manifest. If the students in a class at school like each other, they will encourage each other. An interconnection through Love needs to come about between each of you.

For the disciple, one thing is important: to have the right connection with God. The forms of Love are many, but their purpose is one: the Knowledge of God. To come to know God—that is to say, Love in its Wholeness—is the job of the disciple. The disciple needs to try to come to know God.

It is said in the Scriptures, "If you do not become like these children, you cannot enter into the Kingdom of God."[12] This means that if you do not become pure, you cannot enter into the Kingdom of God. By "children" here—this is understood to mean "purity of heart." Man needs to carry within himself the qualities of a child: that is to say, Divine Purity. The Path to the Kingdom of God is Purity.

The Disciple

On another occasion, the Master said the following about being a disciple:

To live as a spiritual being is the assignment of every disciple. The assignment is difficult, but attainable.

The disciples see the soul within their fellowmen, but not the shortcomings because they know that the soul has no shortcomings.

---

12. See also Matthew 18:2–3, "Then Jesus called a little child to Him, set him in the midst of them, and said, 'Assuredly, I say to you, unless you are converted and become as little children, you will by no means enter the Kingdom of Heaven.'"

Only those who remain one and the same, whether in hell or in Paradise, are able to perceive Divine Love.

Those who can reconcile sorrow and joy within themselves are disciples. We easily become discouraged in times of contradiction. Things might change on the surface, but we should remain unchangeable.

It is expected of you to be self-controlled. Should you be ill-disposed, in order to retain your peace, say to yourselves, "I dwell in the World of absolute harmony. I am surrounded by Sublime Intelligent Beings who are ready to help me."

Man needs to understand one thing: the extraordinary in Life is that which brings joy.

Someone then asked, "What will man do when he becomes perfect?" To this the Master replied:

After man has become perfect, only then will he come to his real work. The disciples carry the New within. Wherever they go, they bring light and a special fragrance. Without speaking about God, all people will recognize that God dwells within them. They never speak about ordinary things, yet whatever they say carries weight. The Bulgarians call such people fortuitous. Within their beings, they carry a great, sublime idea. They are helpful to everyone and wish everyone well.

In the springtime of the spiritual student's life, that person resembles a garden with beautiful flowers, visited by butterflies—the human beings. In the fall, the soul of the disciple is like a garden full of ripe fruits.

Health

Nature is an inexhaustible reservoir of energy from which man can draw in order to maintain his health. The Master provided many rules and methods for making use of the forces of living Nature to become healthful.
He explained:

For someone to think rightly, he should be healthy so that his focus will not be undermined by disease. Tell yourselves, "My body should be healthy; it is a corpuscle in the great cosmic body." When unorganized matter is introduced into it, death follows. Man is healthy when all the matter of his body is organized. The unorganized matter in the human body brings death. For example: you are doubtful, you are angry; and if you are not careful, the doubt, anger, and hatred will introduce unorganized matter into your body.

If you want to make use of Nature's forces to fortify your health, the best months of the year to do this are April, May, and June. These months bring a vast amount of wealth. If one makes use of Nature's forces, one can fortify oneself within a month. During the spring months, it is beneficial for a person to dig and cultivate the soil for some time each day.

When it rains in the summer, one should go outside and, for a while, be soaked by the rain. The rain in May, June, and July is suffused with electromagnetism or prana. One rain shower is worth ten ordinary baths. Four or five such showers can heal a person from disease. After you have been soaked by the rain, change into dry clothes.

The body's pores should always be open. The first task of the disciple is to keep the pores of the body open. This can be accomplished through sweating and drinking hot water. The hot water that one drinks helps to dissolve calcifications of the body. In addition to this, the hot water induces sweating, through which toxins are eliminated from the body. The farmer who works in the field and sweats should change into dry clothes. He should carry a spare dry shirt with him.

It is advisable for an ill person to carry water from the source in an earthen jug. Water that is taken in this way will improve the circulation of the blood, strengthen the respiratory system, and induce sweating. In addition, through the carrying of this water, one will be able to absorb its electromagnetism. A person can be healed of many diseases in this way.

Faith and Knowledge

During an afternoon conversation, the interrelationship between faith and knowledge was explained.
The Master said:

Faith is related to knowledge. We can obtain access to positive knowledge only through faith. Faith precedes knowledge, and knowledge precedes faith. You cannot believe unless you have knowledge, and you cannot know unless you have faith. There is this Law: Through faith in God man attracts Wisdom. Only people of genius have faith; talented people have beliefs, whereas ordinary people have superstitions. As your faith grows, so does your knowledge. As soon as you grow in knowledge, you grow in faith as well. If faith becomes stronger, but knowledge does not grow, this is not real faith, but belief. And thus, as an inner striving of the spirit, faith leads people to the realm of true knowledge. The basis of one's faith lies within the knowledge from past centuries that has been tested, proven, and examined.

There exists a connection between the mind of man and the Consciousness of God. Faith is based upon this connection. To have faith in God means to make a connection with Him, to establish a connection with Him. The Power of God then flows through man. True faith, therefore, indicates the creation of a continuous connection with God. Since a relationship with God is established through this connection, His Powers flow to us. For this reason, I call faith the Law of Nourishment. The Law says: Faith is the connection by which the Divine forces flow into our souls.

What is faith? Faith indicates the opening of my window so that clean air and light may enter. This means that faith makes it possible for man to receive the Divine forces. Through faith, man draws the forces that rejuvenate him.

While we are living on Earth, we are surrounded by the Divine, by the Eternal Life. If you could connect with the whole flow of the Great Life, even if you were on your deathbed, Life would begin to flow within you again. For this, one needs to have faith stronger than the greatest adversity that interferes with the balance of the human organism.

Faith in God indicates that you are connected with the whole of Life. If this were the case, everyone would come and give you help. This, everyone can test. If you are not capable of coping with the difficulties of life through faith, then this is not true faith. If I believe in God, Who abides within me, I will believe in every human being.

The dove symbolizes the Spirit of God: it is a symbol of innocence. The lamb is a symbol of meekness. The grain of wheat is a symbol of patience, and the virgin is a symbol of purity. Innocence, meekness, patience, and purity—these are the qualities of faith through which all the obstacles in the world can be overcome.

A person can walk through life and apply Love only through Faith. Faith has practical applications in Life. If you are in bankruptcy, if you are ill, if you have other hardships, apply living faith and everything will be overcome.

When the rich believes that he might become impoverished, he is unhappy. When the poor believes that he might become rich, he is happy. This Law applies to everything.

Some people believe that faith is a complete and static process. No, faith is a continuous process.

You complain that you lack something. Be glad that you do not have this. If you do not have this or that, have faith in God; you need to have faith in yourself as well.

The slightest doubt that is born in someone's mind with respect to the Divine, has the power to postpone a Divine blessing for at least one day. We are always hesitating. There is a Law that is unknown to people: As soon as doubt enters you, as soon as the slightest doubt penetrates you—even if no one else would perceive it—you lose the Divine blessing. The slightest doubt that might enter your mind will draw the greatest adversity to you.

When someone is ill, if one complains, has doubts, and does not have any peace, then that person will not recover, not being able to bear even the smallest of trials.

There is no heroism in doubt. Doubt is faint-heartedness. Doubt is a setback for those souls who are lagging behind in their development.

Cease to have faith, and you will understand what faithlessness means. When a person attains living faith, that person changes fundamentally: his eyes become clear and his facial muscles become flexible. Something special emanates from him. This person becomes compassionate toward people's suffering, tender and attentive toward all. When one has this faith, Love comes to visit.

Divine Providence

To those who were worried about the next day and were fearful of its uncertainties, the Master explained:

Intelligent Nature has foreseen everything. We need to learn to use what God has created. Today you have satisfied your hunger, and yet you say, "Who will provide for tomorrow?" Tomorrow is provided for. There is a wellspring here, and yet further away there is another wellspring, and over there is a third one. God knows what He has provided, and we need to observe the progression of things.

We need not concern ourselves with when the spring will come or when the Sun will set or rise. We need not concern ourselves with what might happen. Man is the weakest being that God protects; He does this so that man may come to know of the Existence of Divine Providence.

Who would raise the children if it were not for their mothers' and fathers' love? With birds, both the mother and the father keep the eggs warm; then when the chicks hatch, the mother and father bring food until the chicks' wings become stronger. What is it that makes the birds provide for their chicks? It is the Divine.

There exist those who watch over us and protect us. All the Beings who love you watch over you. Often you interrupt your connection with the Invisible World—with those Beings who love you—and in this way, you start to doubt yourselves in life.

You are at school. The air, the water, the light, the heat, and the cold in nature are tools of the great school to which you have been admitted. These are temporary tools. Above them is the Divine Spirit guiding people on the path of their development.

Every human soul you meet is sent by God to help you. All obstacles that you encounter are opportunities for the Invisible World to help you. Be thankful to the Enlightened Beings who watch over you as small and weak beings, helping you constantly. The time will come when all your affairs will be put in order.

Nature employs different methods for every student, but the purpose is one and the same: to strengthen man so that he may endure all conditions and evolve. God has placed man under specific conditions so that he will develop particular virtues. Each virtue is developed under conditions specific for it: one virtue under less favorable conditions, yet another under more favorable.

Whoever wants to develop Love needs to embrace the least important position in the world.

Think of everything in the world as having been created well. Think of everything that happens to you as working for your good. This awareness needs to penetrate deeply into your mind, heart, soul, and will. Often Providence sends some great suffering to someone in order to save that person from an even greater adversity.

Some people demonstrate an aptitude for science, arts, or for some other field; yet in their moral and spiritual life, they are underdeveloped. This indicates that they are behind in their development in general. In such cases, their friends from the

Invisible World will inspire them with more sublime gifts in order to lift them out of this lower condition in which they find themselves.

God provides for everything. Many believe that they are abandoned, that there is no one who takes an interest in them. If they would understand the interrelationship that exists among all living beings, absolute peace and harmony would reign within their souls. This interrelationship, this inner bond among beings, is such that even for the least one, a blessing is provided that uplifts him. God abandons no one. Even under the worst conditions, God has a plan for every being that is still unknown to humankind. It is good that they do not know of the plan that God has destined for all living beings. They need only to know one thing alone: everything that God intends to do is good. What are God's ideas? How will they be realized? This will remain a secret for all times and epochs.

God has foreseen the conditions necessary for your mental, emotional, and spiritual development. Regardless, He has left a specific sphere of activity exclusively for you in which He never interferes. When you work within this sphere, He watches from a distance and retreats immediately afterward. This is the sphere in which man is free; outside of this sphere, man is not free. As soon as he departs from it and enters another sphere, he already feels restricted.

Man is a being who is exposed to great dangers. Every day when you eat or when you walk, you are exposed to great dangers. You need to be grateful that Providence is watching over you. If it were not for Providence, many misfortunes would have befallen us. Every good work in the world has been done by the Intelligent Sublime Beings. Not one good work is done by chance. Many think that things happen arbitrarily. Someone asks, "Who will help me?" There is Someone to help you.

Even when coincidences and chance occurrences cannot be explained, it does not mean that they are arbitrary. These are Manifestations of a Higher World, and yet they are reflected in our world as well. Because they do not occur often, we call them "chance occurrences." They do not follow the laws generally known to people; other Laws govern these chance occurrences.

At present, it is difficult to persuade people that Divine Providence exists in the world. Providence does exist in the world. Even with regard to the greatest contradictions, there still is a Law that determines what needs to take place.

You are royal sons and daughters. The Sun rises and asks every day, "How are you?" The wind blows, the water flows. Be grateful that you travel throughout the Universe like tourists, without money. The Earth is a great ship. At present, it has approximately 50–60 smokestacks and travels at a speed of 29 km per second. And yet, you are dissatisfied and say, "Why am I on this ship?"

Every person needs to rely only upon what God has given him; he should consider other people as additional conditions for him. God's blessing can only come in two ways: He can bless you at the beginning of your journey, and He can bless you at the end as well. We have been given so many blessings by God. To every person, at least one thing on Earth is given; but not knowing its purpose, he suffers.

The good things are in front of us. What we have learned until now are the things of childhood. Man has not yet begun to learn, to attain virtues, knowledge, and artistic mastery.

Someone might say, "If God provides for you, you do not need to work." No, this is incorrect thinking. God will provide for me only after I have planted two or three hundred trees. God will provide for me after I have completed my university studies. God will provide for me when I work in the vineyard and become an experienced vine-grower. God provides for His wise children who work, think rightly, and listen to Him.

In Africa, a traveler encountered a lion that was ready to jump on him. He heard the voice of his mother saying, "You have matches; set the grass on fire." He set fire to the grass, and in this way, he saved himself. The higher consciousness of his mother accomplished this.

There is the case of a man who had fallen asleep in a field. A snake was just about to bite him when a bee stung the man and woke him up. In this way, he was saved, as the bee did him a good service.

A man was traveling and robbers who were stealing from wealthy travelers captured him. When they took him to their leader, he was told, "We do not have orders to steal from you." And so, they let him go. This means that God had told the leader, "Let him go free!"

For God's one desire to be realized, all worldly laws should collapse.

A father who was disabled had only one daughter, and she departed for the World beyond. After her departure, many people began to bring the father food and take care of him.

A young man was left with only one *lev*[13] and said to himself, "What can I do with one *lev*? After I have spent it, what am I going to do?" Meanwhile, a beggar approached the young man and asked him for help. Something said to this youth, "Give it to him!" And so, he gave the last of his money. "I gave it to him," recounted the young man, "and I thought to myself: What God gives… A short while after that, a friend of mine that I had not seen for ten years invited me to his home for dinner." Give and salvation will come from somewhere else.

Visitation by God

The people of the world cannot change the Divine Order of things. In spite of the war and the destruction, spring came again. The meadows were turning green, the first flowers were blossoming, and the flower buds on the apple trees were ready to open. The spiritual New Year, March 22, was drawing near. The small homestead became greatly enlivened. From everywhere, guests, brothers, and sisters started to arrive. A shelter for all was improvised. Temelko's home was filled with people. This was a cordial gathering of friends, and all faces radiated with joy and goodness. The unity of Love, for which all people are longing, filled their hearts and shone on the faces of everyone.

Early in the morning at 5 AM, on the festive day, we gathered in the upper floor of the house. The room, the hallway, the terrace, the steps, and the yard were all filled with people.

---

13. *Lev* (plural *leva, levove*) is a Bulgarian currency.

We all attended the morning sermon, and participated in the prayers and songs. Then the Master gave the lecture, "The New in Life," published later in "The Testament of Love," Vol. 1.

After the lecture was finished, we all climbed to a peak above the village where we performed the morning callisthenic exercises followed by Paneurhythmy. Then, while songs were being sung, everyone greeted the Master by kissing his hand.

The day was beautiful, the sky clear. The Sun rose, and the ground felt its warmth. The life around us pulsated in harmony with the Great One. On this luminous day, we saw the signs of another Spring for which all souls wait and long. We all wished for the New Life of Love, Brotherhood, Peace, and Freedom to come for all nations on the face of the Earth.

After breakfast we gathered again around the Master, singing more songs. Music is a universal language.

Someone asked the Master, "In what way does God reveal Himself to man?"

The Master answered:

When God reveals Himself to someone, He sends him to work. If a person has the desire to live a righteous life, God should be the ideal of his life. Do you think that God will come to live within your heart if disorder and chaos exists within it or if you quarrel with this one or that one? In such a case, He will enter into your heart and retreat immediately.

A visitation by God is the greatest moment in the life of a soul. As short as it might be, it will have significance for eternity.

There is a way in which God reveals Himself to His chosen ones. The great musician reveals himself only to his talented students. The great artist, poet, or sculptor reveals himself only to his gifted students, never to the ordinary ones. Therefore, if we are prepared to devote our energy, life, health, and everything else to God and are able to endure all hardships and suffering without ever doubting Him, God will reveal Himself to us.

The one who has come into contact with the Divine World is prepared to become a martyr and says, "I am ready to sacrifice for God!"

If one of you comes to feel, even for a moment, God's Presence in the way I know it—in the way I have experienced it—with the slightest gesture of his hand he would be able to pacify an enraged mob that is rioting, and all would quiet down and become silent. If, in such an instant, you were to stand in front of an army of one hundred thousand, all cannons would become silent. Such a great thing is the Presence of God!

There is one ideal that you need to attain: to be able to feel, at least for an instance, what the Great Love of God is. To come to know the connection among all beings, from the least to the greatest, this is a great moment. If you had heard the Voice of God, you would no longer be an ordinary individual.

The meaning of Life is to wait for the time when God, the Absolute Reality, will visit you. You have waited for this for years and years. Wait yet a little longer; wait until Love comes.

Life is neither physical nor spiritual. It has physical and spiritual forms, but Life is Divine.

Beauty is not in the forms, but in the Divine Life that is hidden within them. In every life, there is a moment when Reality can be sensed. You will then pass from one state into another. Only then will you come to understand the Great that is hidden within you. Out of the duration of your entire earthly life, only one year—or one month, one week, one day, one hour, one minute, one second—is set aside when Love is able to visit you. If you use this moment, you will attain all goals. If you cannot make use of it, your entire life is wasted. Everything else is only a preparation for this moment.

When Love comes to visit you, it will stay for one-thousandth of a second. In this instant, Love will have seeded something within you. Then what has been sown within you will grow.

The wise person can hardly withstand one minute in the presence of Love; yet for an ordinary person, even one-thousandth of a second is considerable.

What people call love is only a consequence of Love.

When you receive a letter from God, you will have eyes like the Angels have. And whomever you look at with such eyes, an awakening will dawn within that person.

Paneurhythmy

Beginning on March 22, the first day of spring, we start to dance Paneurhythmy every morning soon after sunrise. Paneurhythmy consists of movements set to music as introduced by the Master. It is danced in pairs forming a circle. The movements are flowing, rhythmic, and harmonious, with each one a manifestation of an idea.

In many of his lectures, the Master provided explanations and clarifications for Paneurhythmy. He also suggested other physical exercises for us. Here is a conversation in which he gave some additional explanations:

Do physical exercises for at least 10 to 15 minutes daily. Those who do not exercise now will need to exercise at one time or another.

Our thoughts and feelings should be present in every single movement. Every movement you make influences Nature. The slightest movement of one's index finger, for example, affects Nature in her wholeness. The waves of radiant energy that emanate from the fingers will circumnavigate the Earth. In the end they will return to the person from whom they have emanated, with an increase in the good or bad sense. Knowing this, one should be cautious with regard to one's actions. In addition to this, the activities of the various organs of the human body exert certain influences upon the mind, the heart, and the will of man.

There are movements that develop the mind, others the heart, and still others, the will. One lifts up his hands while exercising and this is an appeal to the Intelligent Forces of Nature for help.

We have close to perfect conditions for Paneurhythmy.

For Paneurhythmy to be performed well, it is necessary that the consciousness be focused.

One should first learn the basic movements and then proceed to the more complicated ones.

Paneurhythmy is a method that deals with the problems of the past, the present, and the future. In the circle of Paneurhythmy the past, the present, and the future come together into a single present moment.

The music for the Paneurhythmy sequence, "Step by Step," is in a minor scale. Taking a step forward or to the side is related to departure—in other words, to involution. Stepping back to the starting position is related to returning—in other words, to evolution. In the exercise, "The Rays of the Sun," moving forward toward the center represents receiving from the Center. Moving away from the center represents giving back what we have received.

The Advanced Beings from Above also dance Paneurhythmy; they make similar movements, and if our movements are in accordance with theirs, we will connect with them and receive their blessing. In order to make this connection, it is not only necessary that our Paneurhythmy movements be correct and rhythmic, but that harmony exists among the mind, heart, and the will of the performer. The performer should possess Love, Purity, and an enlightened state of the spirit.

The way in which Paneurhythmy exists Above cannot be done here on Earth because humankind is not yet ready for it. We are given as much as is possible for us in its most accessible form.

No other music or movement is as accessible as Paneurhythmy. In the future, Paneurhythmy will be introduced and practiced in other countries as well. A Swiss man has studied various kinds of dances, folk dances, as well as movements set to music practiced by different nations of the world. When he visited Bulgaria, he commented that he found the most perfect combination of music and movements in Paneurhythmy.

A special school for the study of the movements and songs of Paneurhythmy is needed.

The First Violinist

Deep bonds of relationship exist between man and Nature. Man needs to safeguard these bonds. The rising of the Sun—especially in the spring—is the most beautiful of moments, and we should not miss it. The Master would go for a walk almost every morning accompanied by friends and disciples. We would meet the first rays of the Sun from the beautiful mountain peak. The

Master had spoken often about the Sun, yet there was always something new to say about it:

The aura of every living being that rises early before sunrise, and works with love, is beautiful. If one does not rise early and does not work, he will be ordinary and "miserably attired." All living beings are expected to do some work. The more conscious they are, the greater is the effort that they need to apply. If someone wishes to be young, he needs to rise early from sleep when Love whispers to him to arise. Love says to him, "Arise before the sunrise."

During springtime, it is important to make use of the renewing powers of Nature. Even one open window will have a certain impact. However, if you are aware of the presence of an intelligent being opening it, then the influence will be of quite a different character. I will interpret this for you: every morning the Sun rises in the east, and in the rising of the Sun, we need to perceive the Intelligent Beings.

To meet the sunrise is always beneficial, even when the Sun is covered by clouds because its energy permeates the clouds. In all cases, the sunrise brings an uplift to man.

This living energy only comes in the morning. For every task, there is a fixed appointed time. Those who desire to become great need to go out every morning and greet the Sun. They need to allow these powerful forces to work upon them.

Get up early! Go out! Greet the Sun! What wonderful things are hidden within the rising Sun! If one goes out regularly in the morning, one will receive inspiration.

The first violinist of Nature is the Sun. The first ray of the Sun is the first aria. If you observe the rising of the Sun without feeling its music and its message, you are in the position of the financier who adds and subtracts numbers—who makes calculations all day—without gaining anything.

Expose your back to the Sun; contemplate upon the Sun that you may receive its energy. During those times when you are ill-disposed, stop whatever you are doing, go out, turn your back to the Sun for a while, and then continue your work. You will receive from the Sun something that no science or philosophy can give you. The light is the Sun's outward aspect, but within the

Light, there is something quite subtle—within it are the vital Intelligent Forces of Nature.

The Inner Work of the Disciple

It was a calm, clear spring evening. We were seated comfortably around our dear Master under the trees in the yard. The stars were visible through the branches. Cricket sounds were audible. There are times which the World of Supreme Consciousness prepares from afar. There are times when the sounds of the world appear to be in perfect polyphonic harmony. We sang a few songs. And then in the silence that fell, someone brought up the question about the inner work of the disciple.
The Master said:

Prayer is the most powerful act of human existence. It brings one's thoughts, feelings, and will into focus. Such a prayer is powerful—it works miracles. Prayer is the most beautiful work! It is a conversation with God. There is no more important moment than when one beholds God's Face! How beautiful it is, upon rising in the morning, to talk with the Immortal One!

Those who are not interested in God gradually lose their vital forces and fall behind. While thinking about the Angels, you are in the Angelic World. While thinking about God, you are in the Divine World. We live in whatever world we are thinking about.

One environment tolerates you for a certain period of time, but after that, you move into another one. Fish were in the water and after a while, the most advanced of them moved into a less dense environment. Because of the great limitations in which the fish found themselves, the idea entered their minds that another, more favorable life existed in a less dense environment above the water. And in such a way, they became birds. When human beings find themselves living under restricted conditions, they also strive toward God. You strive today, again tomorrow, and finally you enter into a more sublime Life. The idea creates the form.

The Law states: If you think about a good person, into your mind, light will appear, and into your heart, warmth. If you think about a bad person, into your mind, darkness will appear, and into your heart, cold. This Law is related to our relationship with God. When you connect with God, Light will enter your consciousness and profound peace, your soul. Should you connect with the Angels, again you will be filled with luminous thoughts and sublime feelings. When you think about the plants and animals, you will be influenced by them as well. The Law states: You connect with whatever you are thinking about.

Through prayer, people communicate with God and the Advanced Beings. God will then tell them about Love and about the Intelligent Light Beings. When you arise in the morning, direct your consciousness to the One Reality. After that, regardless of what you are doing—be it studying or hoeing—ask the Invisible World for help. Conversely, should you immediately begin to labor in the morning, you will forget about the Great Reality, about the Intelligent Forces of Nature. There is a Law that states: When one directs one's consciousness to the Reality, it abides within; and when one directs one's consciousness to the shadows, one lives in the shadows.

Prayer and contemplation are expressions of the soul's striving to ascend to a higher place. In this way, an influx of mental energy will come, and with this, the work of the conscious human life will become easier. Prayer and contemplation indicate the transmitting of your report to that Supreme Center from which you have descended. What will you report on? On the work you have accomplished. In response to your report, a correct exchange between your thoughts and feelings and those of the Beings of the Sublime World will take place. If someone thinks that prayer, contemplation, and meditation are not necessary, that person is on the wrong path.

When you pray, you determine your own status. When you pray, you are in continuous connection with the whole of Creation. Knowing this, do not obstruct that natural process within you.

Through prayer, we acquire energy from the Divine World. The Law of Prayer is similar to the Law of Nourishment.

When deprived of food, one feels that something is lacking. When the soul is deprived of prayer, a need is also felt. Prayer represents the inner necessity of the soul.

Prayer is reality, not a shadow. What at any given moment gives strength to the mind, heart, soul, and spirit is something real.

Prayer is the conscious work of the human soul. When one prays, the soul steps beyond the ordinary consciousness. We can describe this process as the "emergence" from the narrow confines in which one lives.

Prayer resembles the extending of the amoeba's pseudopodia to catch its food. This is a continuous process. For the New to enter into you, you need to direct your mind each morning toward the Great Center of the Universe.

Prayer is similar to the Law of Providing Water. Through it, all good influences are drawn to you. When you are praying, everything around you should grow and develop. When one understands the Great Law of Prayer, that person will become a true human being; he will become one of the Great Initiates.

Are you aware of how the Angels pray?

Prayer is the first method through which we begin to learn the Divine Language. If you do not pray, you will never learn this Language. Through prayer, we study God's Language. We still do not know God's Language.

Real prayer implies concentration and seclusion. Nobody should be aware that you are praying. When the merchant is praying, he should forget about his business and all of his dealings.

On another occasion the Master said:

Prayer is one of the methods through which one comes to know God as Love. It leads to Love, that good and sublime state that you have attained. That you help and forgive your fellowman, that you uplift the fallen one—this is the result of the time you have spent in your secret chamber.

People need to pray so that God does not turn His Face away from them. It is terrifying when God hides His Face from someone! Then darkness and solitude will set in unlike any living experience that person has had.

The saint receives his Knowledge through prayer, contemplation, meditation, and experience. The saint prays for a long time, in order to become inspired and to receive new ideas.

Wherever you are, in whatever situation you may be, take half an hour or an hour to think about God. In such a way, your consciousness expands. For one to think about the Great Origin—about the Great Center of Creation—is worth more than all the material wealth available on Earth. Thinking about God also renews and rejuvenates the physical body because its energy extends to the body as well.

If someone says that one does not need to think about God, one becomes like an orphaned child who, being without a father and mother, goes around in torn clothes, homeless and friendless. Then the vermin begin to attack and one loses one's bearing in life. I am speaking figuratively. I will explain: when someone stops thinking about God, one becomes vulnerable and the dark, inferior beings begin to attack.

One cannot attain anything, if one does not pray. Pray that more Light may enter into your consciousness.

There are no beings more highly developed than the Angels. The next phase that humankind will enter is the Angelic Phase. Then our dense bodies will be transformed into ones that are more dynamic. They will be composed of matter that is more refined. How will these be created? Through prayer, contemplation, and meditation. In other words, prayer is a method of organizing the spiritual body—the new body in which one will live.

I ask contemporary scientists and philosophers how many times each day they think about God. The reason for the misfortune of people today is that they do not think of God. Prayer is the method for resolving the most difficult problem. Doubt, suspicion, skepticism, and many other negative thoughts and feelings are the cause for most of the diseases of humankind. Through prayer, one overcomes these negative conditions. There is a miraculous power in prayer.

If someone recites a verse from the Scriptures with the willingness to understand, that is sufficient for Christ to come and help that person. He will bring Light into his mind and put his affairs in order.

Prayer increases the vibration of the human aura. In this way, we become inviolable to the inferior influences surrounding us. Through prayer, people safeguard themselves from the anxieties and fears of the world. They cannot penetrate them.

When you pray for one of your good desires to be fulfilled, the Invisible World always helps. You are ill, pray to God, and in a short time, you will recover. There is nothing in the whole world that one desires that God has not granted. The world represents the desires of these small beings. God has granted all their desires.

If all people would have turned to God with the supplication, "God, we have used all methods of putting the world into order; tell us the way of doing this," and if they would have prayed from the heart, the method would have come. This is the easiest of methods; but when applied, God will come into the world and help people.

There is no living being in the world, large or small, whose appeal God has not answered. There is no case in which God has not answered your mail, regardless of its disorderly state. Put your mail in order! The mail from the Invisible World leaves on time; but while it is en route to Earth, the letters become lost somewhere and are delayed for months.

How beautiful it is for us to realize that we occupy a place in the Mind of God. When we have this awareness and turn to God with a plea for something, our prayer is received.

Ask God to abide within you and to reveal Himself through you. The only One who transforms people is God.

All people are searching for the meaning of life. The meaning of life lies in one's communication with God.

The most favorable time for prayer is the early hours of the morning—for example, 3 AM or 5 AM. The psalmist wrote, "God, I called upon You at early dawn."[14] This means that I will

---

14. See also Psalm 88:13, "But to You I have cried out, Oh Lord, and in the morning my prayer comes before You."

occupy myself in the morning before sunrise with the most sublime work—communion with the Great Center of Creation—to receive the energy necessary to accomplish my day's work.

Wherever you go, whatever work you begin, you need energy. If you let the world influence you, the mundane affairs of your life will pull you off course. When you arise in the morning, you need to have one essential thought—that you may open like a flower. Christ spent the whole night in prayer.[15] Why? Because during those hours, He was replenishing Himself with energy—as one would recharge a battery—for what He had expended during the day.

You need to pray. You should work on yourself to be ready for the New that is coming into the world. How long should you pray? Continuously. Prayer does not imply that you need to stop and pray the entire day. You can be in motion and pray at the same time. Work does not exclude prayer. You can pray constantly. Only those who abide by the Law of Love, and only they alone, have the disposition to pray. Whatever they are doing, they are always in prayer. In other words, in the life of a loving person, everything is prayer.

A mother says that she has no time left for prayer because of her children. The one who cuts trees says that he has no time left to pray because of his job. The one who writes says the same. People say that they have no time for prayer, contemplation, and meditation. In reality, the prayer comes first, and then all other things follow. First you breathe and then you work. Otherwise, you cannot finish your work.

Those who do not pray are not good students. The laziest, the least capable, and the least talented students are those who do not pray. Give a topic to a student who is limited, and that student will say, "Where did this topic come from?"

You need to pray when you are in good spirits, as well as when you are in a conflicted state or when there is darkness in your consciousness.

---

15. See also Mark 1:35, "Now in the morning, having risen a long while before daylight, He went out and departed to a solitary place; and there He prayed."

Anyone can go into seclusion even when among others. Seclusion is not only an external process.

I will give you a principle: For every person, there is a Divine Wave that uplifts him. When you arise in the morning, do not hurry to go and work in the field immediately. Stop, work inwardly that this Divine Wave may come, and then you may go and begin your work. You could be the most ordinary of people, but when the Divine Spirit visits you, you will achieve something beyond yourself.

If thought, emotion, and will do not take part in prayer, it is not genuine prayer. To go into your secret chamber means to enter into your virgin soul. Then you will understand the deep meaning of all things and the reason for your existence. The more precise a prayer is, the higher the consciousness is.

When you are in difficulty, I say: Pray that you may connect with the Intelligent Light Beings who can help you. Some people say that they are praying, but have received no answer. The reason is that their consciousness is not yet awakened. The human consciousness is similar to a radio that is transmitting and receiving sonic waves from the Universe. Scientists say that there is a belt above the Earth that deflects the waves and obstructs them from rising. This could be used to explain why the prayers of some people are unable to rise sufficiently. The more awakened and the more evolved someone's consciousness is, the greater the possibility is for one's prayer to be received.

What is required of you to connect with the Invisible World? You need to have your own radio. You already have it. When you direct your prayerful thoughts upward, you should safeguard yourself from rapacious waves. Doubt, disbelief, and a lack of Love are waves of an unfavorable character that are formed in the astral world. They have a harmful impact upon the human spirit. The difficulties of human existence result from attacks by these rapacious waves. They have influence over one's prayers and obstruct them from ascending. They obstruct the good aspirations as well.

Praying is better when one is persecuted. When you are subjected to great suffering, trials, and persecutions, then you pray as you should.

Until the furnace of the heart is fired up, a prayer cannot reach God. One cannot pray in an impure place. You need to go to a pure place. Prayers need to be transmitted from a pure place. When one is praying to the Invisible World, one should be exact. Otherwise, a prayer is like the application form that does not state what is being requested. In such a case, it remains without consequence.

If I were to pray now, I would ask God for Strength, Knowledge, Wisdom, Love, Truth, and Freedom.

When someone prays, one should ask for the least thing that is, at the same time, the most essential. A prayer is received, when God's Will is taken into consideration. Conduct the following experiment: concentrate on what is deep within yourself and say, "My Lord, I am ready right now to fulfill Your Will that inspires every living being in the world." Or say, "If I have found favor in You, let me feel Your Joy in the name of Your Love, Wisdom, and Truth." Do you know what you will feel? You will feel such an excitement as you have never felt before. You will feel reborn. In a moment, you can transform your countenance.

Turn to the Lord and say, "Lord, place me in the Fire of Your Love." Or say, "Lord, what do You want me to do that Your Kingdom may triumph on Earth and Your Name be sanctified among all humankind?"

One very important Law states: When you pray for someone, your prayer gains miraculous power only when it is accompanied by Love for that person.

Now, let's concentrate for five minutes and send one good thought throughout the entire world. The Law states: If you send this thought rightly, the work that you will accomplish will be equal to all of the work that you have accomplished throughout your entire life.

Communion with Nature

Wherever the Master might be, some work would always be created. With his presence, he would gradually, imperceptibly, without making plans ahead of time, improve our surroundings. Therefore, quite naturally, everything around him would become more beautiful.

To work with the Master was not only pleasant, but the work would acquire a special significance. Everything we did was imbued with profound meaning. The Master imparted a specific idea to even the most insignificant work. He observed everything that was happening around him: the weather and how it would change, the difficulties that would be encountered in the work and how we could overcome them, how many of us and who exactly should participate. We all had the feeling that he was communicating with the Intelligent World that was invisible to us. Its Language was also unknown to us, but at times, the Master would provide the translation. For him, all things were fine instruments that would indicate which Law of Intelligent Nature was at work in any given moment.

The wise person who abides in the Unity of Life can intervene sometimes to divert certain forces or give way to others, or call upon the action of one Law or another. In such a case, he is acting as a representative of the Great Consciousness. His actions appear to be both prophetic and miraculous. Being able to change the pace of great events, it is not necessary to move mountains to attract a certain Law of Living Nature; it is sufficient to move a small stone if one does it with knowledge and understanding.

While studying the steep slope in front of the house, the Master discovered a small wellspring. The water was barely dripping. He caught it carefully, gathering it all in a small basin. He then built a path to it, complete with steps. He implanted an Idea in this work and named the wellspring, "The Wellspring of Good," the Divine Center that directs Life itself.

When the wellspring was dedicated, the Master said:

Life is a continuous process of revealing the Divine blessings. The whole of Life is a constant discovery of things that have been lost.

We accomplished the work of the day successfully, rejoicing in the sense of completeness that one experiences when working in accordance with Living Nature and receiving from her everything needed, in other words, when one has given rightly and has received rightly.

After completing the work, we gathered around our beloved Master beneath the large walnut tree. We stood in silence for a while, listening to the voice of awakening life that was flowing through every branch, through every bud of every tree. The first birds of spring had arrived and were joyously chirping in the branches.

With an expression of gratitude on his face, the Master looked around and said:

You should be glad for everything that surrounds you—for the wellsprings, the stones, and the Sun.

From Nature, we will learn the Law of Perfection and how to apply it in life. Everything exerts an influence upon us. You stop in front of a wellspring and the wellspring influences you. You stop in front of carnations in bloom and these influence you too. It is important that when you stop at the wellspring or at carnation blossoms, that your consciousness participates and is not distracted by the thinking of other things.

Connect with Nature and receive from her knowledge and energy. You need to connect with Nature; if you make the right connection with her, you will learn in one day as much as you would from a professor in twenty years. Nature is generous to those who love her and to those whom she loves. If a person does not love Nature, she will wait for as long as necessary, until the time comes when that person's consciousness awakens.

I desire that you connect with the Forces of Intelligent Nature and with all good people on Earth. When you accomplish this, energy will begin to flow to you from all directions.

When we are able to perceive and sense things, then Reality is within our reach. When we see things, but are not able to understand them, we are not attuned to them. You see the sunrise. When you come to understand that the sunrise is a manifestation of the Life of the Advanced Light Beings, you are then connected with Reality. Today's beautiful weather is a manifestation of their good thoughts and desires.

Hold all plants and animals in your consciousness as being God's Creation. If you do this, all your affairs will be put in good order. You need to arrive at that state in which you are capable of observing things and being aware of them at the same time. This is a privilege that is difficult to attain and requires great effort. You will then arrive at the Reality of all things.

Those who have attained Reality proceed to helping others. To be connected with Reality means that a person perceives Life outwardly and is also aware of Life inwardly; then one is truly in communion with Nature.

In the evening, go out and give your attention to the stars. Choose a star, follow its course, and see with which of the other stars it is connected. The stars exert an influence upon us as human beings.

When you come to a beautiful and healthy tree, lean against it; make the effort to enter into communion with the Life within. You will then be able to draw energy from the tree, and you will feel renewed.

Whenever man comes into discord with those around him, he needs to draw upon the energy from Nature: from the stones, the trees, the wellsprings, and the grass. Nature is the only thing that can help you. When you find yourself surrounded by Nature, you open your heart to your brethren and your fellowmen. The mountains, too, have an influence on you, and so does every river. A river that flows in the eastward direction has one kind of influence; while a river flowing westward, another.

When you are surrounded by Nature, be observant. For example, how will you find your way when you are surrounded by fog and have no compass? Usually, one finds more moss on the northern side of the stones than on the southern side. But there is also another method: to face all directions. When you turn toward the north, you will feel certain calmness: you are not confused. When you turn toward the east, you will sense that something good comes from there: something is flowing to you. Once you find these two directions, the other two are easy to find.

God loves those who work, who study. When I see a wellspring, I sit down and have a conversation with it. You will say, "What a strange man—to talk with a wellspring." What would you say about your accounting ledgers? You sit in front of them, open a page and say, "This person owes me twenty-five thousand leva; this other one, fifty thousand leva. I should send them to jail." Who is wiser? The one who enjoys the small snowdrop and the wellspring and conversing with them or the one who opens and closes his accounting ledgers?

The Great Substance

The Master said:

The whole world is created by Love alone. Everything visible that exists is an expression of this great Love and of those magnificent possibilities that await the human mind, heart, soul, and spirit. The Origin of all things is Love. It is the Primordial Eternal Substance in which we all live.

Someone asks, "Why is it that people exist without Love?" It is not Love they lack; they live within it. Love is what permeates all things. It reigns everywhere in the world. The first act in the world is Love. The valuable fruit that awakens the human soul, the human heart, is Love. All living beings, from the least to the greatest, move in God's Love. This is the way in which the whole Universe moves. I know Who moves the Universe.

When does someone speak softly, calmly? When he wants to say something kind. The most beautiful things are whispered in the ear, in order that no one else will hear them. The silent Voice of Nature represents the external Manifestation of Love. The Light speaks softly because it carries Love within itself. Can you sharpen your hearing in such a way as to be capable of hearing what the Light is saying? Do you know its language?

Love permeates and embraces everything. It never strays, nor does it emanate. It does not enter, nor does it exit.

People will often say, "I have lost my love." Do not delude yourselves. Those who are saying that they have just lost their love never had any. Love cannot be lost, nor can it be gained. It is a delusion when we say that we gain or lose Love. How can you gain what abides within you? How can you lose that which you are immersed in? We need to understand the words "gaining" and "losing" in a different sense. When you say, "I gained," this means that you have come into harmony with God. When you say, "I lost," this means that you have come into discord with God.

You say, "I do not believe." Whether you believe or do not believe, the Earth is carrying you, the air is sustaining you. Whether you believe or not, you are immersed in the Great Eternal Substance: within Love, within God.

The Two Laws

In another conversation, the Master said:

People of today still live with the delusion of awaiting love from the others. Open your hearts to God for His Love, and then people will love you. They are the multitude through whom God manifests Himself. Therefore, for you to come to know people, you should first come to know the One. This means that in order to understand the multitude, you first need to understand the Unity. I, too, draw close to you through Him—through God.

When people do not understand you, it indicates that you do not understand God. When people doubt you, it shows that you doubt God. Whatever your relationship with God is, such will be people's relationship with you.

The following two Laws exist. The first one states: When people love you, it indicates that you love God. The second Law states: When you love people, it indicates that God loves you. Here we need to give a little explanation. When I say that God loves you, this should be understood in a different meaning: God's Love for you is unchangeable. Yet by the expression, "God loves you," it is to be understood to mean that you are receptive to His Love. Thus, the relationship of others with you depends upon your relationship with God. When you have a good relationship with God, all people relate well to you. If you love people, it indicates that you have perceived God' Love rightly in its fullness.

You can personally come to know a family in two ways: either by loving the children—then the father will begin to love you—or by loving the father—then the children will begin to love you. When you befriend the children—when you are helpful to them—the father will be interested in you. I give this interpretation: your neighbors are God's children. When you are helpful to your neighbors, to God's children, you are connected with God.

The Psychic Causes of Disease

During a lunch conversation, a question arose regarding the cause of disease.
The Master said:

When food remains for a long time in the stomach without being digested, toxic substances are formed, toxins that are distributed throughout the whole organism and poison the blood. The same takes place with the heart. If unattainable desires accumulate within it, they cannot be assimilated and create astral toxins. The same also occurs when one holds onto thoughts that cannot be brought to realization. These remain within the brain for a long time and form mental toxins. The presence of toxins within the body produces the primary conditions for the abnormal development of microbes, the carriers of various diseases.

The Law is as follows: A worthy life purifies blood. As soon as you introduce an impure thought into your mind or impure feeling into your heart, the purity of your blood is lost. The impure thoughts and feelings create disease. All disturbances cause impairment to the mind, the heart, and the body.

Some diseases are due to mental disturbance; others, to emotional disturbance. When the disturbance is of an emotional nature, it affects the liver, the blood vessels, the heart, and so on. Any of these disturbances is due to not having loved.

If someone sinks into jealousy, doubt, anger, or any other negative condition, that person needs to find ways to transform them; otherwise, he will become ill. One should be able to balance any negative feeling or thought with a positive one. This will neutralize and transform it.

Every imbalance of the spirit afflicts the health. The disciple needs to be aware of the origin of his disease and whether it has a physical, spiritual, or mental character.

When Love is missing in people's lives, they can become ill with tuberculosis. The reason for all disease, disabilities, and afflictions in life is a spiritual one. If you would like to be healthy, maintain positive thoughts within your mind and good feelings within your heart.

The reasons for many diseases are hidden within the subconscious. These are the remnants of your past that you need to deal with.

Weeping does not cause the eyes to weaken, but immense sorrow does. Someone loses his health; someone else loses a son or a daughter, and they cannot get over the loss. From frequent, repetitive thinking about the loss, the eyesight gradually weakens. Tightness in the chest is due to discord in the feelings. A feeling of heaviness in the stomach is due to discord in one's actions.

Diseases exist whose origin is due to not having loved; other diseases are due to negligence and not having kept elementary rules of hygiene. Some diseases are caused by a person's dislike for the Truth and his serving of falsehood; still others are due to different kinds of anxiety.

When the frequency of vibration of the organism goes down, man becomes susceptible to different illnesses. In such cases, the slightest reason can cause disease. There is a rule that states: For an organism to be capable of coping with disease, its frequency of vibration needs to be raised.

Remember: every disease is the result of a transgression committed, either in the past or in the present. At the present time, it is noticeable that instead of the number of diseases diminishing, it is increasing. This will continue until people come to realize that they need to seek out the causes of these diseases and eliminate them.

One acquaintance related to me the following experience: "For ten years, I was angry with my father and mother. During that time, I had a boil on my neck which bothered me for a long time. It had barely healed when another erupted. Thus I was tormented by these boils for ten years. As soon as I reconciled with my parents, I was free from the boils." In this case, the energy from hatred that had accumulated in the virulent matter of the boils, surfaced and was released.

Rheumatoid arthritis, for example, in addition to having purely physical causes, also has mental ones. These causes are rooted in the thoughts, the feelings, and the willpower. Every mean-spirited thought, feeling, and deed in life manifests in the form of rheumatoid arthritis, boils, and other diseases. Beware of fear, hatred, worry, envy, jealousy, and other negative states that build up toxins and residues in the organism.

A disease can even manifest when a person has not reconciled with someone who has passed away. An ailing priest came to me once. He was very frightened. He related that a relative of his, with whom he had not been on friendly terms, had passed away. "This disease is because of your relationship with this relative of yours," I said. He confessed that he had beaten his mother, and she later died. I advised him to make peace with his mother, and then he would be healed. "How can I make peace with my mother?" he asked. I told him, "You need to confess to God and to your mother that you have not acted well."

Through disease, Nature gives a person certain lessons. People who are cruel and rude become more pleasant after having been ill. Disease makes people kinder and milder. After each disease, a small improvement comes in the human character.

The Disciple—He Who Is Tested in Life

The Master did not like to be addressed with questions of a personal or material nature. He preferred when profound questions were raised and discussed them always with readiness. The favorite subjects of our conversations were: the path of the disciple, the development of the inner forces, gifts, and capabilities in the human being, and the Laws of the Conscious Life and the methods for their application. The Master perceived Life in its depth and wholeness clearly, calmly, and fully. With simple words and examples, he would respond to the most complicated of questions. One evening, after finishing all of the daily chores, we gathered around him, and a question about the disciple arose.

The Master said:

You are still little children, for whom God has created this great world to explore. God's greatest Blessings are yet to come. What you have experienced thus far is good, but it still is not your purpose.

We can wait many years to accomplish what we strive for: the development of the inner forces. This can be accomplished sooner when we act in a Divine way. In this case, the time is shortened.

Disciples should study Nature and make interpretations of her language. Observe the flowers, the grasses, the trees, the wellsprings, the light. And when you do so, eliminate from your observations all impressions that harm or darken the consciousness. When you make these observations, you need to eliminate all negative thoughts, feelings, and impressions.

Study all that God has created because each and every stone is a result of Universal Intelligence. The trees, the flowers, the water, the air, the light, all these are manifestations of this Intelligence. When you are making your observations, think of this Intelligence, think of the Divine because wherever life exists, there you will find Divine Manifestation as well. By applying this method, you will be able to accomplish what in an ordinary lifetime, would take much longer to achieve.

What calms is the Spirit—the spiritual life. Herein lies the solution to the great work of earthly existence. What oppresses and brings all suffering is the loss of the Sublime Splendor—the loss of the Spirit.

Christ's Teaching is so profound that it can only be applied by the mystics. Should you desire to apply it, you will encounter many diverse temptations, the aim of which will be to divert you from your path. A multitude of desirable things will be promised to you with the sole intent of obstructing you.

As disciples of the Great School, you are given the task not only of acquiring knowledge, but of developing those new organs that are still in the embryonic stage. Without the development of these organs, you will not be able to evolve. This task is a difficult one, but it is unavoidable. The development of one of these organs represents learning the art of swimming so that you may be capable of remaining on the surface and not sinking during any storm on the sea of Life.

If you make wise use of the present conditions, a bright future will await you. Should these conditions become lost to you, you will need to wait for thousands of years for new favorable conditions to come along.

You need to give expression to all of the good that God has implanted within you; otherwise, you will be negligent in your work.

If humans are not prepared to use the natural resources in a sensible way, they will become a burden for them. For this reason, Nature has concealed many of her resources from those who are not ready. To those who are ready, she reveals her many mysteries. No pretense exists within Nature. When you are ready, she will lift the veil from in front of your face and reveal all that is required of you. When you are not ready, she will use ten keys to lock up everything in front of you. For this reason, those who seek to attain the Great Truth need to prepare themselves. If you do not work mindfully on yourself, you will drift into monotony, and this will carry you off into a state of lethargy. One needs to pass on to a higher state of consciousness from what one finds in oneself at present. The fundamental purpose of the Divine School is to prepare the disciple so that he may be ready to receive God's blessings when they come.

A modest improvement in one's capabilities can be achieved by many, but for one to become genuinely talented, preparation is needed. I will give you an example: one person works little, and his violin playing is mediocre; another one works hard and becomes a virtuoso.

Each evening, the disciple should make an accounting of the thoughts, feelings, and actions that he experienced during the day that he may keep what is of value and discard what is not.

Work mindfully that you may be admitted to the Divine University. Here, kindred souls with similar endeavors come together and form a network. This occurs in Heaven. This is how the Divine Schools are arranged. In the image of the Divine Schools, similar Schools are created on the Earth as well. Your status as students is not determined by the Earth School, but by the Divine. In the Divine School, a record is kept for each and every student: when he first became enrolled, how he has progressed in his studies and with his behavior, and how he has completed his education. Should the student experience much adversity in his life, should he be unable to resolve the contradictions, and for this reason has left the School—this is put in his record as well.

Some will ask, "What is the Master's purpose in speaking to us in this manner?" My purpose is to help you become members of the Great Universal Brotherhood.

The Great Universal Brotherhood is not a new association. It has existed since antiquity and continues to exist today. That you may become worthy of this blessing, you need to pray and work arduously on yourselves until your hearts become still. Every storm and every turbulence upon the sea needs to cease. When this occurs, the rising of your Sun will come; a brilliant Day with no clouds or shadows will set in. When the Sun of your Life rises, your hearts will stir because you will hear the Voice of God, the Voices of all the Angels and of all the Advanced Brothers. You will then enter the Great City to dwell among the Advanced Sublime Beings. When you attain this, your Joy will be extraordinary.

At the moment, you are all in the desert where you should pray for many days until that time when you are able to overcome the hardships that you have encountered along your way. Do you think that it was easy for the Angels to attain their present state?

Only the one who resolves his assignments rightly may be a disciple. Remember the following: the favorable conditions are given to man for free, but the effort needs to come from him alone. For one to be a genius depends upon the effort that he has made in past incarnations. The disciple should eliminate everything extraneous still residing within. Only what God has imparted should remain.

The disciple will be exposed to many contradictions and temptations in his work that need to be overcome. The end result will determine his status. When you are admitted to the School, two voices will speak to you. One will tell you, "Leave the School and go on living in the world as other people do." The other voice will be saying to you, "Remain in the School; fulfill what is required of you."

Many old patterns of behaviors and forms exist within a person's life—within his prayers, within his ideas, and so on, that he needs to eliminate. If a person is smeared with honey, flies will be attracted to him and will stick to him. This means: never present the inferior spirits the conditions to be attracted to you; never expose to others that which is sacred. That is to say, never put on display the sublime within your soul.

As soon as you begin to make the effort, the Invisible World will come to assist you. When a disciple has the help of the Invisible World, his affairs will improve. And so, be not afraid. When the Invisible World begins to help you, you will become a talented person.

Many believe that when they begin to walk upon the New Path, their lives will become easy and pleasant. This is correct, but only at the end of their journey. In the beginning, however, they will pass through great difficulties and trials.

All good people are put through great trials while on Earth. When an Angel descends to the Earth to incarnate, he gradually descends into dense matter and forgets his experience in the World Above because if he should remember how it is there, he would suffer.

Job passed through great suffering: he lost everything and became afflicted with boils and scabs all over his body. There are those among you who believe that it will be easy to enter into the

Kingdom of God. Have you ever experienced the greatest suffering? Suffering provides the conditions for you to become truly fulfilled. It is only under such conditions that you can become worthy of tasting God's Love. It is then that something sublime will be brought forth from you. It is then that you will become genuine human beings.

God is continuously testing your love. He gives you money, and then when He takes it away from you, you are saddened. This indicates that you are concerned with the material. You should rejoice when you are robbed. No one can take away from you what is real: the Divine. Who is able to steal the stars, the sky, the Sun, or the Pacific Ocean?

The world is a sea into which, many fishing rods are cast. The fishing lines are the temptations. Once you become entangled in them, you begin to stray from God.

The ordinary believer lives like an ordinary person. For that person, trials do not exist. And yet, the moment in which you become a disciple, trials will begin to appear. Therefore, the disciple is tested, whereas the ordinary person—in this sense—remains free. One's faith is tested in times of greatest trouble. The strength of a ship is tested during the greatest storms.

Someone chooses to take the spiritual path. One prays, helps others, and after a while says, "Now let others do the work; I have worked enough." This is not correct. Those on the spiritual path need to work harder than anyone else. Prayer is required of all people today. Why is it required? Because we find ourselves at the border of a changing world, into which a New Order is coming this very moment.

Those days of trials and tribulations are coming, of which the Scripture says, "The Sun, the stars, and the Moon will darken."[16] This means that the belief systems of all religions will lose their significance and that secular authority will lose its power as well. And so, all disciples of the School should seek to better themselves by putting on their armor and their helmets that they may withstand this Wave of trials and tribulations, through

---

16. See also Matthew 24:29, "Immediately after the tribulation of those days the Sun will be darkened, and the Moon will not give its light; the stars will fall from heaven, and the powers of the heavens will be shaken."

which all of humankind shall pass. The name of this armor is Love. After all, when people pass through this Wave, they will change for the better.

When you find yourselves in the midst of contradictions that assault you from all sides, you need to understand that you are finding yourselves in your natural environment, and for this reason, you are being assaulted. And when you come to the greatest of contradictions, you need to understand that the moment has come for you to return to your own—to your people—that you may show them how to live. Do not question why these contradictions come, but return to the place of your God-given origin. It is there where you will come to know your true self. And once you have come to know yourselves, you will have attained an inner peace as well. In so doing, you will have become your own masters. All of the trials that one needs to endure: this is the work. After the trials come the fruits, the results, and the renewal. Whenever something is sown in the soil, the Intelligent Forces in Nature will work upon it, and it will sprout. In this way, whenever something is sown within your soul, the Invisible World works upon the implanted seed and brings it to life. The main work is accomplished by the Invisible World.

Those who do not learn cannot be admitted to the Divine School. To be admitted—this indicates that one is gifted. However, should a person withdraw, it is not because he is ignorant. Not everyone is admitted. And so, he has interrupted his study for other reasons. Later, when he returns, he will continue from where he left off. The fact that he had begun his study in the Divine School indicates that he is capable, but has been hindered by the external conditions and for this reason has interrupted his study. Later he will resume it.

It has been said, "Narrow is the Way."[17] The "Narrow Way" is given as a general concept, but the Narrow Way is different for each. You should be admitted to the Divine School on your own efforts.

---

17. See also Matthew 7:14, "Because narrow *is* the gate and difficult is the way which leads to life, and there are few who find it."

In the desire to achieve something of note, many neglect the little things that are, in reality, the most beneficial to them. Each morning upon awakening, the disciples need to implant at least one small Divine Thought within their hearts so that their lives may have meaning.

Each one of you should study a science: mathematics, chemistry, physics, biology, philosophy, and so on. The disciple needs to be well-informed about the present epoch. Once you have come to Earth, you need to study. You are students. All living beings need to study—even the least.

Not until people reach the age of 40 will they be able to study the fundamental Law: the Love for God. At the age of 30, human beings pass through a crisis, and their status is determined as to whether or not they will make something good of themselves.

You can determine which grade of the School you are in by the assignments that you are given to resolve.

Perfection of the Human Soul

The Master used every opportunity to teach a lesson to his disciples. The slope in front of brother Temelko's home was steep, rocky, and without water. Observing it, the Master discovered some moisture in one place. He asked us to start digging, and he worked with us until some dripping water was found. We built a basin and led the water to flow into it; the basin began to fill up.

This was the second wellspring that we discovered and the Master named it "The Wellspring of Health." With this, the Master taught us not to neglect even the smallest of Divine Gifts.

The wellspring was made beautiful: a path was made, and beneath it, a small vegetable garden was planted that was irrigated by its water. The lesson was given clearly and with strong imagery. In this way, it would be well-remembered by the disciples. Does not a person resemble a small wellspring? When the work was finished, the Master gave an explanation of the third Law: Love for oneself.

To love yourself means to love God within yourself. To serve yourself means to work on yourself that you may develop the image of God within yourself. To love yourself means not to tolerate any bad thoughts, feelings, or deeds. To love yourself means not to harm yourself or develop bad habits. People who do not respect these precepts do not love themselves. Therefore, you cannot love yourself if you do not love God. To love yourself means to be perfect.

If we cannot perceive the deep meaning of Life, we lose our Blessing from the Intelligent Light Beings who bear Divine Life and give us knowledge. You need to know what the meaning of Life is. It is more sublime than we can imagine. The meaning of Life is the perfection of the human soul!

A man came to see me and asked, "What is the meaning of Life?" I told him: In the Universe, there are about one million suns and around each sun there are twelve planets. You need to visit all of these suns and planets, and on each one of these suns and planets, you need to live for 100 million years. Only then, will you learn the meaning of Life in its depth.

Right Breathing

Springtime had now come. Nature had awakened and her essence flowed freely. The Master used every opportunity to guide us into her realm. He introduced us to the methods for mindful living that give man the opportunity of making use of Nature's bounties and communing with her. The following Law applies to her: The more that one's consciousness is awakened and enlightened, the greater will be the bounties that Nature will provide.

One morning the Master discussed the concept of right breathing.

The air is the most fundamental element of life that we need to study under the present conditions. Each and everyone of us needs to comprehend those Laws that the air obeys.

Right breathing is understood to mean the complete drawing in of the energy that is present in the air. If I can accomplish this, I will have accomplished a certain task, and I will rejoice.

During breathing, one needs to observe the following Law: Love the air, and receive it with joy. This is the only way in which we can receive those blessings that the air provides.

When you exhale, no air should remain in the lungs. The cause of many diseases is the result of leaving considerable quantities of air in the lungs during exhalation.

Shallow breathing shortens one's life. If you were to breathe more deeply, your life would be prolonged. When a person's respiration is rapid, he will die sooner than he would if it were slow. The one who is ill with tuberculosis will have twenty to twenty five respirations per minute; the healthy person should have three respirations per minute; and there are those whose respiratory cycle has only one respiration per minute. And then there are those adepts who have only one respiration for every twenty-minute period, and others, one for every hour.

Those who desire patience should breathe deeply. The longer that you are able to hold your breath, the greater your patience will be. Through right breathing, you can rid of any morbid condition—physical or mental—gradually bringing balance into your life force and, at the same time, becoming revitalized. Once you have achieved internal balance, no external condition, no external influence can deviate you from your path.

In addition to oxygen, man also receives life force—prana—through right breathing, and new ideas as well. This can be achieved by following certain guidelines.

I recommend deep breathing to you. Direct your consciousness to God and begin breathing rhythmically. As you inhale and exhale, repeat a mantra or a prayer in your mind. This will increase your ability to receive more of the sublime forces hidden within the air.

You should have gratitude toward God. The air has been provided by Him. It is required that God enters into you continuously and that you enter continuously into Him. When I inhale, God reveals Himself to me. When I exhale, I reveal myself to Him.

The air is a transmitter of Divine Thought that penetrates first the respiratory system, and then, the brain. This means that one does not receive Divine Thought directly, but through the air. The air is the fundamental transmitter of Divine Thought. I speak of the air's real essence, and not of what the chemists analyze as a mixture of four-fifths oxygen and one-fifth nitrogen. The air is the primordial element that serves us as the origin of our life force.

When you breathe, your consciousness needs to be vigilant because thought—after it has been received from the air—is received by the consciousness. As vigilant as your consciousness is, that much will you be blessed with the life force within the air. In this way, you will be connected with the Sublime Intelligent Beings who you will be helping and who will be helping you.

As soon as spring comes, go out each morning for a walk in the fresh air—away from the soot of the city—and devote at least one hour to right breathing and exercise. If you take these walks, your affairs will be in better order than had you stayed in your room.

Many methods of breathing exist. It is best done through both nostrils simultaneously, but it can also be done through one nostril at a time. I will give you an exercise. Inhale for 15 seconds through the left nostril, hold the air for 40 seconds, and then exhale through the right nostril for 15 seconds. When you inhale through the left nostril, the right should be closed, and vice versa. While you are holding the air, both nostrils should be closed. Then, inhale through the right nostril, and exhale through the left.

If you desire to become a poet, breathe. Real poetry is dependent upon right breathing. As you breathe, so will you write.

The Music of the Future Culture

This afternoon we spent a few hours filled with music. We sang many songs, and after that, the conversation was naturally about music.
The Master said:

Music began very well at the beginning of the involutionary epoch. However, as it gradually descended into matter, the music increasingly lost its depth. What man had in the

World beyond has become lost to him. With the music of the evolutionary epoch, man needs to restore what he has lost.

In their error, people lost their primordial musical Life.

The music of the East descends; it is of the involutionary epoch. In contrast, the music of the West ascends because it is of the evolutionary.

Today uplift for music is coming: the impulse is an upward one from a denser substance to a lighter one. With the descent of music from the lighter substance into a denser one, the tones are of one kind; and with the ascent of music from the denser substance into a lighter one, the tones are of another kind. In other words, the music of an evolutionary epoch is different from that of the involutionary epoch. In its descent, the music of the East moves from a comprehensible melody toward an incomprehensible one. In contrast, in its ascent, the music of the West progresses from an incomprehensible melody toward a comprehensible one.

Our departure from God is in the minor scale, whereas our return to Him is in the major one. In the first case, there is something soft in the voice: there is sorrow and lament in the content. In the music of the East, the melody dominates; whereas, in the music of the West, it is the harmony. The music of the East is music of the emotions; whereas the music of the West is of the mind and will.

I divide music into the following categories: that of the Frigid Zone, that of the Temperate Zone, and that of the Torrid Zone. Slavic music belongs to the Temperate Zone.

At the sunset of one culture and the sunrise of another, the music will always be different. Today something new needs to be introduced into music. It is no longer possible for people to sing as they did two thousand years ago. So how should people sing now? The new music needs to serve as an improvement to what has been accomplished up to now. If we do not add something new to the music of today, what good would it serve?

All musicians and singers will be inspired in the future. Their music will be capable of causing total transformation in the souls who have fallen and will awaken the impulse for science in those who have never desired to study it.

The harmony of contemporary music is a manifestation of the entire modern culture: its optimism, pessimism, materialism, skepticism, and so on. A new Music is coming. From now on, music will begin to evolve. The entire development of music to the present has only been an introduction. The culture of the future will be created through music alone. Those Beings who have manifest themselves through the music of Beethoven, Bach, Mozart, and others will once again give the world something new and more sublime than has ever been given before.

At present, the conditions do not exist for the sublime Music to manifest. It is not easy for a person of genius to incarnate. For this to occur, he should have a perfectly structured body in order to withstand the enormous stress of those forces that will manifest through him.

Music fulfills its purpose only when it serves the uplift of humankind. Man needs to move from the extrinsic music toward the Music of Cosmic Consciousness. The person who has not developed his ear for the Music of Cosmic Consciousness cannot enter into the Divine World. Today God breathes the Breath of Life into our ears; and for this reason, all people should learn to sing.

With the events of today, there will be a greater understanding of music's significance. The impulse to sing will grow stronger. Throughout the war, cruelty has increased, and people have hardened. At present, we can hear the harsh sounds of machine-guns, cannons, bombs, and more. These are the harshest of sounds.

Music descends from the Invisible World to help humankind. In the future, people will be born with a developed gift for music. In the past, music as we know it did not exist.

In the music of the people of Spanish heritage, the feminine principle is expressed; whereas in that of the Anglo-Saxon, the masculine principle is expressed. In the Slavonic music the feminine principle is expressed once again, but to a greater extent.

The Slavs have a good ear for music. Because they have experienced a great deal of oppression in the past, their suffering is expressed in their songs. However, they have accepted their fate in good faith and are now on the upward path.

Whenever one sings the songs of a particular culture, one should have an understanding of the epoch in which those songs came into being. The Russians, as well as the Bulgarian people have endured great suffering, and this is reflected in many of their songs.

The epoch of a new Music is approaching. The Slavic people will give a new impulse to music: they provide the good "clay" out of which better "pots" will be formed.

The Sacred Name

The Master said:

Sacred is the Name of God. Absolute silence should instantly arise within the hearts and souls of all whenever the Name is spoken. All should be filled with reverence and sacred awe.

Everything in the world—except for the Name of God and the Will of God—is transitory. The Name of God should be held sacred within your souls. Remember always the Blessings that God has bestowed upon you. In prosperity and in impoverishment, in health and in sickness, in favorable times and in adversity, He always watches over you.

Those who do not fulfill God's Will are sure to suffer, not because God desires this, but because they have erred against the most fundamental Law of Life. The one who abides by His Will is like iron that has been heated until it glows white. At this temperature, all misconceptions, adversity, and disease will be burned to ashes. Only then, will one begin to feel peace and tranquility deep within oneself.

The mere mention of God's Love, of the Name of God, will inspire you. All irreverence will immediately cease. Sacred is the Name of God. Sacred is the Name of the Angels. One needs to nurture these sacred thoughts and feelings about God.

Sleep as a Process for Renewal

This evening the concept of sleep as a process for renewal was discussed. The Master said:

At night you go to bed. You leave your body. You feel as if you move, but your body remains motionless. Your body has one consciousness, and you have another. You move, but you are afraid that the connection with your body might be broken, and you return. You cannot tell your ordinary consciousness about what is immeasurable or what you have experienced in the higher realm. The ordinary consciousness tells you, "Go. Go, but not too far away!"

In the evening—because the right conditions for work do not exist here—we leave our bodies and go somewhere else to work. Meanwhile, others work on our bodies. Nature is like a prudent mother. When people sleep, she cleans the house—the body—and renews it so that upon awakening, we can continue our work. During the time of sleep, the soul leaves the body. During this time, the Intelligent Light Beings set to work on the body's cells to renew them and restore the disrupted rhythm.

When a person goes to bed, he should pray that the body be protected and shielded from negative influences during his time of sleep. Negative, morbid states can pass from one person to another. This happens especially during the time of sleep. One needs to observe the Law of Psychic Protection. In other words, when you go to bed in the evening, you need to protect your body. On the other hand, be grateful to your Sublime Friends who protect your bodies when you are separated from them during sleep. Otherwise, you could find your bodies possessed and violated.

Sometimes you cannot sleep well because of being overtired, having used excessive energy to accomplish an insignificant task. This is as if you wanted to drive a small nail into a wall by pounding it with great force. In other words, you worry too much over small things. Was it necessary to use so much force for such a small nail?

Not much sleep is needed to be truly rested. Before going to bed, you need to rid yourself of all painful moments and negative conditions you have experienced during the day. Your mind and heart need to be emptied of all conflicts. If someone's body, mind, and heart are not at rest when he falls asleep, he will stray into the astral world and not find the Divine School where the Laws of that world are studied. When he awakens, he is dissatisfied; he has understood nothing. You learn also when you are asleep.

When you suffer from insomnia, you should rise from your bed, rub your body with a cloth and warm water, wash your feet in warm water, and return to bed. Your sleep will then be refreshing.

One peculiarity of the astral world is that events are experienced there in symbols, in images. For this reason, some dreams are symbolic. You dream that you have entered a house and are being chased out. You enter another house; you are chased out again. The house represents the body. During sleep you enter someone's body thinking that it belongs to you; but it is not yours, and you depart. You enter another body thinking it is yours; again you leave, and so on.

When a person sleeps, the bond between his spiritual and physical bodies remains. When a person returns to his body unexpectedly—when frightened, for example—it is possible for it to become entangled with the etheric double of another person.

In order to have a genuine encounter with someone in the higher realm during the time of sleep, you need to have the purest and best thoughts about that person. If you occupy your mind with his shortcomings, you will not be able to meet him.

The Mystical Circle

It was early spring, the day was clear and calm. The Sun was melting the snow, and the waters rushed down into the valley from above. Life was increasing its flow with a renewed rhythm.

We were in the mountain with our beloved Master. Three colors combined harmoniously: the white of the snowdrifts, the blue of the sky, and the new green of spring. The Breath of the Eternal One enlivened everything.

The Master said:

Think of Him Who has given you everything and Whom you have not yet come to know. You should come to know the Absolute Reality, the One Who was the first to give His Love to us.

A deep understanding of a person's inner life is required so that he may bring his human aspirations to right realization. When one does not perceive the Divine within, one's most beautiful aspirations will vanish. In such a case, that person has no pillar of support within himself.

Every thought about God—as small as it might be—is like a spark. Every thought about God will bring you a Blessing. Direct your minds toward God, and the natural state of your being will be restored. A Law states: The moment you make a connection with God, you will receive His Thoughts. For as long as people maintain this connection with the Omniscient Center of Creation, they will be the bearers of Divine Ideas. Another Law states: Whenever you think about God, a powerful flow of energy will pass through you; you will receive the Power of the Divine, and all of your gifts and capabilities will develop rightly.

Whenever you think about God, Divine Power and Ideas will permeate and restructure you. It is the same relationship as that of the mountain peak to the valley. When the snow melts on the mountain peak, the waters rush down, and everything in the valley begins to bloom and bear fruit.

Maintaining a sacred idea about the Great One in your consciousness, you will have Light in your mind and Warmth in your heart. One needs to understand that this idea is both fundamental and sacred; and one needs to build upon it.

Now your thoughts are scattered. They resemble disconnected chain links. And yet, when a thought about God arises, it connects all of the links and makes a chain. The Law states: Let the chain not be broken so that the Divine Flow of Life will not be interrupted. This Divine Flow should never be broken!

All are now in need of the power that sustains Life: the life force that emanates from the Divine. All need the life force coming from the Divine Joy.

You need to connect with God: that is to say, with the Infinite Potential of the Living Cosmos. Only then, you are going to attain the Light bearing all favorable conditions for the development of mind, heart, and will. This is the only way in which you will be able to build up your life and organize your life force. Those who strive to create their character anew and attain an enlightened consciousness need to connect with the Great Intelligent World. When you connect with God, your sky will become cloudless. Strive to restore this living connection. You will attain great knowledge when you are able to maintain this connection. Should you lack this connection with God—with your Teacher—you will attain nothing.

The mind is a mystical wand. Use it to draw a mystical circle around yourself that you may be protected. How will you do this? Only by thinking about God is the mystical circle drawn. When you are connected with God, you are protected; wherever you may be, you will be safe. When you are not connected with God, everywhere holds danger for you. When I encounter a bear, I say, "God dwells within this bear." Then the bear has no desire to cause me harm. I encounter a thief—the same.

How will the New be different? In its connection with the Divine. A Law states: All error will be atoned for when the connection between the human soul and God is restored. This is the Law of the Universal Brotherhood of Light. This connection has not yet been restored. Open the way for the Divine to enter into you that you may have peace.

Because you do not presently have a connection with the Advanced Brothers, with the Sublime World, your spiritual forces are in a dormant state; the forces that emanate from the

Sublime Worlds remain in your lower nature without manifesting. When you connect with God, right use is made of these forces, and contradictions are easily resolved.

Another Law states: Whenever a person connects with God, he becomes reconciled with God. God's blessings will then manifest in such a way that that person will reconcile with all of his enemies. Whatever might happen in the world, maintain your connection with the Great Origin of Life and be not afraid.

Whatever thought you hold about God, so will you become as well. When you begin to doubt God, all gifts that have been imparted to you will be lost.

Even when you are in the midst of the greatest hardship, remember that God remains unchangeable. Should you feel God's Presence—even for a moment—all your adversities will melt away as the ice does. If you have faith in God, even the "hell" in which you live will be transformed into a paradise. This is a great Truth. During times of hardship, one needs to depend upon God. To do this, one needs to be strong. Should your home burn down or should any other hardship come into your life, if this is capable of breaking your connection with the Great Center of Creation, then you are not a person of the Conscious Life.

If a thought is not applied, its form will be destroyed, but the thought itself remains as a living essence, returning to God. It becomes lost to you as if you had lost your children. Should you lose the connection with your sacred thoughts, feelings, and desires, you interrupt your connection with all Intelligent Beings.

A person's sacred thoughts are the substance through which he comes in contact with the Great Intelligent World. Should you destroy your sacred thoughts and feelings about God, along with this, you will destroy the most precious part of yourself. It is only through these sacred thoughts and feelings that you may enter into communion with Him.

When someone keeps sacred one's thoughts and feelings about God, that person will be a citizen in the Kingdom of God. All of our thoughts and feelings are born out of the sacred.

When we do not live rightly, this is of concern to God. He wants all error to be atoned for. When we abide in God, we become channels of His Blessings; God desires the Blessing that proceeds from Him to be passed along. God desires that His Blessing be made manifest.

One thing is required of human beings: to have veneration for God. All things that come from God are made available to us when we are connected with Him. When this connection is missing, one will remain an ordinary human being; nothing will become of that person. When someone comes to know God, the conditions of that person's life will improve; otherwise, they will worsen. I have tested and verified this, and I pass it on to you. When you are connected with God, you will understand the material existence, get rid of error, and attain your ideal.

In reality, even the one whose error is the greatest remains connected with God. At times, however, it would appear that this is not true. In such a case, God loosens the bond, and the person moves further away from Him. Some time later, this person will again have the desire to draw closer to God. God will then wind up the thread on the spool, and the person will be drawn to Him. I speak figuratively, of course, this connection is never interrupted.

The concept of God is the most powerful concept. However, its manifestation is at its weakest right now. Not that it is truly weak, but it awaits for the right time to come for it.

The Qualities of Divine Love

The Easter holiday made it possible for many disciples to come and see the Master. Spring had come; the blossoms of the trees filled the air with a heavenly fragrance. The first birds of spring had arrived.

The small community was filled with life. One could see disciples everywhere, standing both in groups and alone. Some of them worked, others read, and still others were conversing with one another. All people had things they wished to share with their neighbors.

Early in the morning, we climbed to the hill above the village with the Master where we performed callisthenic exercises and Paneurhythmy. After that, we returned to the homestead refreshed and invigorated.

We took our meals beneath the big walnut tree. It was warm, and the rays of the Sun filtered through the young green of the branches making them look as if they were made of gold. The conversations were lively. The influx of

life was felt not only in nature, but also in the souls, minds, and hearts of all people as if the seeds of a New Life were sprouting.
The Master said:

Read page 100 from the volume, "The Eternal Blessing."[18] A person with ordinary comprehension cannot manifest Divine Love. Only if an Advanced Being comes to dwell within someone—be it for merely an instant—can one manifest Divine Love.

I have spoken to you about Love, but the essential I have not yet talked about. I am still in the introduction to Love. If I would pronounce the word "Love" as it should be, can you imagine what would happen to you? You would become luminous, resplendent—and would put on angelic forms.

Everything in the world is a manifestation of Love. But what Love is in reality, only few people know. It is the Reality beyond the physical world. It is beyond your will, beyond your mind, beyond your heart. Love has merely points of contact with these. In the existing conditions, Love acts intermittently from without until the human organism becomes adapted because the body's present composition cannot withstand Love's strong vibrations.

Do not try to describe what Love is, but describe its manifestations. Love is the only thing that man cannot describe. You cannot describe the bread until you have eaten it. You cannot describe the water until you have drunk it. From now on, people will come to know Love. Love is the most sublime force in the Universe. When it permeates people, it brings the most sublime and beautiful manifestations of the Spirit. Love first becomes known to the great Teachers, to the great Adepts, to the great disciples, to the great believers, then to the great converts, and finally to the ordinary people.

There is something greater than knowledge in the world: this is Love.

If you would like to come to the intrinsic purpose of things, to free yourselves from the constraints of life, you need to

---

18. "The Eternal Blessing" (*Vechnoto Blago*) is a collection of lectures given by the Master, published in 1943, Sofia.

love God. In reality, Love is the path that leads to genuine knowledge. Do not concern yourselves with the love that enslaves people. It is of the world and you have already experienced it.

Divine Love does not create contradictions in life. It will make you strong and full of spiritual power. It will make you steadfast in your thoughts. Divine Love begins in the following way. A friend of yours comes to you and reads to you two stanzas that he has written. You should put yourself in his place and be as pleased for him as if you had written them yourself. Instead, you listen, and yet, you are displeased and say to yourself, "Why did this not come from me?" Someone has painted a picture and shows it to you. Be pleased for him. Do not say, "Why did I not do this?" Someone has received an inheritance; be pleased for that person. Someone else has put on beautiful clothes, be pleased as well. You need to consider your brethren's thoughts and feelings as your own, and let them be sacred to you.

Yield to the Love within yourself. This means to place God in the highest place within your soul.

Your fundamental idea should be: to love as God loves. If you enter into the Divine World with your human love, you will attain nothing.

One of the qualities of Divine Love is as follows: the one who has this Love within cannot fall into temptation or enticement. No one can tempt the one within whose soul Love dwells. The person who has Divine Love is absolutely inviolable. Even the wild beasts know Love, and when they meet Love on their path, they step aside.

When Love transits from one realm into another, it creates suffering. He who understands this Law will never become discouraged.

When disciples desire to attain the knowledge that Love bears, they need to shed their old clothing—that is to say, all the unnecessary suffering—and renounce their selfishness.

Love is the primary prerequisite, whereby one determines one's own conditions.

To love means to be in harmony with the Divine World of Love, with the Angelic World of Love, and with the human world of Love, that is to say, with all good people.

One needs to know how to manifest Divine Love. It has thousands of ways to manifest and one needs to know them all.

From a Letter by the Master

> The flower that blossoms,
> The fruit that ripens,
> The Light that makes the soul rejoice,
> And the Spirit that gives all gifts
> For the heart and mind
> Are blessings that come down from God.
> Seek these always and learn from them.
> Above all things, love God
> With all your heart,
> With all your soul,
> With all your will.
> Seek God alone!
> Serve Him, and He will bless you.
> Grow and abide in Love!

He Is Coming

The Master often gave a new insight to those problems that concerned us even if he had touched upon the subject at another time. He would approach this as a great musician might take up a simple melody and play it with a new harmony, unveiling a still fuller and deeper content as he interwove it with other melodies. In this way, the Master would summarize and highlight new relationships and correspondences, opening up an entirely new world that had been unknown to us until now. The Master would lead the conversation away from the trivial and mundane topics that people would often concern themselves with and turn our thoughts toward the essential that we might learn something new, that we might grow and develop.

The Master told us:

To be born again—this is a reference to Love that is now revealing itself in a new way. At present, we are just beginning to be born again in Love. However, the time will come when we will dwell among those whom we love and who love us.

Embrace Love, which is already coming into the world. It will make your heart rejoice. It will lead you to your Beloved Ones. You tell me, "Our hearts are full of sacred anticipation." They are in a stir, but your Beloved Ones have not yet come. Only now are they descending to Earth. What you now perceive is merely their reflection; and for this reason, you are feeling disappointed.

Love is coming and will unite all beings into one as servants of God. Thousands of Beings have worked in the material world and in the Invisible World as well, to bring about the favorable conditions that the Great One may come in the name of Love. What is coming into the world now is so magnificent that all the Angels peer down from Heaven so that they may see what is coming and what is taking place on the Earth. All of Heaven—the Whole of Creation—is interested in this. The Great Day is coming into the world. The Manifestation of the Great One is anticipated by all good and advanced Beings. Those whose consciousness has awakened will perceive the Great Divine Origin and be transformed. The remainder—those whose consciousness has not yet awakened—will continue to sleep. If you miss the Great Wave of Love, which is now coming, you will need to wait millions of years for the next one. In order for this Great Love to be revealed to you, you must pass through the Law of Self-sacrifice and Renunciation.

This Wave of Love will transform the adversity of the past into fertile soil so that the flowers may blossom and the fruit of Love may ripen. All of humankind will be sustained by them.

Humankind is presently passing through a new phase of its development. A new form of Love is coming. We ask, "When will God come and reveal His Love to us?" This Day is coming. For some, this Day has already come. Have you ever raised silkworms? Do all form their cocoon in a single day? No, some do it sooner, some do it later. For some of the "silkworms," this Day has already come.

Through Love, all accounts between people will be reconciled. Someone owes you one thousand leva—you need to close this account. Tell the person who is indebted to you, "So much did I torment you for these one thousand leva!" Then give him an additional one thousand leva. When you give him the one thousand leva, ask him for forgiveness for having tormented him. Let the one who holds some claim against another, give instead. This Teaching is not intended for those who cling to the old ideas. Without Love, man cannot leave behind his old ways.

Let us all repeat the following formula:
"From not loving—toward Love;
From mortality—toward Life;
From the bad—toward Good;
From doubt—toward Faith."
Herein lies the meaning of Life.

The Second Law

The sermons and lectures of the Master are dedicated to the three great Laws of the Great Brotherhood of Light:
1. Love God.
2. Love your neighbor.
3. Seek Perfection.

The Master told us:

A nation that preserves these seven sacred words has a future; if it loses them, it has no future.

These are the fundamental Laws of Life. The Master has given considerable knowledge related to them. In the following conversation, he gives explanations concerning the second Law: Love your neighbor.
The Master said:

Whatever your relationship to God is, such will be your relationship to all people. Once your faith in God is weakened, the possibility exists that your faith in your fellowmen and in yourself as well will become weakened. It is not possible for you to have a right relationship with anyone as long as you lack a connection with God.

The love for God is like a venous flow by which the impure blood goes to the heart and lungs to be purified, to become arterial. The venous and arterial flow of the blood not only exist with the body, but with human thoughts and emotions as well. For example, hatred and jealousy are the venous blood in humans, whereas love and joy, the arterial.

When one has love for God, one transforms the flow of the negative forces into positive, and the impure blood becomes pure. After that, it flows as arterial blood throughout the whole body to nourish all the cells. I am speaking symbolically. This is love for one's neighbor. This means that when you come to love God, you enter into His Heart to become purified. So purified, you go out and properly transport the blood; that is to say, His Blessings toward your neighbor.

The love for one's neighbor is included within the love for God, but not vice versa. Many have love for others, but become easily disappointed by this love. Why? An essential element is missing. That is to say, when people love their neighbors, they need to love the Divine within them. Those who have only loved their fellowmen have attained nothing. Without God, the love for one's neighbor contributes nothing.

Imagine that you fall in love with the Finger of God. If you want to see God, you should not fall in love with His Finger alone. When people perceive themselves as beings within whom God abides, they will then have right relationships. Coming to know my neighbor means that I know that the same God whom I love dwells within my neighbor.

When you meet someone say, "Lord, I thank You that I have encountered You in this person." Everyone that you meet is an assignment because you are to love the Divine within him. Everyone who is God's Creation deserves to be loved.

God's Law works in the following way: Behave toward others as you behave toward yourself. And yet, the perfect act is to relate to others in the way that God relates to you, that is to say, hold them within your mind just as God is holding them within His Mind. The least being occupies a high place within God's Mind. Therefore, my relationship with others needs to be as good as God's relationship is to them. We cannot be like Him, but let's walk on His Path.

Your love for your neighbor creates the conditions for the fruits in the garden of not only your own soul, but also in the soul of the one you love, to bloom and ripen.

When we have love for God, we are receiving. God is then helping us; the Supreme Spirits are helping us. When we have love for our neighbor, we are giving.

Laws of the Material Life and the Spiritual Life

One brother asked, "Master, what can you tell us about this great unrest in the world at present?"
The Master replied:

A person will become depleted and exhausted when using too much energy for the worldly life. The contemporary era is very active externally. Here, time is money. You should allot your time in such a way that one-third is set aside for activity in the worldly life. The rest is for satisfying the needs of the mind, the heart, and the soul.

Another question was raised: "How can we rid ourselves of the negative states?"
The Master replied:

The third Hermetic Law states: Everything in the Cosmos has its own vibration. One needs to understand that good, sublime thoughts have a higher vibration than the inferior, negative ones. This is a Law that you can make use of. For example: should you find yourself in a negative state, increase your frequency of vibration and you will eliminate it. The more powerful vibrations of the sublime thoughts will prevail over the negative state and replace it.

Should someone desire to be virtuous, he needs to connect with those who are already virtuous. For one to become a person of science, he needs to connect with learned people. This is the Law. Anyone who believes that this can be accomplished in any other way has deluded himself. If you were to place a herdsman to dwell among people who are scholarly, he would begin to be like them. Conversely, if you were to place a sage to dwell—over the course of many years—among criminals, nothing would become of him.

Question: "How can one learn from the past?"

Everything in the physical world is recorded. Should Beings from the Invisible World aspire to learn about something in the physical world, about a certain epoch, they view the recorded visual image. In the future, human beings will be able to study the past in this manner.

Question: "Is it possible to increase the capabilities of one's mind?"

For this, hard work is required. People need to subdue their lower nature so that they may be capable of receiving Nature's fine and sensitive vibrations.

Question: "When an atom passes through the human body, does it experience any change?"

Yes, a hydrogen atom that has passed through an animal or a human being differs from another one that has not.

Question: "What is the relationship of the Invisible World to the material one?"

There are Laws that relate to the descent of the worlds into matter. Symbolically, the astral world represents water, and thus it is named the "watery world." The astral world will descend and become like water, intangible.

Question: "Why does the mind become weak?"

This is the result of the accumulation of old ideas within the mind. For example, people are overly concerned with how they will manage their lives. These are old ideas that come from their ancestors. When the balance between thought and emotion is disrupted, this weakens the mind.

When someone seeks to express himself, do not restrain him in this. Instead, direct his attention toward something else—toward the sublime. Should you restrain him, those forces that are seeking expression would be passed on to you. Conduct the following experiment: should you attempt to restrain someone's jealousy by trying to change him, the jealousy will find expression in you.

Question: "Why are Caucasians anxious today?"

It is because of the transgressions that they have committed. People become anxious when they do not live rightly.

Question: "How do human actions affect the life of all humankind?"

The Law states: Whatever happens to the greatest will happen to the least as well. And conversely, what happens to the least will also happen to the greatest. For example, when you give a person one lev, another person should give someone else ten leva. A third one, in turn, should give one hundred leva to someone else. A fourth one should give one thousand leva, and so on.

Everything that you do has an effect on the entire world. What we have done with the wellsprings will affect the events in the world. Whatever you do, thousands of people may do as well. When you turn a key, how can you be certain that thousands will not follow you; and if thousands turn their keys, that millions will not follow them?

Human beings are like interconnected channels; therefore, whenever someone works to improve himself, he works to improve others as well. This Law has another application: Whatever one does in one's worldly existence affects one's inner life as well. For example, when we work to clean up a wellspring, or a path, or the countryside, this will produce a corresponding effect upon the state of our thoughts and emotions. In accordance with this Law, one is held culpable before humankind for all of one's actions. The severity of the transgression is of no significance. The least transgression can produce the same consequences as a big transgression because the individual is interconnected with a multitude of people. When you transgress, you provoke others to transgress as well. You are the "fire-starter" in a box of matches. And when you ignite, the remainder of the matches will start to burn as well.

Question: "Does a person leave his influence upon the place he has visited?"

There are times when you pass through a place and experience elation. This is because a person who had been in an elated state has departed from there. You pass through another place, and now you experience sorrow because a person in a sorrowful state has departed from there. Certain places exist where crimes have been committed. These leave behind a lasting influence that is felt for many years to come.

Every object that has passed through your hands has received a certain influence from you as your nature has become imprinted upon it. Should a person who is receptive touch this object, he will be able to describe through imagery your nature and your existence as well. You lead a virtuous life. Should an object that you have used pass into the hands of another, the impulse will arise in that person—whether it be strong or weak—to live as you do.

A consequence of the above Law is the following precept: The water you have used to wash your face, discard on the flowers, vegetables, trees, but not on places where people walk on or in impure places. If you abide by this rule, you will experience a slight improvement in your existence.

The Gifts of Love

There are days when Nature is in resurgence, bringing a feeling of renewal and inspiration to all.

This morning we all went with the Master to a meadow above the woods. On the horizon, the snow-covered peaks of the Rila Mountains were visible. The shrubs around us were opening their leaves, and below us, the fields that had been sown were turning green. Springtime was in its full glory.

Here it was, among the rocks, that we camped. We lit a fire and placed our constant companion, the red teakettle, upon it. The Master sat down next to a big round stone and opened his traveling altimeter to check the altitude—it was 1,800 meters. Before long, the sisters were serving tea, and we had our breakfast in the all-encompassing silence. The mountain world spoke in its voiceless, beautiful language. The conversation began gradually.

The Master said:

You are hungry, you want to satisfy your hunger. You are thirsty, you want to satisfy your thirst. Love is such a thing. When it comes into your heart, it will awaken within you the desire for work.

What does Love represent? It is the Door through which one goes to God. Hatred is also a door, but through it, one departs from the Presence of God. If you cannot enter into God's Presence in this world, it will be impossible for you to do it in the World beyond.

Only Love can reveal to you what is sublime and noble.

It is sufficient for one to take in a single, minute particle of Love for him to feel an uplifting within his spirit. Within Love, there is light, joy, expansion, life, favorable conditions for growth, and the opportunity to partake of all blessings. Love shares even the smallest of crumbs.

Wherever Love is not present, there suffering and death exist.

If you have love for the Immortal Beings, you will become immortal. Whenever you love, you gain something.

Love brings consolation. If you seek consolation, apply Love.

When Love comes to a poor man, he becomes wealthy. Within Love, you expand and rise upward. Without Love, you diminish and descend. With Love, no one falls. The one who loves ascends.

All people are uplifted through these three principles: Love, Wisdom, and Truth. In this, there is no exception. Throughout the entire history of Creation, not one human being has lived who can say that he has uplifted himself in any other way.

What is Love? It is that which always succeeds. What is hatred?—that which always fails.

If someone loves me, that person benefits. If I love someone, I benefit.

Why is it that you cannot attain your desires? It is because you have not come to know Love in its fullness. When one has Love, everything else is easily attained.

Health is due to Love.

The absence of Love has never contributed to anything. It is power taken away from Love and used in a different way. This absence of Love will cause us to lose our strength, grow tired, and develop a need for rest. The need for rest indicates that we need to apply Love so that we may draw energy from it.

When Love is speaking to you, you have everything. There is no greater suffering than when Love ceases to speak to you. When Love does not speak to us, the reason for this is our lack of understanding.

When Love comes, everything will become attainable. When Love goes away, everything will become unattainable. When the Sun rises, everything becomes clear; when it sets, everything becomes unclear.

In the presence of Love, you should make use of the smallest gifts of Love. Do not ask for the greatest gifts.

The hardest thing is to love; and yet it is the easiest as well. There is nothing easier and more difficult at the same time than this. Someone says, "It is easy to apply Love." For the one who has knowledge, it is easy; but for the one who has no knowledge, it is difficult.

People who apply Love have everything in abundance. It is a wondrous power. As soon as they encounter Divine Love, they connect with abundance and share it with their fellowmen.

In human love, everything perishes.

The only thing that gives of itself is Love. All that we have is due to Love. What is always giving, always flowing, and never ceases to flow—this is Love. Love says, "I take away everything, and I give everything." For you to come to understand Love, you need to give.

In the manifested, revealed, and realized Love of God, the Good sprouts, Justice grows, Truth blossoms, and Wisdom bears fruit. Wisdom and Truth cannot be understood without Love.

Love is what gives impulse to positive ideas.

Love does not concern itself with the external forms alone; for, as long as you only concern yourselves with the external forms, you are in the physical world. When you begin to concern yourselves with the content, you are in the Spiritual world. And when you concern yourselves with the meaning, you are in the Divine World.

You can clearly perceive someone only if you love that person. Only the one who loves can see. Those who do not love see as if in a fog; they do not really see, and they do not understand.

When you go before Love, you should renounce all that is familiar to you. You should not elaborate upon your hardships; it is better to keep silent. Love does not want to be told about the past. Neither does Love want to know about the future.

Every open door speaks about one's understanding of Love. Every closed door speaks about one's misunderstanding of Love. It is said about someone, "His heart is closed." Do not attempt to knock on closed hearts. Someone wishes to be wealthy, famous, and powerful. These are closed hearts. These things have nothing to do with Love. Someone thinks that if he dresses well or possesses considerable knowledge, he will be loved. Knowledge is only Love's servant. Knowledge, least of all, is able to bring you to Love; it is merely a vehicle of Love.

You love someone, yet, that person is only one "word" in Love's language. All people are Love's "words." And yet, because people here on Earth are not good, they cease to be "words" of Love's language. As a result, contradictions arise.

Of all Divine acts, Love is the most free.

When one speaks about Divine Love, courage is required.

What is the purpose of Love? To teach people to live rightly.

Special days of Love exist about which only the Advanced Beings know.

You should love without being carried away by it. I would like to convey to you the state of that being who is filled with Love and alive with faith in God. What beautiful garments such a being is wearing! There is nothing more beautiful than finding the person within whose heart the Love of God abides. This has the significance of finding a precious stone or a wellspring. This is the image that you should have about Love.

If you go into a desert with Divine Love, it will transform it into a garden. Love is the strongest force of all, and is a Power as well. No single external power can oppose Love.

The Angels bow down before Love. When it speaks through a person, that person becomes strong and powerful. Powerful is the one who has Love. You can accomplish nothing if Love does not work through you. Without Love, there is no Power, no Health, and no Life. Depending upon the strength of someone's love, I will know how long a person will remain with me. When someone loves, one stays longer.

Love is springtime; not loving is winter. Not loving can be compared to sunset, and Love, to sunrise. Love is a Fire that no man can extinguish. Once you are kindled by the Fire of Love, you will be afire for all eternity. All previous bonds will disappear. There is one alone that will not disappear: the bond of Love.

Where there is Love, everything will come to pass. Where there is no Love, everything will be destroyed. One needs to dwell in Love in the same way that one dwells in the light and in the air.

A person of Love cannot be tempted, nor is he a temptation for others.

When the weak one stands in the way of Love's Path, Love goes around them in order not to run them over. For all those who do not know Love, God has special ways to educate and transform them.

If a tree comes to love you, it will bear sweeter fruit. When you go to a wellspring that loves you, it will begin to gush and flow more powerfully. Should it not love you, the surging of the water will diminish. If someone's hand comes to love you, is it the hand itself that loves you? Behind the wellspring, there is an Intelligent Light Being who loves you.

The world suffers because of the scant love, but is blissful because of the abundant one.

The meaning of Life lies in one's eternal striving toward Love.

The Still Small Voice

In the calm warm nights, we gathered around our beloved Master under the big trees in the garden. We were singing and talking. We will never forget those evenings. The day would come to its end. The bright colors would fade and the forms would disappear as another reality emerged before our gaze.

The Master spoke:

From inside the Invisible World or from the depths of Creation, God secretly works within the minds and hearts of human souls. He works within every cell and removes every groan and lament in the world. One day, He will set everything right and in order. He says, "Be not afraid. Wait. Be patient. In a while, the pain will cease." You are hungry. He says to you, "Soon you will have bread."

There is no state more beautiful than God's Presence within the depths of your soul. You are ill. From within, God says to you, "Be not afraid; soon you will be healthy." And truly, you become well. Your affairs are in disarray. God says to you, "Do not worry, things will work out." And they do. On the worst days of your life, He says to you, "Do not worry; everything will be all right."

The water that was taken from the wellspring today is of greater consequence than the water that was taken in the past. The Word that God speaks to us now is also of greater consequence. In the past, the mother spoke to her child in one way. Now that the child has grown, she speaks to her son or daughter differently. And yet, there is no contradiction between the mother's speaking to the small child and the grown one.

Who is He that is pushing us toward the sublime, toward the noble? God is—the Divine within us. This still small Voice that speaks within us is God. He speaks within all people. Someone does not want to surrender. The still small Voice whispers, "Surrender. Submit." Sometimes this small Voice tells you, "What you did is not right." You are glad, joyful. This is because God is speaking to you. God tells you, "I am sorry that you committed this transgression. You did not act rightly."

God speaks to all. All hear God's Voice speaking to them. When God speaks to someone, even if He tells him only one Word, this is worth more than anything that person has ever possessed. Only God teaches the human being. I desire that God would tell you one Word every day. It is important for you to be conscious of that moment when God speaks to you. He will say only one Word. If you do not seize it, you will lose everything. When God speaks to people, most of them are "sleeping." When the Angels speak to them, again they are asleep.

Suffering develops our hearing that we may perceive the most tender vibration of God's Voice. We have come to Earth to learn the art of listening to the Voice of God. Only now, does Life begin for us.

Listen to that still small Voice that speaks to your hearts. This is the Voice of God. On the Earth, there is not one human being to whom this Voice does not speak.

If you apply Love, the Angels will begin to visit you daily and bring you a love letter that has been sent by your great Father.

When the Great One begins to speak to us, Light will appear within our minds, and within our hearts—an expansion. We come to love all people, all things: all flowers, trees, and birds. Everything is beautiful.

Listen to what God is telling you now. Be glad for what God has told you in the past. We erroneously think that God has spoken in the past, but not in the present. This is not true. God speaks to us today as well. But when you err, you cannot hear God's Voice clearly, and you start to doubt, to hesitate. God speaks to all beings. He speaks to them continuously.

Everything that we do—what we think, feel, and act upon—is reflected within the Divine Consciousness. Then and there God speaks to us. In this way, the human consciousness is always being reflected within the Divine Consciousness; it is the latter that speaks to human beings. This means that the Divine Consciousness is also reflected within the human consciousness.

The Unknown Love

Someone had left a big, beautiful apple on the Master's table. The Master looked at the fruit, smiled, and said:

An angel comes, brings you a gift, or helps you, and leaves. You do not know his name. You, too, should act in this way.

Love does not have much time to explain to you what it is or tell you its name. Love is very busy, and for this reason, it leaves you a gift and departs.

Love without having people know about it, and this will be beneficial for you as well. The one who gives love does not need to speak about his love; and the one who receives love should not speak about it either. If someone loves, this should be his secret; nobody else should know about it.

Sometimes you have the desire to explain to people how Love has revealed itself to you. Do not do that. Love does not want you to share with others whatever it has revealed to you. If there is a need, Love will tell them itself.

Jacob's weakness was not his love for his son, Joseph, but that he showed his love for him in the presence of his other sons. They did not need to know about it; this was his mistake.

Sublime Love is selfless. You should love someone without his knowing about it; otherwise, Love will lose its quality of selflessness. In this lies the difference between Divine Love and human love. It is difficult to observe the Law of Unknown Love. This is attainable only by the Advanced Beings. Those who can keep this Law are the minority.

When you love, be glad that you are fulfilling God's Will. The Law is as follows: If you say that you love, you will lose your Love. You will lose what you cherish. Love conceals itself. Love will not allow itself to be defiled. When you love, do not speak about this. As soon as you tell someone that you love that person, immediately a conflict will follow.

Keep the following precept: You cannot be truly happy as long as you do not love with unconditional Love. I do not want you to merely believe this. If you would like, test this out for one year: love without anyone's knowledge, thus, you will verify this truth. Be wellsprings that water may flow out of you in abundance and quench the thirst of human souls; do so without their knowledge.

The Conditions for Attaining Real Knowledge

During a talk, the Master said:

Knowledge and freedom are given according to the intensity of one's Love. Only the one who has attained Love in its fullness is able to possess real knowledge. When you unite with Love, you will receive Divine Light. When Love visits you, you will come to possess the knowledge of real science as well. The mind should look through the eyes of Love.

Do not deceive yourselves into thinking that you can be powerful without Love. Someone says, "Even without Love, I can accomplish my desires." You can accomplish nothing. Search throughout history for at least one great reformer or one great Teacher who has achieved his goal without Love. They might have some success temporarily; but all this will be destroyed, and no mention of them will remain. Power manifested without Love is sentenced to destruction.

If you love, your faith will grow stronger. If you love, you might become a poet, an artist, a musician, a scientist—anything that you desire. The conditions for growth and development are hidden within Love. Love develops the gifts within human beings. It gives vision. To be able to see into the Spiritual world, one should be filled with Love.

Should you manifest even the smallest Love, the first indication, which tells you, that you have the Blessing of the Divine will be the revelation of something great. Should a person manifest the smallest Divine Love, a curtain would be lifted from that person's view in an instant, and the Sublime Beings who dwell in the realm of Love would become visible to that person. They would smile and say, "Walk on this Path! This is the Path on which we walk." After that, the curtain would fall again. Can you become discouraged if every day the curtain lifts, and you see what gives Life and meaning to all things?

Divine Poetry

We were gathered around our beloved Master. Some of the brothers and sisters read works of Bulgarian poets and foreign poets as well. A discussion of poetry began.
The Master said:

Art should have two related qualities. Primarily, it is necessary for art to present a model—an ideal—to which one may aspire. Art should represent the Sublime Life so that it may awaken in us the aspiration to come to know God. Secondly, a sublime Divine Idea should become incarnate in the representation, and in such a way, that this Eternal Divine Idea will be born within the consciousness of the one who contemplates on the representation, becoming alive within. In this way, art is able to connect man with the Divine and with the Eternal Ideas.

Poetry should be so sublime that people who are discouraged will, upon reading this poetry, forget about their suffering and attain new insights.

Poets or writers need to align their creative energy with that of the Intelligent Nature that they may write well. Only Living Nature is capable of inspiring human beings toward the great and sublime in life.

The poet whose forehead is broad in the upper part possesses imagination. This broadness of the forehead will be lacking in the one who writes mediocre poetry.

Poetry will indicate the level of consciousness a culture has attained at the time of the writing of the poetry.

According to me, the genuine poet or writer is the one who, even if he or she might have written only a single word, has done the writing with the heart's blood. This single word is a manifestation of the core essence. Whatever you write about should first be experienced.

Every poet, musician, and artist is the collective manifestation of many souls. That poets may begin to manifest their greatness, thousands of very gifted souls need to come together to manifest through those writers. Whenever people write, many Advanced Beings come to assist them. The Advanced Beings rejoice over each word that comes out of those writers' pens. Sometimes when poets are writing, Beings from the Higher Worlds come down and dictate to them.

The hand of every poet who writes libelous and defamatory verse will wither. However, the hand of every poet who writes sacred verse will be blessed. Consider a poet who has written something. If what that poet has written is fruitful, that person will rejoice, not only for that moment, but for many years to come. If what that poet has written is malevolent and causes harm, he or she will suffer.

All poets know—to a certain degree—when their works are read. You are a poet, and you feel joyful. The reason for this is that you have written something good, and when it is read, you experience fulfillment. There are other times, however, that you have written something that is mediocre, and when it is read, you experience distress.

Only that one who aspired to become a poet while still in Heaven will be a poet on Earth. Every individual is destined to become a first-class poet at some point in time. Order as well as other favorable conditions exists in Eternity that enable humans to manifest. In the Divine World, a Law exists for this. However, you should wait for your time—you should not hasten. God has chosen the time for every being to manifest. One should wait for this moment for a thousand or even a million years. Your day will come when you will be told, "Come forth and manifest!" All of the Cosmos will then manifest through you. Are you ready for this moment? Each and every one of you should prepare yourself for this great day!

Tolstoy was a man of genius: he possessed an inner vision. In "War and Peace," he stressed that it was not Napoleon, the individual, who made history on his own, but that other factors existed in Intelligent Nature that were working through him.

At the time when our Bulgarian poets were doing their writing, the sky was dark; there was even thunder. That is to say, the conditions under which they worked were unfavorable. For this reason, they have not written sacred works.

In India, Tagore had a mystical and spiritual environment in which to work that made it possible for him to write such masterpieces. Tagore's father set aside a special time each day for meditation and contemplation. Tagore arose from bed before dawn each day to spend time in meditation. For this reason, he was able to write sacred masterpieces such as "Gitanjali," "The Gardener," and others.

In the future, great poets will be born in Bulgaria. All that has been written so far is merely a prelude.

Poetry and music are two fundamental elements of life. Music represents the external aspect of life, and poetry, the internal aspect.

Receiving and Giving

During a morning walk, the Master said:

Two Laws exist by which human beings must abide: receiving and giving. One receives and gives. Within Nature, an interchange always needs to take place: you need to receive and you need to give.

We want to hold onto things for ourselves. Can you hold onto the air? You can merely inhale and exhale the air. In a manner similar to your inhaling and exhaling the air—so, too, you need to give after you have received. Inhalation represents receiving, whereas exhalation represents giving. If you do not exhale, you will not be able to receive the fresh air anew. Once having given, you have the possibility of receiving.

Suffering occurs when we begin to receive more than we give. Fruit trees give abundantly to people. We need to learn from the trees' generosity. Be generous, give abundantly.

You need to see yourself as a letter carrier. When you are delivering letters, you are giving. You will be compensated for delivering letters as required. If you do not deliver them, you will be held responsible. You will be asked, "What have you done with the letters?" We are merely letter carriers because all things in the Universe—light, air, water, clothes—all things come from God. Hold onto those Divine blessings that come your way for a time and then give them away. Only hold onto whatever you need. Relinquish the rest; share it with others.

A certain Law exists within Nature. Should someone come to me and I have only one apple, I would tell myself, "Either I will eat the apple or the other person will." And so, I will give the apple. A little while later, I meet another person who gives me two apples. Compliance to the Laws of Nature lies in this: what I think, feel, or do for others will come back to me as well. According to this Law, you will receive as much as you have given.

Trials in Love

In each conversation, in each lecture, the Master gave us insight into the many sides of Love. He unveiled before our eyes a beautiful and infinitely varied world, somehow familiar and intimate. Once, when we were gathered around the Master, he said:

Your love is continuously tried that you may better comprehend the breadth of the Love within you. You assume that you love, but your love is not the kind that will improve your existence. Which kind of love is it? The ordinary human kind. You will pass through many trials to test which kind of love is yours. God tests you that He may try out your love. In like manner, He puts your mind to the test as well.

Love overcomes all suffering, whereas the mind overcomes all contradictions. When the love of modern people is put to the test—some will pass, but others will not.

That person whose Love, Wisdom, and Truth cannot be taken away, I consider to be a hero.

Should someone regret that he has loved, then that person's love was not genuine. The love that does not endure all trials is not genuine—it is only a mood, a feeling, a transient emotion. Those who deny Love leave themselves open for adversity to enter, and their existence will become full of sadness and sorrow. You are sorrowful because you have denied a loving feeling. You say, "I love." Your love needs to be tested. When the least thing is capable of offending you, this indicates that your love is not genuine.

All of the experiences that a person endures are tests.

When a person loses moral stability, Love will vanish as well.

There is an old legend that tells of a Prophet who brought a New Teaching to Persia. Many believed in this Teaching. Once the Prophet told them, "God has given me the Commandment that you must sacrifice your life for Him." Only a young couple who loved one another told him, "We are ready to sacrifice ourselves." In the Prophet's tent, there was a ram. When the couple entered the tent, the Prophet slaughtered the ram and its blood poured out from the tent. Upon seeing this, all the others ran away, but the young couple passed their test. Love is often tested in a similar way. This test was given by the Prophet that he would know whose faith was genuine.

Divine Justice

The work on our "Wellspring of Good" proceeded well. The Master himself participated in the work and supervised it. When he turned his attention to something, all gathered around him. Great attentiveness and thoroughness were applied to this work. The basin was enlarged and three granite steps were put in place along the path. A platform paved with stones was made, and a flume for the flowing water as well. There were workers all about and bystanders too; some were coming, while others were going.

The Master was thoughtful, as if he were solving a difficult task. He worked like a mathematician dealing with number values, both known and unknown. Everything possessed significance: what kind of people were coming and when? Where would they stand? What would their part in the work be? Which initiatives and ideas might arise and how would they be implemented? On this day, everything had a substance and meaning that had never been present before. Phenomena came together in accordance with strange and unfamiliar Laws to form a whole, in the way that individual letters and words come together to form a sentence. These phenomena formed the dynamic and mystical language that was known only to the Master. The Intelligent World took part in our work, as these were the most difficult and fateful days for the Bulgarian people and all of humankind as well.

When the work was completed, the Master evaluated everything once again and saw that it was done well. Afterward, we gathered around the Master, and he began to speak about the Law of Justice:

Justice should be applied to the human existence—Justice in respect to the resources that have been provided.

If there needs to be a religion, it should be a religion of Love. If there needs to be a public social system, it should be a system of Justice.

There exists today a new direction in the Universe for all. The outmoded precepts need to be replaced with new ones. New precepts are required. One of the new precepts states: Love others, as you would like to be loved. Every person should know that the good he desires for himself should be good for others as well.

According to Mosaic Law, the social problem of integrity is resolved as follows: Whatever one receives over the course of 49 years, one must give back on the 50th year. In that year, everyone will become equal again. The 50th year is a jubilee: all celebrate it. Then all give back to their brethren what they have taken from them. Forty-five jubilee years have passed to date without being celebrated. Now 45 jubilee years should come one after the other, that Justice—the equitable distribution of resources—can be restored. Because 2,500 years have passed without the jubilee years being celebrated, these 45 jubilee years will be celebrated together. This is "the end of times." The end of times began in 1914. During the 45 years that come after, all should give back everything that they have taken to everyone that they have taken from.

According to the Mosaic Law, a person that has been a slave will become a free individual after 49 years. Those who have dominion over land received from another must give it back after 49 years to the one from whom they have taken it.

If the people who govern do not equitably resolve all issues in dispute among nations, the world will experience cataclysmic change in the years to follow. Over the course of 45 years, people will need to become free of everything belonging to others, in order to balance the old accounts.

Everything and everyone created by God and set on the Earth is entitled to an equitable life. No one may take away this entitlement.

The Great Omniscient Cause regards all people equally. Oppression is intolerable to God. God is patient, and yet retribution will ultimately come.

No one can take away the bounties that have been given to you. Should they be taken away from you, sooner or later they will be given back to you.

Every human being is born with certain Divine rights. No one has the right to take away the Divine rights that have been given to you. I am referring to those rights that God has given to you. This is the new consciousness that is awakening. All should honor the entitlements of all people.

You have a book that, although it might be plain on the outside, you love it because of its content. In the same way, one should honor the Divine that is imparted to all: all human beings, all animals, and all plants. The Law of Justice requires this. From this point of view, if someone commits a transgression, do not say that he is bad because you will put into discord the Law of Justice—that is to say, the honor you owe to every living being. This person is like the fruit that is in the process of ripening: He has not ripened yet, but he will.

To be able to act in accordance with the Law of Justice, we should be thoughtful and considerate of others. It is Justice that defines the relationship among people.

The Good is what benefits all and not just one. Justice requires that everyone should benefit from God's bounties. To desire to receive and hold these resources for ourselves, this is not right. We should distribute them to all others as well.

Children grow and their expenses grow comparable to their growth. In their first year, the expenses are few; in the second, they will be greater, and so on. The same is also true for nations. They also grow, and their food supply, shelter, and clothing need to increase as well. The resources provided by Nature should be available to all, which means that all should be able to benefit from them.

Love in the future will be dramatically different from love in the present. The new kind of Love will be characterized by the following: what is good for one will also be good for all. Abundance has always been sent from the Invisible World. We live in a world of abundance. There is sufficient food, clothing, and everything else, but these are not properly distributed. If people lived rightly, there would be enough for all. Their error is in the desire of some to possess more resources than is their due. Everyone should possess only as much as is needed.

In the human order, phenomena are not properly organized. In the Divine Order, there is an abundance, but not excess; there is no need for one to make provisions for the future. The wealthy and the poor are both provided for so that they may be assured of having air and light. They are not deprived of water either. Who can deprive a human being of water that flows from the mountain? Humans' great delusion comes from the unwillingness to subject themselves to the Divine Order that is implanted within them. People desire to build their own system in order to impose their own laws. Human laws are useless. We do not need to teach the stomach how to digest food—it knows how to do its job. We need only to chew our food well. The same is also true for the heart. If you interfere with its action, you will disturb its normal functioning. Divine Laws exist for this, but we need to apply them.

To give to all according to their needs, this is the requirement of the Divine Law of Justice. Less is required for the small child, more for the adult. Equity does not mean making people uniform. It means that each should be given the necessary conditions and rights according to one's level of development.

We desire wealth. This is a misunderstanding. Everyone needs to work. All may receive as much as they need from the Divine Wellspring, but none may draw more Water than they need. The accumulation of resources is not tolerated.

The Law states: All may receive as much as they can carry. One night a wealthy man had the following dream: he came upon a wagon loaded with gold that was led by three pairs of white buffalo, and everyone received some of the gold. This man carried a large trunk and asked to have it filled with gold. He was told that everyone could receive as much as he could carry on his back. And so, they strapped the trunk to his back and started to fill it. They put in one shovel-full, two shovels, three, and he would always say, "More! More!" Eventually the trunk became so heavy that the wealthy man could no longer move and suffocated from its weight. Upon awakening from his dream, he realized that his wealth was greater than his need, and so he began to share it with others.

You pass by a tree, you are entitled to pick some fruits and eat them. You go on a journey, if there is a wellspring every five to ten kilometers, do you need to carry a canteen with water?

Justice is the essential Law that is responsible for the distribution of Divine resources through all sectors of society. In order for peace to exist in a country, there must be equality among the people, without exception. The wealthy person is afraid of being robbed; the poor one is afraid of dying from hunger. Let the wealthy person give half of his wealth to the poor one. The resources are to be made available to all people. They need to be removed from those places where they are in abundance that they may be distributed to those who have little or none.

I meet a person who tells me, "My sack is empty; I do not know what to do. My children are dying of hunger." I meet another person with a full sack, who says, "My sack is heavy. I do not know how I will be able to carry it home." Let the one with the heavy sack call to the one with the empty sack and tell him, "Brother, both of us are facing death. Take half the contents of my sack that both our conditions may improve."

Someone says, "God has determined the fate of both the wealthy and the poor." I ask him, "Have you spoken with God?" He responds, "One of the prophets three thousand years ago did." I ask him, "Have you spoken with the prophet?"

The social problem of integrity needs to be resolved. The foundation of its resolution should come from the process of breathing. Resources should be distributed rightly in order that giving and receiving may be regulated. In this way, people can be alleviated of their constant concerns for food. When God made bread, He forbade its sale. A great curse hangs over humankind. Why? It is because you sell bread, which is life's greatest bounty. It is absolutely forbidden to sell bread or flour.

Bulgaria needs to become the first country to apply the Divine Law of the land: bread should be given for free. Only the one who applies this Law is pure and free from transgression. God tells us, "You are not entitled to sell or purchase the bounties that I have provided." This Truth—to distribute bread, free of charge—needs to be applied now on Earth. It is not permissible to sell bread to your neighbor. This is part of the resolution of the social problem.

There is a Law that states: The one who does not freely share his resources needs to eventually share them according to the Law of Coercion. This means that if you do not share them freely, they will be taken from you by force.

A prominent, wealthy man walked along a road. A poor man saw him and told him, "Do not take this road: there is a precipice further on." The rich man only replied, "That is not of your concern." And so, he continued to walk, and he fell into the precipice and started to call for help. The poor man came to his rescue saying, "I warned you!" After this, the rich man who had fallen came to his senses. This means that because he had this experience, he began to appreciate compassion.

When we speak about Divine Order, we need to visualize a world of abundance. Wherever abundance exists, crimes are not committed. Will it be a problem for me to give an abundance of water to all if I am standing by a lake?

The Divine Order is an Order of Love, the Love that bears abundance. All need to enter into the Divine Order that we may build a new way of life.

Humility

The Master told us:

When man is descending—that is to say, in involution—he is prideful, living with his memory of higher existence. When man is ascending along the path of evolution, he has humility because he sees the heights to which he aspires and seeks to reach. The one who is prideful descends, whereas the one who has humility ascends. The one who is prideful descends that he might explore the depths; conversely, the one who has humility ascends that he might explore the heights. When a prideful person descends, he will say, "How deep this well is!" And yet, when the person with humility reaches the summit, he will say, "How high this summit is!"

Humility is the first condition for connecting with God. This is the Law of the Universal Brotherhood of Light. Humility is the primary quality required of the disciple. You should go before God not as a righteous or knowledgeable one, but as a humble one.

When you feel that you have power, this is because many Beings connect with you inwardly. However, when you believe that this power is your own, that you do everything by yourself, these Beings will make no objection, but they will withdraw from you. You will then remain alone so that you might comprehend how weak you are when on your own.

Many people study and busy themselves in many ways, but they do not achieve success because they have many ambitions and seek prominence.

You need to understand that humility is required by Law for the preservation of one's life force. The one who has humility is able to accomplish good work with only a little energy.

Humility is the root of the One Real Knowledge. Pride is the root of transient knowledge. You might possess considerable knowledge, but if you are prideful, you will be in the state of one who has been deluded by the forces of darkness.

When you abide by Divine Law, even if you are the least evolved, you will ascend. Should a person desire for Heaven to take an interest in him and bless him, he needs to have humility.

Both in the elevated and ordinary sense of the word, humility fosters all those Divine virtues aspired by the human spirit and soul. Only the one who has humility can be spiritual.

Only through Love, can you begin to comprehend humility. Through humility, one begins to realize that there are many high peaks.

Only a great person, a saint, and a Self-Realized Teacher, have humility. They understand that even though they are evolved, nothing can be attained without the power of the Sublime World. The one who has humility says, "Lord, let Your Will be done, not mine." The most sublime manifestation of humility is one's desire to fulfill the Will of God.

Happiness and Eternal Bliss

During a morning walk, the Master said:

Only when all people attain true happiness, will we attain the utmost happiness. Until all have happiness, none will be fully happy. All search for personal happiness, but herein lies the misunderstanding. If the entire world is suffering, but only one experiences happiness, I ask: Is life meaningful? The issue concerns whether the one who searches for personal happiness will find it. In other words, one finds happiness not by searching for it, but by being sought after.

Seek not happiness in the present conditions. Everyone today searches for happiness outside of God. Herein lies their error. Do not search for happiness in another person, seek it within the Divine. A fundamental bond exists between your soul and God. Re-establish this bond and all will work for your good.

People of today desire happiness in life, but they do not understand its Laws. Happiness includes the following elements: faith, wisdom, imagination, and love. It includes also an understanding of the natural laws—those of solid, liquid, and gaseous matter—as well as those of light, electricity, and electro-magnetism.

Happiness is not the only way for humans to resolve their life's tasks. Animals are capable of having a good life as well; they can be happy without ever having resolved the tasks of their lives.

Do not search for happiness in the material, but seek for it in the Eternal Bliss. I speak of the great process toward perfection. We did not come to Earth for the purpose of achieving happiness, but to study. True happiness cannot be attained on Earth in its present stage of development, it is for the future. Humankind should prepare the necessary conditions so that everlasting happiness may come in the future.

Eternal Bliss exists in that place where all virtues are present. Happiness can be found only when none of the virtues is missing.

The Law of Love

Regardless of the many achievements that have been accomplished by people today in the fields of science, arts, technology, social welfare, and the distribution of economic resources—one thing is still missing: Love. Only through Love can all these accomplishments be beneficial, of great value for all. Only through Love can these be used in such a way that they have significance. If people do not embrace Love, they will lose everything and will experience ruin.

The Master preached about Love as the path of salvation for all humankind. He revealed its manifestations, qualities, actions, and Laws, as well as the infinite wealth of the perfect World from which he came. He bore witness to this World with his life, his Teaching, and every deed.

The Master always had something new to say about Love. One day, he told us:

The moment in which we attain Love, we will be one with God. When I speak about Love, you need to understand that I am speaking of the only way of coming to know God. If we do not come to know God, He will not be able to give us His Knowledge.

The Law states: When you speak about Love, speak with your softest voice. Speak so softly that you are hardly able to be heard. And speak softly about Light and Wisdom as well. Speak as softly as the dawn.

Divine Virtues have their fragrance. If Justice comes into your heart, Truth into your mind, and Sacredness into your will power, you are going to emit an inner fragrance more pleasant than the floral one. This inner fragrance, this sublime aroma, is called "nyuks." There is not a better nectar than the nyuks created by Nature. The alchemists have sought after this element for centuries. When you work it out, you will be a happy person, and your joy will be beyond words. Love is the main component in this nectar. For example, you know who loves you, even when this person has not uttered a word. Love has a strong fragrance like the carnation; you can sense it from far away.

There is a Law in Life, the Law of Diversity, by which everyone can manifest Love according to their understanding, and they will never do wrong. Therefore, it is not necessary to teach people how to love.

Another unique characteristic of Love is that you cannot express love in the same way to everyone. Your love toward each person is unique. Because every person is a unique manifestation of God, each manifests his love in a specific way. You can sense this subtle distinction. Your Love has a unique intrinsic quality that no other person possesses. It is this that makes each person unique.

Love first manifests to God—to the Sublime—then to the weak, the needy, the abandoned, and finally to like beings. This last manifestation of Love is called "the Love of like beings." In this Love an exchange among the souls exists. This is Love in its state of ascension, through which souls are able to evolve and the consciousness is able to expand.

Should a good person with a weak character become enamored with one who is in darkness, the good person will begin to err and will take on the other's faults. However, if a good person experiences Divine Love, this will not happen.

To dwell in the presence of Love, one should take the ascending path; that is to say, one should come into union with the Invisible World and with God. A good person is the one who is united with those who are powerful, with those who come from on High. If he is not, he will be taken advantage of for being good. And yet, when you are united with the Ones who are powerful—with the Divine—all of your wealth will be deposited in the Divine Bank and you will become protected; whereas here on Earth, only your savings book is held.

There is a Law that states: When two people either like or despise one another, they will receive from one another the most positive and virtuous character traits at first, and after this, the most negative and immoral character traits. This is an inextricable Law. Regardless of whether you like or despise a person, you will begin to behave as he does. You ask, "What can I do to free myself of this Law?" You cannot free yourself of this Law. But you can love the Divine within every human being. Therefore, love God within whomever He manifests Himself, that you may begin to love as He does. For this reason, begin loving the Divine within all beings.

Another Law of Love states: When you love another, you will receive half of his good or bad state. Should he become impoverished, you will become poor as well; should he become wealthy, you will acquire half of his wealth.

Another Law states: Even when all despise you, there will always be one who loves you. When all begin to love you, there will always be at least one who does not love you. This cannot be avoided. This Law is based upon our present level of development.

You meet a person who appears to love you. Why does he love you? There had been a time when you wanted him to love you; and so, now he loves you. Incomprehensible are the ways of God.

A Law is stated as follows: When you perceive whatever is the most sublime within someone, that person will become attracted to you.

Another Law of Love states: He who abide in Love will have the power to attract others to himself. Should he pass by a person, this is sufficient for him to be followed. However, the person abiding in Love will only be recognized by those whose consciousness has been awakened. But for those whose consciousness has not been awakened, he is considered to be an ordinary person. The one who abides in Love can be compared to a flower in bloom that attracts the bees. Why are they all attracted to this flower? It is because there is something that they can receive from it. This is what Love represents, the ideal life. Should the Law of Love be imparted to us, we would have the power to attract others. One of your assignments is to receive from God and pass on to others what has been received. When you love someone, it is because other people love you, and with this Love, you love him. This is the Law of the oneness of Love.

When I tell you that I love someone, it is because I am aware that this Love has already come to realization. It could have come to realization in the physical, in the spiritual, or in the Divine World.

A brother asked, "How is love able to become contaminated?"

The Master replied:

All thoughts that reach you, these become your personal environment. When love enters this environment, it absorbs the influence of your negative thoughts and becomes contaminated in this way.

One Law of Love reigns supreme: The one who loves you rejoices over the least thing you offer. The one who loves you may give you a small seed, and you should rejoice because from out of this seed, something great will be brought forth. Only Love is able to create something great from the least of things. Whenever a person lives outside of Love, the greatest of things will diminish. And yet, when a person abides in Love, the least of things will increase. We all need to test these things.

The First Impulse

We rested and talked with our beloved Master on the summit of the mountain. The grasses and first flowers were just coming up from the earth. A warm and fragrant wind was blowing. Flocks of birds flew high in the sky, and above them white clouds floated on their way to some unknown place. We all listened to the song of life that was present in the stillness. After a time of silence, the conversation started up again.

The Master said:

Someone says, "I pray." In prayer, as well as in everything else, we need to act out of Love. It is our first impulse. The second impulse is toward Divine Wisdom, the third toward Divine Freedom.

Love is the collective manifestation of all Intelligent Beings who have completed their evolution and become one with God. If love is not the collective manifestation of all Intelligent Beings, then it is not true Love. Your love is theirs and your joy is theirs as well. Conversely, their Love is yours, and their joy is yours as well.

God and all of the Divine World participate in Love. The quality of Love depends upon the number of beings who take part in it. The greater the number of beings who take part in your unconditional Love, the higher the vibration it will have. Love will then be uplifting, healing, and helpful under all circumstances.

Someone claims that he does not love. This is not completely correct. As long as this person is like the wheat in the granary, his love cannot be demonstrated; but when he has been sown in the field and germinates, he can begin to love.

A person's profession and social status is of no significance. Social status is a transient thing. One may be a poet, an artist, a man, or a woman—all need to love. To love means to give expression to God's Love. We need to come to know the person apart from his profession or role as mother, father, physician, and so on. We need to come to know each person as the manifestation of his soul.

Divine Love

The Master told us:

We grow old and decline. Our perspective changes, but our aspirations remain unchanged. They do not grow old, but endure forever and give the human soul the impulse to move forward and upward. This motivating force is Love. It is the Eternal Origin within the human being that creates and builds.

Love is the greatest power. Although you may receive only a small dose, when you begin to embrace it, Love will increase. Love is the only Power that continuously increases. Do not search for Love in large dosages. Even a small dose of Love will increase in just a little while. Should your love not increase, then this love is not genuine.

Love is that power that nothing can resist: the Sacred Fire through which all of your thoughts and desires should pass. All things that have not passed through this Fire are contaminated.

Just as the chick follows its mother, so should you follow your Great Mother: Love. Do not obstruct Love from manifesting through you. The one who errs against Love will find it difficult to establish balance and harmony within. The consequences for those who defy the Law of Love will be similar to those of the buffalo that stood in opposition to a train and was overrun. Every being who carries within the desire to resist the manifestation of Divine Love will be overrun like the buffalo.

Love is a wellspring. The flow of a wellspring cannot be obstructed. Should you attempt to obstruct it, this wellspring will sweep you away.

Do not delay loving. Now is the time you should begin to love—in the present moment, not in the future. If the pressure of the steam boiler is not released, it will eventually explode. Only Love can save man from this explosion.

Do not deny the least loving feeling that arises in your soul. Some will say, "This feeling is of little significance." This is not correct. This small feeling of Love will bring you great blessings in the future. These small feelings and thoughts of Love are like the sparks of light that flicker here and there in the darkness. This light in the darkness awakens joy within you because you have found the Path. People today disregard these thoughts and feelings and search for happiness and success in the external.

For the least sublime thoughts, feelings, or actions that are concealed within your soul and known to none, God will bless you.

Love is beyond human laws. Love should be given free expression. Love—in and of itself—is a Law. When you abide in Love, you are completely free. God gives people total freedom. Those of us who are in the world limit one another by saying, "You should not love this one or that one." Whenever someone attempts to express his love, leave him be. Do not impose any restraints upon him, lest adversities come. People should never interfere with someone's feelings of love. This sacred ground belongs to God. Do not concern yourselves with the question of who loves whom—this is none of your concern. It is a question that belongs to God and God alone.

All good and virtuous people serve as transmitters of God's blessings so that they may be received by all. Every particle, no matter how small, is infused with a great energy; and if we were to live according to the Laws of Love, this energy would manifest.

No deprivation exists with Divine Love: it provides for us in every way. Wherever Love abides, so does abundance. When a loving person enters a home, he brings the blessings that he carries within.

The Divine excludes all jealousy, doubt, mistrust, thoughtlessness, and violence. The love that is jealous is not genuine. When you begin to comprehend that Love is indivisible, you will no longer be jealous. When you desire to rid yourselves of the misery of human love—from jealousy, envy, doubt—drink from the Divine Wellspring. The negative expressions of love result from a misunderstanding. You cannot bear it when someone loves the person whom you love: these are human concepts. Jean Valjean had not yet become Jean Valjean because he was enamored with Cosetta.[19] Yet, she loved someone else, and for this reason, he suffered. So, he had not yet become Jean Valjean [the true man].

When you abide in Love, you are protected: evil thought-forms cannot penetrate you. The inferior beings of darkness are unable to influence you.

A brother asked, "What is the connection between personal love and human existence?"
The Master answered:

When you love, all of humankind benefits. When you hate, all of humankind loses. The Law of Love states: Whenever one loves, this Love will be transmitted to all. That Wave of Love that descends from on High and manifests within you, permeates and washes over all the Earth and all of Creation. When you begin to love, others will begin to love as well. Many souls are then awakened by your love. In this way, you are able to assist all of humankind.

---

19. These are characters in the novel, *Les Miserables* by Victor Hugo.

The Universal Language

The apple trees in the garden were in bloom. The air was fragrant and the bees hummed the song of the nectar. As he stood next to a tree, the Master held a branch covered with blossoms.
The Master said:

Every being is infused with Love. The tree, too, perceives that it is loved. Trees possess a language with which they express their gentle feelings. And yet, their speech is silent. Even the smallest beetle perceives Love. There is no being in the world that does not know Love. It is the one phenomenon in the Universe that all perceive.

Guidelines for Earthly Existence

At times, the Master would give us rules to live by. All should attempt to apply them. These are the jewels from the Great Knowledge of Life.
The Master told us:

One needs to come to the realization that he will always be in school. After finishing one school, he will enroll in another. One might complete high school or university studies, and yet, there is another University that has no beginning and no end. Human earthly life prepares for another and greater Life. Earth is a laboratory in which different experiments are being performed.

You need to think about beautiful things; to possess beautiful thoughts, feelings, and actions so that you may build the valuable qualities of your character.

Whenever a sublime thought arises in your mind, do not disregard it. Welcome it instead, that you may bring it to realization. If you do not accept it, a negative thought will come in its place. In such a case, inferior beings will vandalize you through their psychic vampirism.

You need to have discrimination with your thoughts, feelings, and actions.

When a Bulgarian places a duck's egg under a brood-hen and the duckling hatches, the hen does not become its mother. Those thoughts that you disagree with are not your own. Eliminate the ducklings, permit only the chicks to remain.

The Master told one of the brothers:

Your deceased mother and father are working through you. Sometimes they suggest negative things to you. You need to educate them. Someone offends you, and your father tells you, "Do not tolerate this! Rebuke him! You must defend your honor!" Your mother whispers similar things to you as well. Tell your father, "What good would it do if I were to quarrel with him? It would become a scandal. The result would be regrettable; and in the end, should he tell me that I am a so and so, nothing will have changed." Tell your mother, "He is not such a bad person. He said those things when he was agitated. When he gets over it, he will be good once again."

Scripture tells us, "You will tread on vipers and scorpions."[20] This means that you need to become the master of all of the negative elements within you. The least transgressions conceal, within themselves, the potential for larger ones. This indicates that transgressions can multiply. It is of no significance whether the transgression is large or small; it is only significant that the seed of error is not found within you.

In correcting your error, your will can become empowered. The one who cannot correct his error has a weak will.

The Master told one of the sisters:

You are quick-tempered. When you feel that you might become enraged, take up a watering can and go water the flowers. In this way, a change in the flow of energy will occur.

Should a person be impatient, let that person go to a mountain region, upstream of a crystal clear river.

---

20. See also Psalm 91:13, "You shall tread upon the lion and the cobra, the young lion and the serpent you shall trample underfoot."

When you listen to people who are arguing, an imprint of this image is recorded. Time passes, but the tape remains within you and, from time to time, it plays forward and it hums. For this reason, it would be better that you did not listen or give your attention to the negative words and actions of others so that these will not be recorded by your consciousness.

Imagine that your pocket is filled with coins. Yet after a little while, you reach into your pocket and discover that it is empty. Your heart should not stir; it should remain silent and calm. This is how the Advanced Beings educate you. Some Beings will tell someone to put some money in your pocket. A little while later, they will tell someone else to take the money. Or perhaps you are given health, and a little later, it is taken away. The purpose for all these experiments is that you become strong and grow.

You pass by a beautiful and well-furnished house and tell yourself, "I wish I had such a house!" This is incorrect. Rejoice that this person has such a beautiful house. Another time, you say, "I am not such a bad person; I am not like that person!" Again you are mistaken.

Scripture tells us, "Resist not evil."[21] This means do not resist the negative within yourself; instead instill the Divine, and the negative will vanish.

One needs to eliminate all knowledge that is not of significance that one might not harm one's innate gifts. Adversity often besets people today because they do not know which things are of significance and which are of little significance.

When your disposition is good, you build your world, whereas, when your disposition is bad, you destroy it. When one does not give proper expression to the spiritual forces within, that person will eventually harden. Someone will say, "I am not well-versed." In such a case, sing or play an instrument. Use the gift with which God has blessed you. For example, you are a tailor. You might not be handsome, but make clothes for people, and they will befriend you. If you are a farmer, go to someone's garden and plant. If you are a violinist, play for people, and they

---

21. See Matthew 5:39, "But I tell you not to resist an evil person. But whoever slaps you on your right cheek, turn the other to him also."

will befriend you. If you are a shoemaker, make shoes for people, and you will come to know them.

There are some beings who lack warmth and when they pass by us, they draw our warmth. There are others who are cordial and warm—when they pass by us, they take away our coldness. If you emit warmth, then wherever you go, you will be well-received. But if you emit cold, you will not be well-received.

Do not speak about those things that you plan to do: speak about them afterward. Should you speak about things ahead of time, you will meet with opposition.

If you desire to express your opinion, do not hasten—contemplate on it until you have found a more sublime mode of expression.

I will suggest to you a guideline: Each time you have a book to read, you should extract an idea of significance that you can apply.

Be gentle and considerate to one another because Divine thoughts and feelings only grow where there is reverence, respect, and thoughtfulness. When you are approached by a person who is gentle, you have a good feeling. You have a good feeling because that person is enveloped in warmth. Health is dependent upon suppleness. If one loses this, one will become brittle and will become ill easily. When I say "suppleness," I refer to the manifestation of the soul in the physical world. When I say "gentleness," I refer to the manifestation of the soul in the astral world.

Should you offend someone, you offend the Divine within that person. You will make amends for this with suffering.

When you see a withered flower with its head hanging down, attempt to discover the cause. Should you feel despondent, you will then have something in common with this flower. Seek a way that you may help it. Should you perceive that it needs watering, go and get some water for it. The moment that you do this, the flower will raise its crown and joyously look to God's Domain. If you are conscious, you will know that water is a symbol of Life and is capable of improving every living being.

Therefore, should you become discouraged, hesitant, or full of doubt instill Divine Life within yourselves.

If you are able to transform negative states into positive, this means that you are a person with awareness. What do these negative states represent? The Universal Law for Transformation states: One must rise above despair. If one who is sorrowful would elevate oneself into the World of the One Reality, that person's sorrow would transform into Joy. In the World of the One Reality, there are no contradictions.

Cosmic Consciousness

The shrubs and the grass were covered with the dew of the night. In the first rays of the morning Sun, the dewdrops glistened with all the colors of the rainbow. The Master cherished the early hours of the dawn in which one can hear the first song that heralds the new day.

When we finished our prayers and giving of thanks, we sat down in a meadow that was filled with the fragrance of flowers and herbs. After we sat in silence, contemplating on this day—so sublime and so unique—someone asked the Master about the different kinds of consciousness.

The Master said:

The minerals and plants have a subconsciousness, the animals have conscious awareness, and humans—a self or ego-consciousness. Within each higher level of the natural kingdom, the lower degrees of consciousness are included as well. Man, who is characterized by his ego-consciousness, has a subconscious and conscious awareness as well.

The subconsciousness is a complex Divine process that includes also the guidance of the Angelic hierarchy. The thoughts and energy of the Angelic hierarchy manifest through all beings. It is what creates the subconsciousness: the treasury of the past.

Ego-consciousness is a singular process of the individual. Whenever a person thinks or desires to comprehend the meaning of life, he makes use of this consciousness. All degrees of Consciousness above the ego-consciousness are referred to as the "Higher Consciousness." There are moments when a person is in communion with the Cosmic Consciousness, which is one of the levels of Higher Consciousness.

Ego-consciousness does not yet exist in animals. Human consciousness is different in that the human being is conscious of himself as an individual. When someone is inspired by the Cosmic Consciousness, that person will experience the Oneness of Life. Then we begin to look at Nature as one living organism, the cells of which are vital. The plants, the animals, the human beings, altogether, these constitute One Body.

When a person first enters into Cosmic Consciousness, new centers in the brain with new capabilities will begin to develop. One's level of development is determined by one's level of consciousness. Until human beings develop the ability to commune with the Cosmic Consciousness, they will be elated one moment and sorrowful the next. The mere fact that they have entered into Cosmic Consciousness does not indicate that they have attained or comprehended everything; levels of understanding exist there as well. And yet, one will be able, at least in part, to eliminate some of the hardships of one's existence. For as long as people live by their ego-consciousness, they will continue to live in constant fear and anxiety of what will happen to them. People have lived by their ego-consciousness for many years. The time has come for them to enter into Cosmic Consciousness.

Scripture tells us, "And God will create a new Heaven and a new Earth."[22] The "new Heaven" and the "new Earth" will be for those people who dwell within the Culture of Cosmic Consciousness. Today, the Light of Cosmic Consciousness is increasing. People are more aware of their faults today than they have ever been during any other time. People should rise above their ego-consciousness that they may enter into Cosmic Consciousness. Should they not, their existence will remain incomprehensible to them. Now it is time for the human beings to raise their consciousness to a higher level. Should they continue to live by their ego-consciousness, they will never manifest those sublime thoughts and aspirations that abide within their soul and

---

22. See Isaiah 65:17, "For behold, I create new Heavens and a new Earth; and the former shall not be remembered or come to mind."

within their spirit. People need to develop those organs through which their sublime thoughts and feelings may be manifested. The moment in which they attain Cosmic Consciousness, they will begin to realize their aspirations.

A sister spoke about her perception of Cosmic Consciousness.
The Master continued:

Cosmic Consciousness is an extremely dynamic state. One enters into that state of Consciousness when one begins to embrace all beings—from the least to the greatest—and becomes a transmitter of Love that all may be uplifted.

All should work to attain Cosmic Consciousness. The one who is "born again in the Spirit" is the one who abides in Cosmic Consciousness. All can be in communion, in harmony, with such a one. And yet, certain essential conditions are required for this time to come. What kind of conditions? Internal.

People are just now beginning to comprehend that they belong to the Great Body of Life. Thus begins the awakening of Cosmic Consciousness that strives to make all of humankind into One Family, capable of working together and living in harmony.

Divine Science

We were conversing on the subject of modern science. One brother spoke with much enthusiasm about the wonderful achievements of the biological sciences, physics, chemistry, and technology.
The Master explained:

We are only beginning to make use of Divine Science. From this time forward, we will begin to study its Laws. We will learn how to free ourselves from our mental and emotional weaknesses that we may attain enlightened minds, pure and steadfast characters, and wills as hard as diamonds.

Science is a product of the human spirit. The science of today will vanish. Only those things that are most beneficial will remain. Everything else that was like a children's entertainment will be forgotten. Do you believe that the Angels concern themselves with contemporary, mundane laws? Do you believe that chemistry and physics will remain at their present level?

Do other Laws exist in addition to the natural laws? Indeed, other Laws exist that have yet to be discovered. Today's science is based entirely upon empirical investigation. Someone stands in front of a wall and says, "There is nothing behind this wall." Not so. Behind this wall, many things exist. Just because you cannot see them does not mean that they do not exist.

Contemporary science is merely an introduction to Real Science. This does not mean that the authority of modern science or its scientists is not of a value. Today's science has provided the data on which people can ponder that they may develop their minds. The objective mind needs to be developed. It cannot be developed without this data.

Human knowledge is limited—it relates to the material world alone. Modern science is concerned with the study of minerals, plants, animals, and so on. I do not disregard this science, but a new Science with a new Knowledge is now coming into the world.

One who lacks knowledge and focuses one's attention on the external observes only how the book is bound. On the other hand, the disciples should direct their attention to what is written inside. Real Knowledge is not only found in the forms, but in the knowledge of the Principles.

Some knowledge is required for human existence; other knowledge is an adornment to this existence. Yet another is the blessing that gives power and vitality to humans.

You should complete your study of life on Earth that you might enroll in the Divine School. When I speak of Divine Science, I am referring to the Science that studies the Essence of Life. Divine Science is a Science that is concerned with the Intelligence behind Life itself, with the external and internal conditions of this Life and its organic development. The one who is fearful cannot be a student of Divine Science. For it, great courage and fortitude is required.

Divine Science is vital. The words "Divine Science" refer to that community of Living Beings who have real Knowledge.

You need to discover them. Then you will do something for them, and they will do something for you in return. Each day I meet and commune with these Beings.

Why does one need science? In addition to its practical applications in the external existence, it develops a person's gifts and capabilities and shapes the human head as well. By examining a person's cranium, one can determine the science with which that person has been predominantly occupied.

Divine Science provides the means for building a strong and healthy body, for restructuring the human thoughts and emotions, and for stabilizing the nervous system. This can be applied to the individual and to entire nations as well. Study Divine Science and its methods so that you may apply these methods in your daily life.

Great Wisdom awaits you in the future. Today's knowledge is beneficial as well. And yet, you need to be the student who progresses from one grade to the next, from one level to the next, from the present one to the future one. I have not yet spoken of this Science because it should not be debased. Divine Science is only for those souls who have come to Love.

The technology of today is very limited compared with that of the people of Agartha 60 thousand years ago. The vehicles with which they traveled through the air were called "dragons of fire." Their knowledge, however, was available to only a few. In contrast, the technology of today is made available to all of humankind.

It is not possible to comprehend the material world if you are not connected with the Ideal World. In other words, you need to be united with God.

We need to strive for the right understanding that the Divine Science provides.

The adepts of antiquity made use of a magic wand or staff that they would carry in their hands. However, real adepts carry no staffs or wands.

There exists a science for children, a Science for the Angels, and the Science that belongs to God. You say that you know a lot. I am glad for you, but this knowledge is only of the material. Have you studied the Science of the Angels? You will study the Science of the Angels in the future. Have you studied the Science that belongs to God? I do not begin with the Science of the Angels. I do not begin with the Science of the saints. I begin at the Summit with the Science that belongs to God. This is one of the most essential of all the methods. I begin with the Science that is the most difficult.

Divine Science is required for humans to learn the great art of living. However, this does not mean that one should neglect one's study of the material world. Everyone on the spiritual path should be knowledgeable of mathematics, anatomy, physics, music, and so on. These are the introductions to Divine Science. Study the material world. After you comprehend it, you will begin to comprehend the Divine as well.

The level of development that one has reached is determined by one's status in the experiential school of the material world. When one begins to master the conditions of the material world, this indicates that one has begun to master those of the Divine World as well. The understanding of the Divine World determines how well one will live in the material world.

You have come to Earth to study in the experiential school, and now you are being tested. A professor explains a problem to you. You tell him, "I understand," but you have not understood. You need to solve this problem on your own. One is able to understand only when one has solved the problem on one's own. In the natural world, only whatever you solve on your own leads to knowledge. The remainder is merely a helping aid.

Realization of Human Aspirations

Once the Master told us:

Should a person who is ill tell you, "I shall not die; I shall live for an additional 50 years that I might complete the work for which I came to Earth," that person has addressed the task rightly and will have good results. You ask, "Is this possible?" Everything is possible for the one who comprehends the Laws.

However, for the one who does not comprehend them, everything is obstructed.

Something happens to you, and you ask, "Why did this happen to me?" It is because you asked for it.

When you desire that your aspirations be brought to realization, you need to focus your thoughts. A strong focus is necessary for resolving the great assignments of life. By focusing your thoughts you will draw the thoughts of all similar minds. In such a way, your thought becomes the focus of the thoughts of all who think as you do. This is the way in which great ideas manifest. Every great idea, even the one that is born out of the mind of a single individual, is collective. Many minds focus their attention on this thought before it becomes manifest through a genius.

Someone aspires to something good—to become a musician, a poet, or some other thing—and yet, one becomes discouraged. Those who aspire to a great goal in life must begin to work today that they may prepare the conditions. However, a time limit should not be set for this. Whatever one cannot accomplish today, can be accomplished tomorrow. Opportunities will be greater in the future than they are at present.

Do not feel discouraged when your aspirations are not brought into realization immediately: they might become realized 10 years from now. Conversely, an entire lifetime might pass without realization. When you aspire toward something, you should, at the same time, be willing to make the efforts. Always be assured that you are being supported by the Intelligent Nature.

The Law states: When you rejoice that a person has realized his aspirations, you will realize your own as well.

Should you desire to realize your aspirations, you need to understand the Plan that God has already set in motion. When you walk on the Divine path, you will attain all your aspirations.

The Senses

One of the brothers related the following experience, "One afternoon I was laying down, fell asleep, and dreamed of a friend of mine who was starting out toward my home from the center of town. I followed him the entire time until he came to my door and knocked. Indeed, at this moment, he knocked on my door. I awoke and let him in."
The Master explained:

In the present century, there is a lot of insight. The radio sheds light on the Spiritual world, and the television on clairvoyance. A school that addresses clairvoyance is needed. However, this would not be for everyone.

All people do not develop at the same rate: the gifted will learn more readily. For example, you can teach a person to play an instrument, but that person might not have the gift to become a real musician. The gifts are given to all, but the degree of their development will differ from person to person. One needs to learn. The nervous system in the human being needs to adjust in accordance with the development of these gifts. A more sensitive nervous system is needed. The nervous system of a spiritually advanced person is more sensitive and is able to receive the short waves, to receive transmissions from afar.

One sister shared her fear of visions.
The Master said:

Your fear indicates that you are not yet ready for the other World to be revealed to you. The centers for communication with the other World have not yet been developed in humans. These need to be developed. We are already capable of connecting with the Invisible World. The Invisible World has already installed its latest device.

You need to learn to deal with the two great Powers: Cosmic Intelligence and Love. If you have faith in these, your eyes will open. I have the desire that your eyes will open. But when? When you become strong—strong enough that the New World that will appear before you does not cause you fear. For example, an Angel appears to someone and instructs that person what to do. Such a person can resolve all contradictions and can heal all disease. Because an Angel has appeared to that person, he has become strong.

As a clairvoyant, you will experience great suffering. You will see not only the good things, but the bad as well. Knowing this, the Invisible World does not awaken within you those abilities for which you are not ready. For this reason, do not desire that your eyes be opened prematurely. Begin with the following: to see within people only the good, only the positive.

The method of the Brotherhood of Light is as follows: You need to develop the twelve basic Virtues, before you will be ready to develop clairvoyance. If you have a beautiful corridor adorned with beautiful paintings, but it is dark, what significance can it have for you? However, when the light comes in, the beautiful paintings and the beautiful hallway will become visible. If the light should come in, but the hallway is not adorned—if there are no beautiful paintings in it—then the view will not be pleasing; it will be dull. It is appropriate for the hallway to be adorned and well-arranged before the light comes in. I speak symbolically.

Should you desire to unite with the Beings of the Invisible World, you will need to awaken your spiritual senses. Within the body, especially within the brain, powers are hidden that need to be developed. It is sufficient for a person to contemplate for one hour each day on the great spiritual questions, in order to begin seeing beyond. That is to say, it is sufficient for you to enter into a state of inner peace detaching yourselves from the physical world for you to be able to perceive the spiritual. Everyone is able to become a clairvoyant; but for one to do so, one needs to detach and isolate oneself from all impressions of the physical world. Otherwise, in that moment in which you would see something from the Invisible World, something from the physical will distract your attention, and you will see nothing.

At first, when you set aside all things external, you will pass through a dark zone. You will find yourself in total darkness. If you are not fearful, then after a short while, you will perceive a faint light that will begin to increase. This means that you are entering the Invisible World. The one with the sixth sense can see from behind, from in front, from the sides, from all directions. That person can see for thousands of kilometers and he can see also through walls. If your sixth sense is developed, you will even be able to see through solid barriers. As you can hear with the help of the radio whatever is being said in far away countries, so too with the help of the sixth sense, will you be able to see what is taking place in them, at that very moment.

In the future, people will be able to perceive thoughts. The soul and the spirit will then be visible. Today they are invisible, but in the future, the mind, the heart, the soul, and the spirit will become visible. People of today say, "The visible will remain visible, and the invisible, invisible." I say: When we meet in the future, you will see my mind, heart, soul, and spirit, and I will see yours. This is the New Teaching. The world will undergo a great transformation when all error and transgression come to an end. Everything old will remain in the archives.

We can learn about someone not only from the features of the face, but also from the colors that surround that person. This is accessible to the clairvoyant, but not to the ordinary person. For example, if one nurtures within himself sublime and noble feelings, he will be immersed in a soft pink color. The more that one's feelings are of a lower character, the more that the color will darken. Not only do feelings have specific colors, but thoughts do as well.

The experienced clairvoyant reads from the color, as anyone would from a book. From the colors one is able to discern the degree of human intelligence. If a person is loving and kind, one can see a particular, soft nuance of the pink color that emanates an agreeable glow from the person's heart. When it comes to the will, a white light emanates from the human body. It is the color of virtue.[23] All other colors are interwoven among the three main colors: white, pink, and that of light. These interwoven colors form the human aura. From the aura, the clairvoyant can discern the point that a person has attained in his spiritual and mental development.

---

23. The Master speaks about other color correspondences in such transcribed works, as "The Testament of the Color Rays of Light."

If you have developed clairvoyance within yourself, when someone speaks the truth to you, you will see a beautiful blue color emanating from that person that is not comparable to anything else. Simultaneously, you will also see a beautiful pale yellow color emanating from the person's body. If someone is lying to you, you will see darkness emanating from that person's aura; the person will be surrounded by darkness.

If your ability to see increases, you will observe that the eyes of some people emit dark unpleasant rays that can cause harm to anyone toward whom they are directed. These appear as red flames, similar to those from a hot furnace.

Should you become very sensitive and direct your gaze upward at a 45 degree angle, you will see Sublime Spirits; and at 45 degrees downward, you will observe a dark color permeating the ground in which the inferior beings move.

For a clairvoyant to be able to withstand seeing those who have passed beyond, he or she must be able to withstand their vibrations. For one to withstand their vibrations, one needs to consider them as living beings.

Those who work toward the development of clairvoyance will often have the following experience. In front of them, a ball of light with many different colors will appear. It rises up, and when it reaches a certain place, transforms into a beautiful smiling angelic face, which then disappears. The Angel is saying, "Go and learn. I will study at another place. Farewell."

In the future, when people are using their sixth sense, they will read the Book of Nature and will comprehend it.

According to some philosophers, one is able to perceive through the five senses alone. Those who have Knowledge say that the human being has 12 senses, that is to say, 12 doorways. People have five senses at present; the remaining seven are locked away from them. When I say that the human being has 12 senses, I refer to those senses that will be first developed over the course of human evolution. According to Divine Science, the human being has 49 senses altogether. In addition to these, people have others as well; human senses are innumerable. Not until you have developed all 49 senses within yourself, will you come to know God, as God knows you.

I told a young man, "Tomorrow you will meet a wealthy person and you will talk with him. He will like you and will help you to continue your education." The young man asked me, "How is this possible?" I told him, "You will see for yourself and will believe my words. I do not tell you about something that will come to pass in a month or in a year but tomorrow." For the one who can see, all things are possible.

The ordinary tunes that are accessible to the human ear have approximately 35 thousand vibrations per second at the most. And yet, tunes have been discovered that have as many as 300 thousand vibrations per second; these are "the ultrasounds." That is to say, many sounds exist that the human being is not able to perceive.

The Law of the Whole and the Parts

We worked the entire day in order to impound the water that was flowing into a nearby ravine and collect it in a pool from which water for the vegetable garden could be drawn. It was the Master's idea to use this water. At the end of the day, when we had finished the work, we gathered around him as he began to speak about the Law of the Parts and the Whole.

The Master said:

Some people say that the world is bad. This is a misunderstanding of life. This is an incomplete consideration of things. As soon as the hand renounces the body, the hand becomes ill-favored—it begins to lose integrity. If we look at the world as a whole, it will be beautiful. One needs to perceive the whole of Life, to look at each phenomenon as a part of the whole. The world appears to us as being disorganized because we see it not as a whole but as separate parts.

Among all things, an intrinsic connection exists. Each question regarding humankind needs to be addressed from the viewpoint of the whole. Humankind is one great organism. The nations are its systems, the communities are the organs of these systems. Man needs to understand his destiny as a part of the whole organism that he may find his assigned place within it.

What would happen to the organism if each cell would like to live for itself, independently of the rest? It would disintegrate. This idea is drawn from the Scriptures in the verse, "All are represented in the Body of Christ."[24] If one leaf of the tree falls, would it retain the same relationship with the tree, as the others which remain on the tree? The whole of humankind is the tree and each individual is a leaf on this tree.

Each change in the whole is reflected in its parts and vice versa. Much of human suffering and joy is the result of a change in the Universe, in the joy and suffering that other beings experience and people absorb.

All people need to perceive themselves as a part of the whole organism that they may work for the good of this organism.

The individualistic life gives rise to wrongdoing. If only one finger of the hand wants to participate in a task without the participation of the other fingers, it can accomplish nothing. Do you understand the significance of isolation? There is nothing more terrible in the world than this. Those who live only for themselves can be compared to the finger which is cut off from the hand and thrown away somewhere. No greater misfortune for a finger exists. Conversely, no greater fulfillment for a finger exists than to be on a hand and to do its work in service for the whole.

If you put into your mind the idea of living only for yourself, you are initiating your own death.

Beautiful garments are made of fine threads. Should you separate the threads, they will represent nothing in and of themselves. But if the threads are well-woven together, the result will be something beautiful. Each being makes sense only as part of the life of the whole. You should live for the whole of humankind, for the whole of the Universe; that is to say, a higher ideal exists than that you now live for. In striving for this ideal you will then be of benefit to all. Should people stray from the Path, they will be abandoned and forgotten. Those who would

---

24. See also Romans 12:4–5, "For as we have many members in one body, but all the members do not have the same function, so we, being many, are one body in Christ, and individually members of one another."

like to be benevolent, let them direct their energy for the uplifting of the whole of humankind: that is to say, for the good of all. In this way, you will connect with the Intelligent Beings who are helping you. And so, write, play music, work, not for yourself—not for your own glory—but for the Glory of Him Who has provided the conditions for you to manifest yourself. If you do not work with this idea in mind, you will lose everything.

You expect, upon completion of a task, to receive a large compensation and recognition. But this is in the mundane life.

When you share your apples with others, keep the smallest for yourself. If you should set aside the biggest—the most beautiful apple—for yourself, great adversity will befall you even after thousands of years.

The Path toward Love

During a morning walk, the Master said:

Study Love as an intrinsic Power. You all need to strive to learn about it. Today's science, and that of the future—this is the Science of Love.

Which is the path that leads to Love? A disciple went to his Teacher and told him that he desired to comprehend Love. His Teacher took him to the river, grasped his neck, plunged him into the water, and held him there for a while. Upon taking him out, he asked, "What did you feel while in the water?" The disciple answered, "I felt a great need for air!" The Teacher said to him, "When you come to feel such a need for Love, it will visit you."

In order that Love may visit you, take the position determined by Intelligent Nature for you and wait. Otherwise, Love will pass you by without visiting you. You say, "How will I know which position is mine?" When you take the position, you will feel that you are at peace with the whole Universe, that you are ready to forgive everyone. Each and every imbalance that you feel indicates that you are not in your position.

A Letter to the Master

The Master received the following letter from a sister in France:

In these days of trials, I am with you and experience within complete peace and joy.

We sing, pray, and work in Divine joy. In spite of everything, we have the profound belief that the suffering of the world will soon come to an end. All your children feel your protection and the Love that envelops them in Divine Light. I think only of the day when I will see you face to face. I believe that I am born to experience this great moment.

For such a long time, you have watched over my soul as your little daughter. I feel your call through the Sun, the stars, and the wind. When I see you in my mind, I feel in my soul the same joy that I experience in springtime when the garden is full of flowers. In all my trials, you are always close to me. God grants that I will come to you one day. This will be a great day.

With great patience and with all my energy, I work every day on my development. I trust you completely, Master. I open my soul to you. Only through the most sublime poetry and Divine music, is my soul able to express my love, my gratitude, and my reverence for you.

With all my heart, I greet all of my Bulgarian friends.

Love Will Be the Organizing Principle of the New Culture

The Master observed this Law in Life: Wherever he was, he improved the conditions—not all at once as if according to a pre-ordained plan, but gradually, naturally. Everything he worked on corresponded to the inner life. He used every opportunity that arose in the ordinary workplace to teach a lesson. No better method than work exists for people to come together, become better acquainted, and grow closer in harmony. The Master encouraged every good initiative and supported all to participate in it. He was pleased when the disciples manifested resourcefulness, mindfulness, and focus.

The yard and the entire farmstead were gradually cleaned up and put in order. The paths were repaired. On the steep slope where the path led down to the house, a retaining wall was built. The stones were arranged in such a way that they represented the rising Sun. The idea for this came from the disciples. The Master gave this explanation:

The rising Sun is a symbol for the Sun that will arise in all awakened Bulgarians, in all awakened human beings.

Stone steps were built, a seemingly simple task, commonly done everywhere, but in the presence of the Master, it gained profound significance. After finishing all of the work on the homestead, the Master said:

In life, there will always be improvement.

Then someone asked, "How will the New Culture be organized?"
The Master answered:

At present a human order exists in the world. However, this order will be destroyed. From the way in which people have worked in the past and how they work today, the world cannot be improved.

Someone will say that God has created some people to be masters, others, servants, some rich, others, poor. This is a misconception. This world and this order in which some go hungry while others eat lavishly has not been created by God. Others will say, "Why does God allow all this wickedness, all this social injustice, to exist in the world?" All this is done by people, but they blame God.

The Scripture's verse, "All things were made through Him, and without Him nothing was made that was made,"[25] refers to the Eternal, the Great Works in the world. But the temporal, transitory things are not of God. Everything that man does of his own will is not from God.

Some cite the Scripture which states that all authority is given by God.[26] In this verse, something has been omitted. It

---

25. See John 1:3.

should read: All righteous authority is given by God, and all righteous authority is based on the Law of Love.

Modern culture is being put to the test. The culture that is built on sand is not stable. People do not know how to live, how to eat. They do not know how to build their homes, and so on. What can you expect of such a world? And yet, everything will be transformed.

The New Teaching provides the right methods as to how the future society should be structured.

Those cultures that have been based on power have perished.

The Teaching that I bring to you has been tested. Within it, the basic methods are hidden that show people how to live. I am bringing to you that Divine Teaching upon which the future order will be based. This Teaching is upheld by the Law of Living Nature.

When the right time comes, the caterpillars will say, "For so long now, we have been eating and drinking; we need nothing more. We will leave the leaves for the others." They will cocoon themselves. From out of the cocoon, the butterfly flies into the wide world and begins to feed off the sweet nectar of flowers. When will the world improve? When all of the caterpillars transform into butterflies.

Society's problems can be resolved in a very simple way. They will be resolved when the new consciousness enters into people.

You may say that all people want a new order. This is well, I agree with you. But what will happen if you have a new order, but your nature—your shortcomings—is preserved? It is easy to destroy the old, but what can be attained with your negative character? How would you benefit if you tear down your old home, but cannot build a new one? Nature does not permit this: she destroys and builds simultaneously.

---

26. See also Romans 13:1–2, "Let every soul be subject to the governing authorities. For there is no authority except from God, and the authorities that exist are appointed by God. Therefore, whoever resists the authority resists the ordinance of God, and those who resist will bring judgment on themselves."

The moment, in which you err, you are in darkness. People's tragedy is that they desire to do things in the darkness.

It is not the external conditions that create hardship for people, but the internal. God created this world with all the right conditions for human existence. Everything that one desires is provided for. That is to say, with regards to the external conditions, everything is favorable, but the internal conditions are missing: the new consciousness, for example, is missing. The cause of this lies hidden within the spiritual realm. Your mind and heart need to pass from their present state into a higher one.

Some seek to bring organization to people. The world has order. Every person whose consciousness is awakened belongs to the World of Order. However, this world whose consciousness has not been awakened has yet to begin to prepare itself to enter into the World of Order.

People of today would like to build, to re-organize, first the whole of humankind, then society. After that they would reorganize the home and finally the individual. However, this way is not correct. I will give you the following explanation. Take the most prominent musicians who have completed their education in music; they have mastered their art. With them, you can put together any kind of orchestra that you wish. Within 10 to 15 minutes, or a half an hour at most, you will see that you have the best orchestra with the best performers. Why? It is because each one of them knows the score perfectly. But should you bring together people who have no knowledge of music and try to set up an orchestra with them, even if ten of the best conductors come to conduct them, nothing will come of it.

People seek a material improvement in the order. But a spiritual improvement needs to take place as well. Someone will say, "For the world to be a better place, a material improvement is necessary." Make an experiment and you will see.

What kind of consciousness am I speaking of? People should set Love as the foundation of Life, and through Love, create the new consciousness.

The suffering of people of today is greater than it was at the time of Christ. The resolution of the most difficult problems will come through Love. Love will come in a real, living form and will sweep away everything old.

The nations of modern Europe exist in the phase of destruction. They do not apply the Teaching of Christ, but the teachings of a distant past. War is a remnant of the most ancient beliefs. This is the old culture that is appearing in new forms.

My basic idea is as follows: all social problems should be resolved through Love. How are we to resolve the social problem of injustice? We need to replace the absence of Love with Love. Love resolves all contradictions—mental, emotional, and social.

The Future Order

These were the difficult days of war. The future was unclear, disturbing, and filled with danger. Many of our friends were asking the Master where all this would lead, what would be the outcome of this situation.
The Master said:

The Earth now enters into the new, Divine conditions. The whole world is awakening. The one who desires to remain in the old conditions can do so. The whole world, the whole Solar System, the whole Universe, everything is moving in a new direction. The human consciousness is expanding. You will be witnesses to that Great Expansion; you will be witnesses to that Great Transformation for which God now prepares the whole of humankind. The world will come to know that God shall not be mocked.

Some will say, "Once the world is set to order, all other things will fall into place on their own." This is not so. You cannot wait for the world to improve, but should enter into the New Life this very moment. If someone wishes to wait for the whole of humankind to improve, a long period of time will be required.

Many hermits have lived in the woods for 50 or 60 years, then, after reaching enlightenment, have returned to their fellowmen to demonstrate that Love is the only path that leads to the real Life.

The future culture is of the heart. For this reason, we need to be attentive to our hearts and nurture them.

You will say that you know Love. In reality, you do not know it. What kind of love is this of yours that does not endure all trials?

Those in whom the Divine is made manifest, these are the ones who belong to that great New Culture, which is now in preparation. When we enter it, we will be as free as those who are our Advanced Brothers: the Angels, the Archangels, the Cherubim, and the Seraphim. Love will provide the essence of Life for the New Culture. It will provide the material that will be in accordance with the forms of the future order. Today the old forms are falling away, and new ones are being created. When this great Culture comes, all will have such freedom as they did when God first gave it to them.

That culture which has not created the bond of Love among all people is not yet the genuine Culture. In place of Love, people have set laws, money, torment, and power first and foremost. In the future order, money and power will serve Love. All things will serve Love. It will teach them what they need to do. Love is the lever that moves all things: it may appear to be the least of all powers, but in reality, Love is the greatest power.

If only you were able to perceive the world of the Advanced Beings! At present, you are a part of the humankind that errs, but at one time, you belonged to the humankind that knew no error and now desires to participate in bringing order to the life of humankind today.

In the world of secular law, there is little freedom. In the world of money, there is but a little more freedom. At present, we are departing from the world of money and entering the realm of Love. It is God's Will that laws and money should become our servants; we should instruct them in what to do. Under the rule of secular law today, you are being ordered. You are being told, "Move along!" And so you move along. Money, too, gives you orders: you are offered a certain amount of money to do a job, and so you do it. With Love, however, you have freedom.

Man has a lower nature and a higher one. When the lower nature begins to serve the higher, the world will then become a better place. Love destroys the marriage union between good and evil. You need to break this union. Love destroys this contract.

Today contradictions exist everywhere in life: in the individual, in the family, among the nations. In the end, Divine Love will resolve all problems and all contradictions will disappear.

As long as you work in accordance with Love, everything will be resolved: you will expand and become free. Otherwise, everything will be constricted, condensed, and limiting. It is difficult to move without inner freedom.

There exists no better order than that of Love. It is the most natural order and the greatest. And when we are woeful and sorrowful, it is for the Paradise lost: the World of Love. We should rely upon the Divine, which is within us, rather than the cash register, which is external.

Abundance will contribute to the resolution of social problems because abundance is connected to Love. If Love is missing, you are outside of the Law of Abundance. The nations have many laws, but have they used them to improve life? They have improved it in certain respects, but the Divine within man remained undeveloped and so the nations have lost faith and have become totally materialistic. Life has become mechanized. Due to the absence of Love, error came into the world. And because of Love, the Good comes into the world.

At one time, the consumption of alcohol was prohibited by law in the United States of America, but people found ways to obtain it and drink. The conclusion is that the law is not the answer. The human laws are not the way to educate people. A new way is needed for the human development. Laws exist in Nature, which we need to discover so that we may improve life in accordance with them.

If a culture cannot uplift the human heart, is it a genuine Culture? We need to come to that Culture that satisfies the needs of the mind and of the heart. This is the Law of Nature. You give a certain kind of food to a child and he or she becomes ill.

Instead, you need to give the child such foods that will provide the required nutrients.

If we set Love as the foundation, life will change radically. The contemporary social order is obstructed: there is sediment, sand, stone, and so on in its pipes. A new system of drainage for this public order needs to be installed.

Suffering will force people to take up the path of Love.

No culture can uplift humankind; but the Divine can, and its foundation is Love. Therefore, instill Love as the foundation of your life and it will rightly resolve all your problems.

The New Teaching can be verified by experiment. Let them give me a village of 100 homes in order that I may apply the Law of Love. Then let them see what the result will be after 10 or 20 years. Let the Bulgarians see such an experiment.

I would consider that a society has applied the art of how to live if it meets the following conditions: when you enter a town, you will only encounter people who are satisfied and fulfilled, and you will hear no complaint nor see a single tear. Try to find such a society in this world. We cannot boast of such a thing. Throughout the world exist suffering, sorrow, and misfortune. Let those people with the greatest wisdom step up now and begin to instruct humankind in the new path.

People want to know what the future order will be. The future order already exists. You take in as much air as you desire; you take as much light as you desire. This is the Divine Order. The same will be with the bread. In the future order, the strong will be the servant of the weak.

We concern ourselves now with the most important issue: the issue of Love. All are discontented because this most important issue of Love is not yet resolved.

God is telling you, "Go out and bring this Light into the world. Tell all that the Omniscient Love which comes from Above is now descending to Earth. Love is the soil out of which all good seeds shall sprout." And so, we will tell the people, "There exists a Love that is like the air we all need to breathe, like the light we all need to take in, and like the bread we all need to eat."

All contradictions in the world result from the absence of Love.

Order will come into the world only through that Word which is Love! What can set the world to right in one moment: this is Love. With it, all things proceed rightly. If you do not have Love's power, nothing can be attained. No Teaching can be applied without Love.

For someone to contend with the Divine, this is represented by Jacob wrestling with the Messenger of God.[27] How can people contend with God's Will? What has any nation achieved by this? What all nations desire is influenced by human nature. Should a nation desire the Divine, this is a different matter. But all desire that which is of human nature.

The Divine Order is Eternal. No one can stand against it. People can oppose it, but they cannot stop it. It shall be realized!

Unity in Love[28]

A question was raised about the future of humankind, its social problems and struggles.
The Master said:

God's Love is now coming, that Love which will unite all people into one. All are searching for the One Great Law that will unite all people, all beings. This Law is Love. Other than Love, no other law, no other system, exists that can improve your life. You can apply it in practice, but it must be applied rightly.

In the world, only one power exists: the power of Love. I recognize no other authority. There exists no other government greater than Love. Every other power bows before Love. For the building of the New Order, the Law of Love must be applied.

The second Law is the Law of Wisdom. Love brings Life, whereas Wisdom brings Light and Knowledge.

---

27. See Genesis 32:24–29.
28. This title is chosen as more appropriate than the original "The Great Connection."

The third Law is the Law of Truth, which brings Freedom.

Apart from these Laws, no society or nation can be built. They are the fundamental principles upon which the future life will be based. Apart from these no teaching exists. They have their application in the whole of Nature.

The Bulgarians have a motto: "Unity makes the strength." Two words are missing in this motto. It should read as follows: "Unity in Love makes the strength." Love unites. Unity without Love is mechanical. People desire unity, but unity without Love is impossible. The Law states: Love creates a universal bond among all beings. There exists a fundamental link that connects the whole of humankind—this is Love. A few merchants can unite for a common work. If business interests have brought them together, this union is temporary and will fall apart. This is not a genuine association. If, on the other hand, you are united with one another through Divine Love, then no power exists that is able to destroy this bond. If this connection is absent, then everything you do will turn to dust and ashes. Until Love comes to dwell among people, they will continue to speak to one another in alien tongues.

The Two Paths

At times the face of the Master expressed boundless sorrow. It appeared that the pain of all suffering passed through him. The Master knew the human stubbornness in his violation of Divine Law and the consequences which it carried.

Once he said:

You need to understand these two Laws: violence begets violence and Love begets Love. The genuine Divine Culture knows no violence. Today the entire Earth is filled with violence—among the animals as well as among humans. Only among those who lack mindfulness can oppression exist. All oppression, regardless toward whom it is directed, is a crime toward God and His Divine Spirit.

It has been said, "You shall not murder!"[29] But if this commandment is not applied with respect to all beings, then it is not a commandment.

You are asking me for the cause of so much misfortune in our lives. One of the fundamental causes is the indiscriminate killing of mammals. In addition to this is the indiscriminate killing of people. When the souls of those who have been killed pass onto the astral world, they create conditions for the diseases and disorders of the nervous system in people. You think that when you kill a lamb that you do not bear responsibility. The lamb is guided by the Advanced Beings, and the caregivers of the lamb will ask for an accounting of its life. Today these Beings may keep their silence, but one day you will become accountable for all your actions. The suffering of mammals for their extermination is great: more than one hundred million of them are destroyed each year. Great oppression exists in this—there is no law to protect them. The nervous disorders of the Caucasians today are a result of the killing of animals. At the time of their slaughter, fear and repugnance develop in mammals. As a result of this, unfavorable conditions for human development are formed in the astral world.

The day will come when all animals will free themselves. You kill an ox: does this express your appreciation toward this ox for its 20 or 30 years of service to you? Let it graze in its old age. This ox has been a blessing for your home. You yourself destroyed this blessing. You alone chased away those Invisible Beings who were responsible for the ox.

When you cut down trees, you uproot those blessings that they have provided for you, and, at the same time, you chase away also the powers which have been helping you through these trees. To renew an ancient forest of old trees, which have started to decay and fall down, this is a blessing. In your renewal of them, your conditions will improve too. But whenever you destroy a forest, you destroy yourself as well. As its life force withers, as its water dries out, your life will also ebb.

---

29. See Exodus 20:13.

The Americans cut down their rich, beautiful pine forests in order to populate these places. What is the cause for the neurasthenia in America? No other country exists in which neurasthenia is so widely spread. Its cause is namely the cutting down of the forests. The Bulgarians also cut down the forests indiscriminately. What they are doing is not good. When you walk through the woods, you should know that everything in this world has a life and a consciousness. You should not tear off leaves because these leaves are breathing. You should not pick flowers either.

You will say that you kill a criminal because he is dangerous for the society. You do not realize that when he is outside of his body he becomes more dangerous than when he is in the flesh. Then he moves freely among those with a weak character and suggests to them thoughts and feelings of revenge. The question arises today if there should be a death sentence. According to Divine Law, the death sentence is not permissible. As long as people are in dispute and are violating one another, they are acting in a human way. A person should not be put to death. Even as a minute particle of the universal organism, he will impede its movement. People do not understand that the execution of a single person will result in great evil in the future for humankind. For this reason, it is better to put a criminal to work. Instead of jailing the criminal, let us give him farm tools and require him to work. In my opinion, any teaching that makes use of killing is but an old teaching with a new name. What God has created, we have no right to destroy.

The one whose heart is without Love will be cruel.

How can you persuade modern people not to use execution if they think that someone deserves it? Each being whose body you have taken away will claim it some day. You may believe this or not. If you can accept this idea, you will gain from it.

I spoke with an old man from the town of Sliven. Looking at his face and head, I noticed that he had the face and the head of a criminal. I told him, "You have killed many people. Your face and your head have changed to a certain extent, but your hand carries all the signs of your crimes." He answered me, "All of this is a great burden to me. We have been fools. We thought that in such a way we could put the world in order. But the world was not changed by that." He is 70 years old, and mellowed by time, but he has killed so many people and now they are following him. He now sees that he has impeded himself in his existence. He said, "Wise people did not exist at that time to teach me, to show me the right path."

You ask how one can apply the New Teaching when we are surrounded by people who are looking only for revenge. The New Teaching hides such a power within itself that when you encounter an enemy, you need only to wave your hand, and he will fall asleep. And when he awakens you will feed him and send him on his way. How can your enemy fight with you when he knows that you will make him sleep? Those of the New Teaching possess a power that nobody else has. Someone asks, "What will you do when someone draws a gun against you?" That person's hand will remain in the air and he will need to do much work in order to bring it down.

People of today think that the world will be put in order through violence. Violence destroys people; it does not change them. Violence is similar to a hammer or an ax. What has the hammer contributed? After hitting stones for many years, it has become worn out; it has destroyed itself. The same happens to bad people: they destroy themselves. You are still under the law of idolatry because you are under the order of man.

Be aware of the following: not all are interested in the same ideas. Therefore, do not impose upon another those ideas and forms which he shows no interest in. Christ did not desire for people to come to accept the New because of the law of compliance. It is important that we are fulfilling God's Will and, whether or not the others are fulfilling it, we should leave them free. Do not make use of force or put pressure on people!

In the world, power without Love brings disappointment and suffering, but power with Love brings great blessings.

People have killed each other for thousands of years, but what are the consequences of that? The entire Earth is littered with cemeteries. There is no place that is not bespattered by human blood or that of animals. The Earth is so contaminated and stained, that as a result, some of its continents will probably submerge. The New Culture cannot grow and develop on this impure land. A purification of the Earth is necessary. People of today are not aware of the dangers that they live among. Everyone has sublime desires and noble impulses, but they lack insight; they do not know how to live.

The All-embracing Love

The Master addressed every human being and every living being with attention and respect. He revealed to his disciples the great unity of Life, pointing out the place and significance of everything in the whole of Life. In this manner, he gave us a guiding idea with which to study Nature.
The Master explained:

Each leaf needs to love all of the other leaves on the tree because of its dependence upon them. An interconnection exists among all beings. You need to have an intrinsic relationship with all living beings. We are searching for those relationships that have existed among all souls in the Beginning.

Within every being—plant, animal, or human being—you will find at least one good quality for which you can love them. For as long as some people are agreeable to you while others are not agreeable, you will regard things from outside of Love.

Even within the least form, an Angel is hidden who after thousands and millions of years will transform this shape and reveal to it the knowledge that it carries within itself.

Now you will study the unconditional Love toward the whole. This is the Law that God will teach you. By yourselves you will not be able to learn this Law. Someone else is going to teach you. Who? Only the One who has Knowledge can show you how to love the whole. Who is this scholar? God. If you do not learn from Him, you will remain ignorant.

What does a river need to do while it passes by the trees? It needs to leave something of itself. What does someone need to do when passing by other people? One needs to leave something of oneself. If they are dead, he should awaken them, ignite them, and set them aglow. When you enter into the all-embracing Love and find yourself in Nature, you will listen to the singing of the birds, the humming of the insects, and the flying of the butterflies. And you will rejoice. You will then look at the flowers in bloom, the trees that bear fruit, the Sun that shines, and again you will rejoice. And lastly, when you go among people and listen to how they speak, you will again rejoice.

In the all-embracing Love, all beings will become your friends. The reptiles, as well as the frogs, that are looked upon with revulsion, will become your friends. You will look at them with sympathy rather than revulsion. When you encounter a turtle, a frog, or a snake you will know why the turtle carries its shell on its back, why the snake crawls, why the frog is cold. To apply this Love, this Knowledge, means to become a sublime, great spirit.

In my opinion, every heart that is not open from morning until evening, giving everything it has and accepting everything that falls upon its lot, is not a true and genuine heart.

When you enter into the all-embracing Love, you become connected with the whole Universe. You will then feel the suffering of all living beings.

You love one person; God desires that you love others as you do this soul. This love you have for one is a model for God to show you how you need to love the others as well.

If a grocer has only one customer, that person will go bankrupt. If you love only one person, it means that you are like a grocer with only one customer. If you love one hundred people, you are like a grocer with one hundred customers. The more people you love, the more profit you will have. The greater the number of souls which you are connected with, that much more your consciousness will be invincible, and your memory stronger. One's success depends upon the number of souls with which one is connected. If you love one person, your knowledge is equal to one. If you love two people, your knowledge is equal to two. The number of people that you love will define the degree of your knowledge.

In the all-embracing Love, you will feel an intrinsic joy. The consciousness of all beings forms one unity, and you will communicate with this collective consciousness.

The great Love is like a great body of water. The great water is not murky; it does not produce silt. The small water is murky and does produce silt.

The Teaching that I give is not a teaching of ordinary morality. It is a Teaching of great Love. Love can improve the health, enlighten the mind, expand the heart, and give impulse to the spirit. To whatever party you may belong, from whatever nation you may come, make use of this Teaching.

When I meet someone, I do not wish to know any details of that person's past. This is not my concern. Why impart any negativity to myself?

The one who plays music or sings—be it before an audience or one person—should be loved by them.

One soul who loves you is sufficient for you to be supported in the times of hardship in your life. Imagine then what can become of someone when not only one soul, but countless souls direct their love toward that person. Such a one can become a singer, a musician, an artist, a scientist, whatever he wishes, he can become.

We can imagine then what progress, what sublime Culture, will exist on Earth when the Love of all toward all does come.

Steadfastness

The Master guided our sight toward reality, freeing us from life's illusions and shadows. In this manner, he guided us in the right direction.
The Master said:

Love forms the most steadfast union. There is no power that can separate the two elements united by Love. Whatever people call "love" is not Love because the two elements that are brought together by human love can be separated. Wherever Love creates a union, no dissolution can exist. Every union in which God is not present is unstable, is falling apart. Divine Love can never die. How can you recognize Divine Love? It forms steadfast unions.

Someone says, "I have had love, but it died." How is it possible for a lamp that God has lit to go out? This is impossible.

I consider as a friend the one who is my friend not only in one life, but who is my friend from the moment of my departing from God to the moment of my returning to Him.

The Love manifesting among souls today is the result of relationships that have existed throughout many lifetimes. It has been in preparation for thousands of years. With this understanding, you will look at Love as a sacred act of Life.

The qualities of Divine Love are constancy and steadfastness. If some people change in their love for you, they have never loved you. When someone says that his love is abating, that person has in mind those transient moods which people incorrectly call "love." Someone says, "There was a time when I had love, but now I have aged and have lost my love." No, this is not love. This is only a temporary graft. Love is never lost, but the current of Love that passes through the person can become interrupted.

Those who understand the Law of Love can restore their original connection with it and acquire it again. On the other hand, those who do not understand the Law of Love will regret having lost it. In reality, they have not lost it: they only need to restore the interrupted current.

When observing the manifestation of Love in people, you will see that it is constantly being interrupted. This, however, is only apparently so. It relates to one's outer consciousness and not to this person's essence. External obstacles—clouds in the consciousness—exist, which seem to interrupt Love.

The higher the realm to which one's consciousness rises, the less one's love will be interrupted. I will give you an analogy. You are sitting in your room and look out of the window. At this time, your friend passes by. You follow his movement and can see him up to a certain distance. After a while, he disappears from your sight. This occurs because you remain at the same level. If you had risen to a higher level, you would have been able to see him constantly. The higher the level on which you stand, the more your love will be without interruption.

We have known righteous people who have led a high principled life and later say, "It is not worth it to live like that." Why? It is because they lacked a profound understanding of Life.

You love someone and are ready to do everything for this person. But it happens that this person burns the food, and you utter a scornful word. Then the Advanced Beings who have come to live within both of you go away. In this way, the love between the two is lost—but apparently, only temporarily.

If your feelings are inconstant, one day you will suffer because of that.

The Future Perspective

During a morning walk, in a conversation, the Master said:

For as long as man does not know how to live rightly, God will not allow him to manifest himself. But when he learns, God will make him the bearer of His great deeds.

We are now entering into a new phase. You will not remain in this position. A great future awaits you. For those who fulfill God's Law, great opportunities await them. One day every one of you will receive an inheritance, which has awaited you for centuries. All human beings need to develop the latent powers within them so that all the endowments, which God has bestowed upon them, may be fostered. God has imparted to all people one primary gift, which they need to develop. Their fulfillment depends upon this gift.

When people develop their radio, they will be able to enter into communication with the Advanced Beings from the Invisible World.

When people develop within themselves the organs for breathing in the ether, they will be able to live in the ethereal world.

Many secrets exist within Nature that remain locked away because people are not yet ready for them.

People of talent and of genius are collective beings. The time will come when every one of you will ascend to this level. One needs to be prepared. The hour for each will strike, and you need to be prepared to greet this hour. When you meet a person of talent or genius, rejoice. After that person, many more will come. Your turn among them will come as well.

A great future is written out for you. The Earth enters into new conditions. The new in the world is coming. Be prepared for the new conditions.

We wish to live on Earth the life of the Angels. We want too much. Their world is far away, but we are moving toward it. There is nothing more beautiful than to have inner peace, to be connected with all people living on the Earth and to converse with the most intelligent of them.

One brother asked, "Will this happen?"
The Master answered:

This already exists.

Relative and Absolute Reality

In a conversation, one brother asked about the relative and absolute realities.
The Master said:

The caterpillar represents the materialist; the cocoon is the idealist and the butterfly emerging from the cocoon—the realist. I use these words symbolically. Imagine a room in which someone lives. This room is closed up on all sides. The room is illuminated. The person who is in this room is exploring it. This is the materialist. Another person makes a hole in the wall and explores what is outside. This is the idealist. The realist is the one who freely walks everywhere—inside and outside the room.

When we say that matter is not real, we merely imply that the material things are the result. This result could not exist if at least two to three powers were not at work. When observing the material, one should not separate it from the Divine and the spiritual because the material is a manifestation—a result of the spiritual. The material and the spiritual are one and the same thing. They are two currents of the whole Life. If you are not able to understand the material life, you are not able to understand the spiritual, and vice versa.

We consider what we see to be reality. This is correct, but what we do not see, that, too, is reality.

The World beyond and this world are one and the same world. This one is a small sector, a small projection, of the other World.

The Angelic World is more real than ours.

How is the Universe created? This question in and of itself is irrelevant because the Universe exists. But when I say this, I imply the Real World; the physical world is but a shadow. When one speaks about the creation of the physical world, this is not Creation, but a Manifestation. It is because the Real Light, which exists eternally, is beyond the physical world. The shadow can appear, disappear, then appear again, and so on.

We now live in a transient world. Someone sleeps for seven hours; he dreams that he has graduated from the university, has received his diploma, has been appointed as a teacher, and then awakens. How is it possible for him to complete his education and become a teacher within seven hours? In the dream, this is considered to be reality, but actually, it is an illusion. On Earth, illusory things exist; and when we awaken to the World of Reality, we see that all existing on Earth is illusory. Not that it is an illusion, but it is less real.

The World as God perceives it is the World of Absolute Reality. The way in which the most enlightened people perceive it, this is the relative reality.

In the Mountains

Today with our beloved Master we went on a springtime hike, which we all loved so much. We departed at early dawn, climbed the steep path while it was still cool and met the rising Sun high up in the mountain. We performed our exercises, after which we sat down near the brook that flows through the young greenery and the flowers. One could feel the closeness of the mountain peaks from which a fresh coolness was descending upon us. The big snowdrifts were glowing in the sunshine here and there. Everyone was feeling the pulse of the great life, the surge coming from Nature.

In conversation the Master said:

When climbing in a high place—because the path varies and there are flat and steep places—all organs are activated and one becomes healthier.

In the early spring, observe the violet color of the snow on the mountain slopes. This is a result of the influx of prana; this is its color.

Many people are climbing the mountains today.[30] The young generation in Bulgaria visiting the mountains is to be relied upon.

The high peaks are dynamic centers. They represent a reservoir of power, which will be utilized in the future. The mountain peaks are connected with the Earth's internal forces and the cosmic forces as well. At the same time, they are pumps that suck up toxins. If you feel indisposed, climb a high mountain and you will feel refreshed and invigorated.

When we built the fountains in the Rila Mountains, we instilled in them the new ideas. Whosoever drinks from this water will perceive something from these ideas.

There was a time when elephants, mastodons, lions, and tigers walked here on the Balkan Peninsula.

All of the mountains of the Balkan Peninsula are undergoing a certain leveling, and after a time they will become fields, while the fields will become mountains.

In the past, Mount Vitosha was higher than at present.

---

30. The organized tourist movement in Bulgaria was initiated in 1895 by Aleko Konstantinov (1863–1897), a well known Bulgarian writer and prominent politician.

When you go onto a mountain, remain in that place to which you feel drawn.

When impure people try to go to pure places, they are not admitted; the weather worsens and they are forced to return home.

If you are walking in the mountains, keep only one thought within yourself. If three or four thoughts come into your mind, you will stumble. Never think about bad or negative things while in the mountains.

Places exist where when one takes time to sit and rest; one receives inspiration. There is a great benefit to such time spent.

Ideas and thoughts exist that manifest at an elevation of 3,000 meters. Others manifest at an elevation of 3,200 or 4,000 meters. Every one of you can verify this Law!

Should you climb the Himalayas to a certain elevation, and through your mind, pass those ideas characteristic for an elevation of 5,000 meters, then you can say that the elevation at which you are standing is 5,000 meters. For example, a meat-eating person climbs in the mountains and suddenly the idea not to consume meat any longer comes into his mind. This indicates that he has reached the elevation at which this idea was born. This elevation is 8,000 meters. When one reaches the elevation of 9,000 meters, one forgets one's nationality. The higher you climb the more sublime are the ideas that occupy your mind.

Beautiful are those places where no one has set foot. Seek out such places. There exists in some places in the Rila Mountains some of this primordial element, and if one walks in such a place, one will instantly rejuvenate. Some day you should walk in such a place. At that moment a new epoch in your life will begin. Living vortices exist in Nature, which transmit the sublime forces to you.

If we climb a mountain in order to perceive what God wants of us, such climbing is meaningful. And when we descend into the valley in order to bring to the people whatever we have received on the mountain, this descent is meaningful.

We have come to the mountain to enjoy the domain of our Father. Since you have come, forget everything old. A transformation in your outlook needs to take place. The one who comes to the mountain should set oneself free of a bad habit, shortcoming, or pain.

The Divine World is far more beautiful than the most beautiful mountains and the most beautiful places in nature.

All spiritual centers in the Rila Mountains, the Alps, the Himalayas, and other mountains are interconnected. In the Rila Mountains, great diversity exists. There are places there upon which no man has ever set foot.

Thousands of years ago, the Advanced Beings knew that we would go to the Seven Lakes in the Rila Mountains and they prepared them for us. The Rupite[31] peaks are beautiful. They look like a big city. The Rupite are the most sacred places in the Rila Mountains. The word "Rupi" has in its root "ruh," meaning "the dwelling place of the Spirit." In the Rupite there is an esoteric School.

The region from the River Beli Iskar to the Rupite—the so-called Skakavtsi—is the sanctuary of the Rila Mountains. Inaccessible places exist within it.

The oldest esoteric School is situated within the Rila Mountains. The Himalayas are young-fold mountains. From the Himalayas, initiates are coming to the Rila Mountains to study. There is an ancient University in the Rila Mountains. The initiates from the Himalayas come to study in the libraries of Rila. A School exists in the Alps as well, but the oldest School in the world is in the Rila Mountains. The Beings who dwell there have ethereal bodies.

Knowledge is stored in the Rila Mountains. The cultures of Egypt and India originated from the Rila Mountains and later became widespread. The future holds much to be learned.

What is the significance of these sacred centers? They are working for the New Culture. These Luminous Beings dwelling in the mountains do not appear to people, except when people have Love for them.

---

31. Rupite is the name given by the Master to a section of the Northwest part of the Rila Mountains (Elenivrah, Orlovets, Dvuglav, Zli Zab, Popova Kapa, and Golyam Kupen).

The Master pointed to the great valleys and peaks in front of us, and said:

If your eyes were open, you would see pictures here from "A Thousand and One Nights." Intelligent Beings are present here. You should make contact with them. Address them and greet them with the following words, "Luminous Brothers, we greet you and desire that God blesses you!" They will then answer you, "What you have said to us, let it come back to you as well."

The Divine Teaching

We were in the mountains with the Master. Someone asked what the New Teaching is about.
The Master answered:

The New Teaching is coming now into the world to bring the New Culture and reveal the internal side of Life. The New Teaching comes from the Invisible World and will come to be established. There are things that have been tried millions of times, and now they need to be applied. The Teaching of the Brotherhood of Light is founded upon their testing: the Principles, Laws, and Methods of the Divine Teaching can be tried. How can you prove that an object is sweet or to what extent it is sweet? Can you describe its sweetness alone? You can, but with that alone it will still not be understood. Yet, if you taste it, you will immediately gain knowledge about its sweetness. This means that the experiment is authoritative. One needs to try things—to test them that one may understand Reality.

Love brings Life, Wisdom brings Light, and Truth brings Freedom. These are the fundamental Principles of the New Life, of the New Teaching. This Teaching is not our own: it is Divine. First, it is applied in the physical, then the spiritual, and lastly the Divine.

What is the New Teaching? It is method for managing one's obsolete habits. What does the New Teaching consist of? It consists of the correction of the transgressions of past centuries. The New Teaching, which I profess, has the purpose of eradicating all conditions for error and disease in human existence. At least seventy-five percent of all diseases need to vanish. If the New Teaching cannot do this, then where is its power? If it cannot balance the forces of the mind and the heart—if it cannot give people peace—then what can one expect of it?

If the Teaching being taught to you gives meaning to your life; gives you health, wisdom, illumination; and sets you free—then follow it. It is that Teaching which every soul bears. It directs people to the real Life.

There is no "teaching of Mr. Deunov." There is only the Divine Teaching that has been made known to me. It is the Great Teaching of Life. I have been acquainted with it since time immemorial. Christ said, "What I speak, my Father has taught me. As for myself, I speak nothing."[32] This means that He did not preach His own teaching.

The Divine Teaching is recognizable: it brings Joy, Peace, Light, and every sublime inspiration. Which teaching is right? The Teaching that gives expansiveness to the mind, the heart, the will and gives impulse for growth. This Teaching is Divine.

People exist who are paying off an old debt and are not concerned with the present. Power lies not in the old but the new understanding. People need to understand that yesterday's knowledge cannot help them. Today a new Knowledge, a new Science, is needed for the people.

In the future, people will have the need for new ideas. I will give you an example. A colonel had an aide who was a well-read, erudite man with a science degree. The colonel always treated him abusively. The aide endured this. Once while traveling, the colonel fell from his horse and dislocated his foot. The aide said to him, "I know how to heal this." The colonel asked, "How do you know?" "I have graduated. I have knowledge in this field," answered the aide. He fixed the injured foot. Since then, the aide became equal to the colonel because the

---

32. See also John 8:28, "Then Jesus said to them, 'When you lift up the Son of Man, then you will know that I am He, and that I do nothing of Myself; but as My Father taught Me, I speak these things.'"

colonel understood with what kind of a person he was working. The colonel never abused the aide again and did not permit anyone else to abuse him. After the colonels understand what knowledge we possess, they will come to study with us. They will correct their relationship with us.

The New Teaching will travel to people like air, like water, like the light. When someone asks what the New Teaching is, give them "The High Ideal"[33] to read. In it is shown in a practical manner what Nature's method is. The deep mystical questions will follow later.

What is the New Teaching? To eat without a sword hanging over your head.[34]

Some old people have lost their teeth, and when apples and pears are offered to them, they cannot chew them. People exist who do not have teeth for the new ideas. One needs to give them baby food. The New needs to be given to the people a little at a time.

Whosoever declares himself against the Divine will lose favorable conditions. Everyone who does not desire to serve Truth, Justice, and Good, who goes against the service of God, will receive retribution.

Our friends should exert care in their lives and hold only to the sacred, the Real, that they will not suffer.

All who listen: prepare yourselves for the New and teach the others as well. Now you need to work with a profoundly awakened awareness that you may serve and work for God. And while working in this way, be glad that you are fulfilling God's Will and everything else will work out by itself.

We need to keep the eternal Fire. From your candles, all people will light their candles.

---

33. The High Ideal (*Visokiyat Ideal*) is a lecture given by the Master Beinsa Douno to the General Esoteric Class in 1923, Sofia, Bulgaria. First published in Bulgarian, in Sofia, Bulgaria, 1923. First published in English by the Sunrise Press&Books, USA, 1969 and a second edition was issued by Byalo Bratstvo Publishers, Sofia, Bulgaria, 2012 in a collection of lectures entitled "The Blossoming of the Human Soul."

34. This phrase comes from a story about Damocles who had to eat his food with a sword hanging over him which was tied up by a single hair.

Some people threatened us: "We will chase you out of Bulgaria!" When it comes to banishment, who is it that you will drive out? This land is not the Bulgarians': it belongs to God. England does not belong to the English: it is God's.

Our Brotherhood has passed through the greatest obstacles.

The Invisible World considers our spiritual settlement Izgrev[35] to be an oasis. At Izgrev, you have the most favorable conditions for coming to know and apply the Divine Teaching. There is no better place on Earth than Izgrev. Izgrev has the most favorable combination of conditions, a unique combination.

I would like that Izgrev be a model so that whoever comes here will begin to understand what the New Teaching is. During the evacuation you went into the country in order to appreciate the value of Izgrev.

A disharmony in our brotherhood is mirrored in the world situation. For this reason, peace and harmony should reign at Izgrev.

Bulgarian Folk Songs

The Master worked for years on Bulgarian folk song until he restored its purity of melody, rhythm, and text. In this way, he gave a number of models of folk songs. One day at lunch, a brother performed a few of them. In connection with that, the Master said:

Bulgarian music is very original, but within it there is incertitude, a latent wavering. Few people sing the old folk songs well. Now a kind of modernization exists in them, through which they have lost important things.

The Bulgarians sing well, but they lack performance skills. We need to work in this regard. There is a need for change

---

35. Izgrev, meaning Sunrise (1927–1956) is a settlement built near the Bulgarian capital of Sofia as a spiritual intentional community of Beinsa Douno's followers. There he gave regular lectures to his disciples and Sunday sermons open to the public.

in the consciousness of the Bulgarians in respect to music. There exist some beautiful Bulgarian songs.

Bulgarian music moves within a closed circle. A great pessimism is found in it. The Bulgarian uses traditional instruments: *kaval*,[36] *gadulka*,[37] *gaida*,[38] and ocarina flute. The Bulgarians cannot complain about a lack of musicians. The folk songs, revolutionary and ancient, have had historical significance at one time; but now they have become obsolete.

Songs that awaken the mind are needed today. We want to show what the Bulgarian song should be. New ideas need to be instilled in the folk songs and the character of the lyrics should be changed as well. Many of the ideas in the lyrics of our folk songs are antiquated and obsolete. With regard to this, great work is eminent.

I have chosen as an example, two folk songs: *Tatuncho* and *Blagosloven da e* (Blessed It Be). The lyrics for these two songs are completely negative. Negative characteristics are given in them.

The Master invited a brother to perform these songs with old lyrics and then with new lyrics given by the Master so that the difference could be seen.

The Master said:

Sing these songs to the Bulgarian people with the old lyrics and the new, and then they will see what the new moral values are.

The old folk songs were given during the old culture of winter. The revival of the folk songs with the lyrics we give now represents the beginning of spring, which is already within the Bulgarian.

---

36. *Kaval* is a wooden chromatic end-blown flute traditionally played throughout the Balkans and Anatolia, primarily associated with mountain shepherds.
37. *Gadulka* is an ancient, bowed stringed instrument also known as the rebec.
38. *Gaida* is a goat-skin bagpipe.

Entering into the Great World

The summer rain passed through like a whisper, cleansing and refreshing the air. One could breathe with ease. Above the valley, appeared the bright arc of a rainbow. We gathered around our beloved Master under the big walnut tree in front of the house. The pungent fragrance of its leaves hung in the moist air. Large droplets from the rain were still dripping down from its branches.

Someone asked, "Master, you are constantly speaking to us about Love as something new and unknown to us, yet we think that we have a perception of it."

The Master said:

People cannot receive the true Love because the organs through which it is experienced have not yet been developed in the human beings. Not all silkworms form a cocoon in one and the same day. In this same way, each person will come into Divine Love at different times. At the moment unconditional Love is accessible only to people of a higher evolution. People of today do not understand Love. It is a power that is not yet known to them.

By reading the New Testament, you will see that because of the difficulties faced in life, the love of many will cool down. That is to say, many will not have the strength to endure.

To begin loving someone means elevating that person to a great height. To stop loving that person means dropping him or her down from that height. There is no philosophy here—this is the nature of human love.

Some people are asking what this Love that I am speaking about is. This is the Infinite Love, not yet manifested Love. God abides in it. He manifests Himself through it. Life has validity in the Infinite and the Unmanifested. Divine Love is an Infinite World.

When I speak about Love, I am not referring to human love. Love is something sublime, which only few have experienced. Unless the human beings come to experience the true Love, they feel emotions.

People can be truly loved only as souls. When you come to love someone as a soul, you will not pay attention to one's weaknesses and faults, just as a mother does not pay attention to her child's mistakes. If you succeed in attaining this state, you will have resolved one of the most important tasks in your life: you will have attained the level of fulfilling God's Will.

A distinctive quality of Divine Love is that what you attain through Love cannot be taken away from you. In addition to this, the further away you are from the one you love, the nearer you feel to this person and the stronger your Love is. With human love, it is the opposite: only when you are close to the one you love is your love strong, and when you are far away, it disappears.

You are still in the shadow of Love.

People are in need of this extraordinary, all-embracing Love.

A great and sacred Life exists of which you have no knowledge. Something great and glorious exists for which you have not the slightest idea. Through Divine Love, you will enter into this great World.

The New Relationships

The Master said:

In the Spiritual world there is no criticism. Why do you need to look for other people's faults? This is like poisoning. Enter the house of a person as a friend and look for the treasure he has hidden within. Do not concern yourself with evil. If you accuse someone in not being good, you do that person harm. Maleficent thoughts are like decaying meat, which disperses its bad smell far away. Everything that begins to smell bad is a presage of death. Every negative thought is an omen of death. Speak about the positive things in life, not about the negative. What does it mean to speak or think badly about someone? It means that you prepare bad food, which will make that person sick.

When you get up in the morning, say, "God, teach me to think of my brothers and sisters as You think of them." To think well of people is to be strong. It is important to maintain a good opinion about everyone.

One of the most dangerous situations in life is to see the negative qualities of those around you. All people need to concentrate their attention on the unchangeable, the good and the Divine in others. To see someone's flaws is not science. In my opinion, it is a great science to see the good in a person and to address that. What do you gain if you know other people's faults?

When you come to the perfect Life, you will not reprove anyone. It would be good to form a group of ten people who would not see people's faults. Do not hold in your mind someone's defects and faults: thus you will become defiled and will lose. To speak badly of someone is not moral. It is moral to not allow any negative thought into your mind.

One of the sisters was telling me about the faults of one of the brothers. I said to her, "Your conclusions are not correct. This person is not bad." Until a fruit is ripe, it is tart and bitter. Yet when it ripens, it becomes sweet. You should wait for people to ripen. If someone has made a mistake, do not worry, but say, "The fruit is not yet ripe. We will wait until it ripens." The negative features of a person cannot characterize that person because the human being is in a process of development. One day nothing will be left of these negative characteristics.

How can you criticize a flower bud for not having blossomed yet? The time has not come for it to blossom. Do not tell someone that he is not a good person, but say, "The painting is still unfinished." If you would like to have a correct relationship with someone, you need to keep in your mind his good characteristics and not deviate from them. Then goodness will manifest in him.

The one who loves you sees everything in you as good. What is Love? The one who loves you does not see any faults in you. Love does not see faults. When people see faults in others—when they judge them—they act according to the law of human justice. For thousands of years, people have lived according to the law of human justice. Not only has the world not improved, but the Earth is covered with dead bones.

Even if you do not love someone, try to find positive features in him, and as a result, you will begin to love him. Many years ago, a young woman, very intelligent, came to me and told me how she regarded people. She accepted all people well with a good disposition. She would first attempt to find the best feature in a person. Then she would hold onto it, and after that, she would forget whatever negative she saw. She had made the following observation: When she held the good characteristics of a person in her mind, that person would open to her.

You meet one of your friends and say, "I know my friend well." No matter how well you know him, there is always something new and some good feature in his character, which you will discover today. He should do the same regarding you. Only in such a way, you both can achieve something precious in your life. The price of love needs to increase. If you cannot find one good feature in the person you love every day, your friendship will soon be over. That is the way it was thousands of years ago, and so it is at present. If this does not happen, I can determine after how many years your friendship will end.

If you would like to reform someone, do not hold onto his faults. If you keep his mistakes in your mind, you will never correct him. The only way to reform someone is to keep in mind the good and the noble in this person.

The True Human Being

This morning we climbed the solitary peak of the mountain. We performed morning exercises high up in a clearing surrounded by rocks. The Sun suffused the Earth with a joyful light, warming the rocks, and enveloping everything with radiance. As we talked, a question about the true human being arose.

The Master said:

There is a World that you do not see. It is necessary for your eyes to be opened in order to perceive it. You are a shadow of that World. You, its shadow, need to believe that there is one Real World from which you originate. You are only a projection of that Reality. There is one inner Light in the human being. This Light is the Divine Origin, which awaits for the time of its awakening. Man is something more than his mind, his heart, and his will. These last are servants of the human spirit. Man in his origin, in his essence, is something great.

If you love people, if you believe in them—and not in that which they manifest externally—you would see how great the human being is. You say, "Man is a being who thinks." But people are more than their thoughts. People are neither their thoughts, their feelings, nor their actions. The human being is Divine. You possess hidden within all the possibilities for a high-principled Life. What you have lost, you will find. When? When you realize that God has implanted untold riches within you. All possibilities exist for a person to become an artist, poet, scientist, and so on. Malice in people is on the surface. It is something external. The Divine in human beings is unconquerable. No matter what trial a person passes through, in the end, he will return to his original state.

When someone brings you a precious stone wrapped in a few layers and placed in a box, the first thing you do is to open the box, free the stone from all the wrappings, and, after you observe it carefully, appraise the stone. The Divine in the human being is a precious stone that you need to take out from its wrappings.

Trust in the Divine within you! The only genuine thing in us is the Divine. It is eternal and unchangeable. Those who want to evolve rightly need to accept the existence of the Divine Cause within themselves as an axiom. With Its assistance, you can develop your talents and abilities.

Trust in the Divine within all people. Upon this rock, you will build your great future. People can manifest themselves in their wholeness only when they realize that God abides within them and within their neighbors. Would it not be nice to perceive the Sublime World within your neighbor? When everyone becomes convinced that the Divine dwells within others, then the correct relations among people will reign.

The Eternal Home

The summer night was descending upon the mountain. Crickets were chirring in the meadows. The noise of human activity quieted down. From the sky came the last radiance of the passing day. We were sitting around our beloved Master and talked.
He told us:

Human beings cannot manifest their true essence on Earth. In order to say that someone is ideal, you need to perceive what that person is in the causal world. When you perceive a person in the physical, in the astral, or in the mental world, you can always find some flaws. When you come, however, to the causal world, you will see there the human soul, which does not have any flaw.

It is said that God dwells within human beings. God does not dwell within the human body, but dwells within the human soul. The human soul, which dwells in the causal world, does not dwell continuously within the physical body, and as a result, one often feels empty in the physical world.

Human beings with their ordinary consciousness live in the physical world, and the human soul visits them only from time to time for one-hundredth of a second. Then a person feels complete, rich, and inspired. During that time, he receives impulses and directives for his work. After some time, the soul visits him again. As long as a person can maintain this connection with his soul—with, in other words, the Divine within—he will have the desire to work. When people interrupt this connection, their forces will abandon them; their lives will become meaningless, and tribulations will follow one after another.

When people live an outwardly life, they are not completely incarnate within their body—something is missing. As a result, one is not a master of one's conditions. After thousands of years—when the human being is ready—the soul will come to dwell forever in the body. That is the true incarnation. Then one will become a master of one's life and will become immortal. At present, the body is still not perfect; therefore, the soul remains outside of the body. There is no home for the human soul; the same is valid for the human spirit. From now on, a temple is being built in which God will come to dwell.

You feel it when God visits you. You feel His Presence and His Influence. Then something inside of you ignites and you are ready to reconcile with the whole world. When this moment has passed, you say, "Was that reality? Was that only a dream?"

There is a beautiful inner side of the human being. You have not seen it yet. There are events, though rare, when someone's face becomes illuminated and others see the person as they have not yet seen him until now. Even when people know what they are in reality, they still need to be humble.

What interests you in a poet? The poet, too, has eyes, ears, and a nose as do other people. You are interested because of what this person has created. What interests you in a violinist? You are interested in what the violinist plays. From every individual, Light emanates. Everyone is a Divine potential. The Divine that someone bears is what interests you.

We are under a delusion. We think that we see Ivan, Stoyan, and so on. You have not seen Ivan. You have seen his car, his airplane.

Someone asks me, "What flaws do I have?" I reply, "You know your flaws. I will tell you what good qualities you have."

Human nature is silt that can deceive you. You need to wash away this silt in order to see that there is something precious in the humans being. There are extraordinary thoughts, which are like precious stones. Who perceives these beautiful thoughts, which are hidden deep within the human soul? There are clear-sighted people who perceive them.

We need to abide by the Laws that are inscribed within our souls—this is our life's mission.

Very often we have been taught what we have known, yet have forgotten. We come from a more Sublime World. There we know many things. When we come to the Earth, we learn them as new; but in reality, this study is a recollection.

You will say that some individuals are sinful and others are bad. Neither one of these is true. These are temporary manifestations that do not determine the human character.

When bad people come home in the evening, they say, "We do not live rightly. We should not live like this." There is some regret in them.

The true human being can be recognized when the soul awakens within beginning to think about God. Then you resolve easily your tasks, helping yourself and your fellowmen as well.

All negative human characteristics have the property of the snow. When the Divine comes, they melt: they disappear. We have put on masks, and we do not recognize each other. When you were a child, you had one mask; now you have another one: of an adult or old person. That you become older—that is a mask. Why do you come with masks? In order to be free.

Reality itself—Life itself—is invisible. There another vision is necessary. Therefore, Reality remains unknown to people and only the forms that have been made manifest are known.

Do not say, "Nothing will become of me." Thus you violate the Divine Plan. Say instead, "God will uplift me. He will fulfill His Plan for me."

God has created all beings. They are necessary for God. You do not know what will happen with some beings in the future. In the plants and in the animals there exists something noble, which is similar to that in humans. There is something incorruptible in them. In addition to ordinary life, something extraordinary also exists in them, which has not been made manifest.

The Invisible World

One sister asked where the departed souls are now.
The Master said:

The three worlds—the physical, the spiritual, and the Divine—are one world. When you are asked where is the World beyond, say, "The three worlds are one." The stomach, lungs, and brain correspond to these three worlds. One carries these three worlds within oneself.

Today there are more ways to explain the Spiritual world. We have radio waves; through them one can understand how it is possible to transmit a thought from one person to another and thus the Spiritual world becomes more understandable. When one dies, that individual simply changes place without disappearing. If people think that their friends and relatives die, this shows that they live in the transient world. When someone dies, only the assets of the company die, but the company itself remains. Why are you crying for your departed daughter? She is in another World. You can talk to her; she will write to you. She writes to her mother, "Mother, the World where I am now is very beautiful. Also, there are universities here, and professors who teach us."

The World beyond is more real than the physical world. You have a friend whom you love. One day he dies. You ask yourself, "Where has he gone? Where is his consciousness?" Your friend is alive. Nothing is lost in the world, only the relationships change. When we die, we pass from one state into another. In fact, there is no aging. When the creative forces project from this world into a more Sublime World, the form is destroyed. Here there are no conditions. The form can be destroyed, but the consciousness, never.

Do not be afraid of death! No one can kill another. The most dreadful thing comes when the human consciousness is not awakened after death. Then one lives in darkness and deep sleep. In order to be saved from that darkness, Nature sends that person suffering.

Someone says that God has arranged for humans to die. This is a misinterpretation of the Truth. Death is the result of not understanding the great Divine Laws. When someone dies, this resembles traveling by car. The car breaks down in the middle of the journey. When one realizes that the car is beyond repair, one starts to walk, realizing that it is possible to travel without a car. The same happens after death.

A woman came to me. She was crying that her husband had died. I said to her, "I see your husband near to you; he is happy now."

When someone passes beyond, one takes along the essence of the brain. The human being has a material and an etheric brain. After death the material brain is left behind and the etheric brain is taken along. It is the etheric brain that organizes matter. In other words, one takes with him that which is valuable. People of today deny life after death. I am sorry for those people of genius whose disembodied spirits haunt the funeral place. Some rich man wanders after his death, moving about his big house, which he has built, regardless that the house is now occupied by other people. With such ideas he will not evolve.

What do people know about those departed to the World beyond? You call for your father, asking him what is in the World beyond; he does not know anything. You call for your mother; she says that she sees nothing, darkness all around. This is understandable. As much as they knew on Earth about the World beyond, that much will they know about it after their departure, at least in the beginning. There are some departed who perceive and understand, but they are few. They have worked on the Earth consciously and they continue to work in the World beyond.

Those who do not live rightly will find themselves after death at first in complete darkness, only with a bare, stripped consciousness. This is hell. After death, everyone will be convinced that there exists another World as well.

Our departure for the World beyond is an unrelenting Law. This Law is valid for the present phase of human evolution. After death, when one begins to become aware of his errors, he will gradually begin to organize himself and will come again to the Earth as a small defenseless child.

After death, one is still in contact with the physical body; one has been buried and yet can see how one's friends and relatives cry at the funeral. The consciousness of someone who has committed crimes remains connected to the body after death and is present for some time during the decomposition of the body in the tomb. And afterward, in one's next incarnation on

Earth, when one is taught again how to rob and lie, one says, "Have you been where I have been? Because of that, I cannot steal or lie anymore."

Those who have departed to the World beyond, already have vibrations of a different nature. There is nothing dense in them, similar to water in a cooking pot that when brought to boiling, is transformed into vapor. The one who has departed to the World beyond differs in one's vibrations. I was told that one brother was not alive. I performed some investigations. I compared his vibrations with the vibrations of another whom I knew had departed for the World beyond, and I observed that there was a difference. I said, "This brother is alive; he has not departed."

When you go to the World beyond, you will not forget the Earth because you have related souls here. You will feel their needs, and because you will be rich there, you will come to help.

A man has departed. His relatives give a luncheon in his memory. To give a luncheon, this is all right, but nobody prays for the departed. Then the person comes to me and says, "They gave a luncheon for me, but no one prayed for me." It is necessary to send the departed souls a good thought. Our prayers help them. Our good thoughts toward the departed are food for them. They feed on the juices contained within the thoughts and feelings.

A departed person can sometimes manifest oneself through other people. For example, one can manifest within someone for a year; within others, for two years, three years, or ten years. Still, sometimes the person manifests oneself through someone else for only a few hours. One example: I was in the city of Varna when two of our brothers from Sofia passed away. In the morning, around 10 AM, I was visited by two boys of 18 years of age from the villages. They stayed with me for two hours. One of the departed brothers was known to be witty and the first boy expressed himself in such a way. The other departed brother has also been witty, but in a specific manner. Such was the behavior of the other boy. I did not ask the boys where they came from, what their names were because the disposition of the departed would have been destroyed. One who has departed prematurely stays to work on the Earth until the time comes when it was planned for one to depart.

Artists, musicians, poets, philosophers, and so on are sent here, to Earth to be in training. Afterward, in the World beyond, they will perform their true work as artists, musicians, poets, philosophers, and so on. In other words, in the World beyond they will continue to work in the same field, but with greater opportunities and under better conditions.

One's entire earthly life is recorded and will be shown at one's arrival at the World beyond as a living experience movie: childhood, adulthood, and old age.

A bud blooms into a flower. A fragrance comes out of the flower. Then the flower chalice drops off, and only the small seed inside the fruit is left. Where are the bud and the flower? Everything is in the fruit. The bud is the first phase, the flower is the second phase, and the fruit is the third phase. Inside the fruit is the seed. This has an analogy with the human life.

Our world is filled with evolving souls from the World beyond who need to be enlightened. At our spiritual gatherings, for example, around each one of us there are many undeveloped souls from the World beyond who want to evolve. Sometimes you are in a pessimistic mood. It is from those souls who would like to be helped. There are souls who do not know that they are departed. As the living are attracted toward the fruit gardens, the wellsprings, so the departed souls of our relatives are attracted to our spiritual meetings, prayers, and lectures. For them, these meetings, prayers, and lectures represent fruit gardens and wellsprings.

One of our brothers who had departed for the World beyond let us hear from there and told us about his condition. He said, "From the World beyond we are sent to work, to help others. You work the whole day over some who are incarnated on the Earth. You go from place to place. You teach people, but only a few understand you. You visit someone who lives on the Earth, whisper to him from inside as to how to act. Yet he waves you away; he does not want to listen; and you come back indisposed, dissatisfied. If you do not want to help someone on Earth, you lose."

A departed soul from the World beyond will be sent to a pub to influence some good person who drinks to stop drinking. Another departed will be sent to some big house where the wife is squandering money and tormenting her husband. The departed soul will whisper to her not to spend so much money, to be more modest.

After the departure, one's existence is a continuous ascent into the higher Worlds, according to the level of awakening of one's consciousness. And when he goes to the higher Worlds, a curtain lifts in front of him in order for him to enter the Divine World, and to perceive the Great Reality.

The Divine World is in such a harmony that when you enter it, you will forget all your difficulties and suffering. Things there have meaning and depth. Everything lives in Love. There exist such arts that you cannot imagine and such variety that a special work exists for each and every one, which he will like. When you live with Joy in the Divine World, you can study without becoming bored; Life there is not monotonous.

The Spiritual and Divine Worlds are a thousand times more beautiful than the physical one. The prophets have visited the World beyond, but the World beyond has changed from that time until now as well.

The Two Fundamental Laws

We welcomed the sunrise on the open clearings. We said our short morning prayer and did the morning exercises.
The Master said:

Love for God and fulfillment of His Will are the two fundamental Laws of Life. To abide in God means to never go against the Divine with your thoughts, feelings, or actions. You should serve God above all things. The Scripture tells us, "You were bought at a price; do not become slaves of men."[39]

---

39. See 1Corinthians 7:23.

One Authority exists in the world, and this Authority is God.

Someone believes in God. This means nothing in and of itself. Of what use would it be if you were to believe in a head of state, yet did not abide by his laws? The one who is blind cannot see anything. The one who does not think is mentally blind. And the one who does not accomplish God's Will is spiritually blind.

You ask, "What will happen to us?" Visit the poor section of the city, visit the cemeteries, visit the hospitals, visit the surgical wards in the hospitals, and visit the battlefields. Then you will see what will happen to you if you do not fulfill God's Will.

A Law states: When one does not fulfill God's Will, one makes a place for the darkness within oneself. That is to say, one becomes vulnerable to the negative forces in the world.

The Great Universal Brotherhood

We celebrated the feast of spring equinox in the mountain. We had been there for a couple of days, staying in the small mountain hostel at the foot of the peak Ostritsa[40]. Every morning we climbed the peak where we met the sunrise, prayed, and performed our exercises. After that we would choose some sunny clearing and sit around our dear Master. One morning, a question arose about the Brothers of Light, who guide humankind.

The Master said:

There is one Divine Community. There is one Divine Nation. I advise you to bind yourselves strongly to it in order to perceive the new Light in your minds, hearts, and souls. I say to everyone: We will triumph! God is with us. There is no force in the world that can oppose the great principles which we serve. All good, honest, just, and wise people—men, women, and children—are with us. All these people who are supporting the three great principles of Love, Wisdom, and Truth—independent of which church or party they belong to—are with us.

---

40. Ostritsa is a peak in the Mount Vitosha near the village of Marchaevo.

We are asked, "Who are you and how many are you?" We are one Great Brotherhood, which the world has never seen before—a Brotherhood that has branches on Earth, in Heaven, and in the whole Universe. The one who is serving God is a citizen of this Great Universal Brotherhood, which we call the Brotherhood of Divine Love, of Divine Wisdom, of Divine Truth.

You will say, "We would like to become members of this Brotherhood." Yet I would like you to become students of this Brotherhood. To study with God means to pass through the School of the Universal Brotherhood of Light. The best professors, the best teachers, are in this School. Each one of you needs to find it. This School is not like our universities. In it there are no hypotheses or theories.

When you finish this School, you will be given difficult missions that you need to fulfill correctly. For example, you will be given the task to visit primitive fierce tribes and live with underdeveloped people. After that, you will be sent among both good and maleficent people, among the plants and the animals, and you will be watched as to how you interact with them and how they accept you. Upon completion, you will be given one precious and one common stone, and they will observe what you do with them. If you use both correctly, the common and the precious stone, the Brothers of Light will accept you as a member. They are very strict toward everyone because each will be a master of their powers. Once they accept you among them, they will help you always. Great prospects, great future, and great accomplishments are ahead of you.

John the Baptist, who came a little while before Christ, was familiar with the Divine Knowledge, the Divine Teaching. He had not been an ordinary man—that is, ignorant. He had been initiated. He had studied in one of the ancient Schools. The new in the world has always been given by this Great Brotherhood.

The Brothers of Light brought the good into the world through Christ. If two thousand years ago Christ did not come, what would be the status of humankind? All the good in the world has been introduced by the Brothers of Light, who have worked for the uplifting of nations.

Those people within whose souls and spirits God lives are the Great Souls, people of genius, Teachers of humankind who have given the highest manifestation in music, poetry, art, in all fields of life in general. These are the souls who help humankind to progress. This or that nation, this or that person, are not the factors for the human historical process of development, but the Invisible World. They are the Forces that conduct the events, namely the members of the Brotherhood of Light. The only leadership in the world is that of the Great Universal Brotherhood. All other people—public figures, writers, priests, ministers—are servants of the Brotherhood of Light. All manifestations of culture and justice in the world are inspired by the great power of the Brotherhood.

The Great Universal Brotherhood is not something fictional. It is neither a church nor a cult. It is something alive and beyond these corrupted conditions in which people live. The one who completes his evolution will enter into this Universal Brotherhood.

Good people are inwardly connected with the Brotherhood of Light. A good person deposits whatever he acquires into the Great Brotherhood. We are sought after for the capital that we possess.

There are people who have walked around the backyard of the Universal Brotherhood, but have never entered its sanctuary. What can a student know who has not listened to a single professor?

Some say that in order to attain initiation, you need to go to India. You could have gone to India, you could even have passed tests without having become initiated. The one who would like to be initiated can get this everywhere—in India, as well as here.

Members of the Brotherhood of Light know the Laws of Nature. They know how to condense and thin the matter of their bodies and transport themselves wherever they want.

Brother is someone who has been a brother to you from the point of leaving God until his return to God and throughout all his reincarnations. Under all life's conditions, he has been ready to make a sacrifice for you; and he is doing all this not because of being forced, but with the great consciousness of the Divine Spirit that is living within his soul. If every one of you has this ideal, you will be students and servants of this Great Universal Brotherhood.

The Divine Teaching of the Great Brotherhood was not born now. It has existed since the beginning of the Creation of the world. It has existed ever since the Universe existed. The Brotherhood of Light has taken part ever since the Creation of the world, of the whole Universe.

Every member of this Brotherhood is a manifestation of God. They have achieved this through hard work. If you study the lives of these Brothers, you will see what they have sacrificed for the world. If someone could be found to portray their lives in a novel, you would follow their path. Until now, there has been no poet or writer who could write such a novel. Why? It is because he could not find such beautiful images in either his mind or his heart. Only that person who can connect with the Great Brothers and follow their path can know this new philosophy of Life.

One brother asked, "Why is the expression 'Brothers of Light' preferred to the expression 'Advanced Luminous Beings'?"

Because when you say "Brothers," it is understood that they are related to us, that they are our brothers. In some quite common events are hidden things that you do not suspect. You meet a person who you consider to be ordinary, yet he is one of the Luminous Brothers.

"Will these Luminous Brothers appear among people in the world in the future?"

Some of them already have appeared. The Angelic Hierarchy leads humankind. Angels have representatives on Earth.

The School of the Great Universal Brotherhood is on the Sun. Every year, the Brothers of Light gather there. And representatives of the Brothers of Light on Earth have meetings as well. Where? On one high peak of the Himalayas. Where is this peak? I know it, but I cannot tell you: it is not allowed. It is then that the Great Brothers manifest their Love toward their representatives on Earth in all its fullness and with all of their energy that is sent to the entire world. This same energy is the reason for the advancement of religion, sciences and arts, for the reformation of societies and improvement of the social order and government. The enlightened and sublime days of our lives are due to the convocation of the Brothers of Light on the Sun.

When one of the Brothers of Light on Earth receives consecration, that is, passes through initiation, he should pay attention to be sure that this takes place during the days of the solemn convocation on the Sun because it is then that the Rays of the Sun send something new to Earth.

One sister asked, "Could we visit the Brothers of Light where they are living?"

It is not a question of their not wanting you to visit, but that people are still not ready to understand the Knowledge studied there. Moreover, they are not in physical bodies such as ours. They live in ethereal bodies.

After some time, the Great Universal Brotherhood will give more support to humankind and an epoch of Light will come. There is one Plan in Nature that no one can change. This Plan will be applied and people will be free.

One brother asked, "Did the movement of the Bogomils have a connection with our movement?"

We have never been an outgrowth of any teaching. We are a wellspring that has come from God. Other streams have come out of us, but we have not come out of another stream. The Bogomils have similar features to our stream because both the movement of the Bogomils, as well as our own, came from One and the same great Center of the Universal Brotherhood of Light.

In the past we have manifested in one way. In the future, we will manifest much more perfectly.

The Master

It was the longest day of the year. The Sun was descending in the west, golden and content after being given generously to everyone. The rocks were warm. From the forest, a balsam aroma was rising. We had been seated around our dear Master on the top of the mountain. All around us, it was as clear and light as in Paradise.

While sitting in silence, one brother asked, "Master, tell us something about yourself, about your work."

The Master was silent for a long time, then said:

I use a natural method. I do not say which ingredients the bread contains, but will advise you to eat this bread and you will benefit.

Whoever wants to force his teaching upon people gives them water from a bottle, but instead he should lead them to the source, to obtain it from there.

People say about me, "You are a holy man." Forget this; it is not important who I am. You need to be concerned with how you can best benefit from me. Be thankful to God that you have found this wellspring, which is flowing, and as of myself, I do not speak anything. Someone asks, "Is this wellspring from God?" If you can benefit from this wellspring, it is indeed from God. I desire that those deeds of yours that have been worked upon shall begin to shine through.

There is something unusual in the world, and this is the Divine; I would like to acquaint you with it. This is what I am preaching about. In order to understand it, you need to step on the ground of Love.

I have no personal considerations; I would like to fulfill God's Law. I speak and do only what God tells me. When God tells me to go somewhere, I know that people there need me. I would like to fulfill God's Will, as God has ordained it. May His Name be sanctified!

God has been so good to me that I would like to repay Him with all my gratitude. I would like that you, too, follow my example. Do you know me? You will say that I have preached to you; yet, at present, I am only preparing you. You say that I know many things. This is true. I live simultaneously in this world and in the World beyond. When I go to the Sun, I am traveling at a speed greater than that of light. At night when I would like to study the worlds, I go out and visit where no human foot can step and no human eye can penetrate. After that, I come back again. I have a device with which one can observe the most remote of suns. Everyone can try these things. When? When you develop within yourselves the talents with which God has endowed your souls. In order to be able to accomplish that, you need awareness. I perform spiritual experiments that need special conditions. This is a science—an art that can be passed on only to those who are ready to serve with Love and selflessness.

It is a delusion to think that it is possible to exist without a Spiritual Teacher. Without a Spiritual Teacher, the student can accomplish nothing. If you love your professor and he loves you too, he teaches you his knowledge and you understand him. If you do not love him, no matter how much he speaks to you, you cannot understand him. He can love you, but if you do not love him, he cannot pass on his knowledge to you.

If you could apply a one-hundredth of this Teaching, you would be fulfilled. I do not expect more than a one-hundredth. Today, all of you can be fulfilled. How? When you come to believe my words. Being one year around me will be enough to learn more than only listening to me. But if you want to perceive God's Mercy, you should follow me for thousands of years so that I could teach you and make you ready. This is not an easy task.

When I go back to Him Who has sent me here, He will ask me, "Have you accomplished the task which I gave you?" If there should be something I had not finished, I would come again. If I should not finish my work the second time, I would come again and again until I would be told, "You have accomplished your mission well."

If you are speaking about earthly love, I do not love you with this love. If you say that I do not love you as your Angels love you, you are wrong. There is no one on Earth who loves your souls as I love them. I would like that you, too, would love human souls in this way.

Someone asks me, "Do you know Christ?" I know Him; I speak with Him. I have spoken with Him many times.

In order for a great Teacher to manifest himself, all Enlightened Beings must be united within him.

The king should wear the most humble of apparel in order to remain discrete.

Some people would like to oppose the new ideas. This is what I will say: When the Divine Teaching is applied everywhere, a Fire with a temperature of 35 million degrees centigrade will appear. This is the last Plan given by God that I have brought from the World above.

Once one brother asked, "Master, why were you interned during 1917?"

The Master said:

More than 30 years ago I said that there would be a war in 1914 and that Germany would lose it. Later I warned the government to sign a peace treaty as soon as possible, but instead they interned me. I said that a Second World War was coming and also told them which cities would be destroyed. I was summoned to the public security department of the police and I told them that if I had wanted, I could have not come, but that I respect the laws and therefore I came. By following the present course, nothing will remain of Sofia. You violate God's Laws and you will see that I am not speaking from myself. And if I speak the truth, you will bear the consequences. Something terrible is coming for the Bulgarians.

Now the same will happen with Bulgaria that has happened with a certain priest. He was traveling by a horse-wagon when the horses became frightened. The wagon turned over, and the priest fell on a molehill. Because the molehill was soft, he was not hurt. There was a stone nearby. If his head had hit the stone instead, he would have died. The same will happen with Bulgaria. Bulgaria will go through hardship, but as with the priest, the nation will fall on a molehill and will pass through the hardships more easily.

A big catastrophe had awaited Bulgaria. Great misfortunes would have come upon the country if I had not been able to help until now. If the people of Bulgaria had listened to me, if they had listened to the Divine, Bulgaria could have been without even these hardships. I took upon myself nine-tenths of the trials that had awaited Bulgarians. For them, only one-tenth is left. Therefore, the Bulgarians will pass through more easily. Only God has the right over the remaining one-tenth of the trials of the Bulgarians. These cannot be reduced anymore.

One brother asked, "Master, last autumn you walked to the Mount Vitosha every day, independent of the weather. Why did you climb the mountain with such consistency?"
The Master answered:

In order to build roads and bridges for Divine Justice to come into the world. In this way, I am building the New Path—our Path toward God.

The Truth

The one who is able to comprehend the Law of Love will be able to comprehend one-third of the One Reality, the one who is able to comprehend the Law of Wisdom will be able to comprehend two-thirds of the One Reality, and the one who can comprehend the Law of Truth will be able to comprehend the Whole of the One Reality. That one will become a Magus capable of attaining anything at will. He could take up the magical wand and resolve all hardships in life.

Some people are in their first stage of life: Love. One needs to begin with Love. Others are in the second stage: Wisdom. A few are in the third stage: Truth. People will continue to suffer until that time when they are able to comprehend the Laws of Love, Wisdom, and Truth.

What is Truth? Truth is what makes Love and Wisdom accessible and comprehensible. To point out the transgressions of others, this is not truth. Truth offers Resurrection. What brings resentment and death, this is not truth. Truth is what offers Freedom.

The one who is not truthful will continue to experience death and reincarnation. You have known the Truth in another time, but you have forgotten. Truth abides within your souls. Learn to speak its language. Unless you know its language, Truth cannot speak to you. It can speak only to those whose hearts are filled with Love, and whose minds are filled with Light. When one's heart is in discord, and when one's mind is disturbed, one cannot perceive the Truth.

One brother asked, "What is the significance of the elimination of falsehood for human existence?"

One who lies brings suffering upon oneself. No one who lies has advanced. Lying is the only thing that does not produce a gain. For example, if you pay someone with counterfeit money, you will be paid back with the same. In this way, you bring suffering upon yourself through falsehood. Whoever lies is foolish because that person does not comprehend the consequences. This person may deceive and outwit you, but he does not understand that one will be discovered and will bear the consequences.

Why should you not lie? That you may not die, that you may not lose the whole Blessing of Life. If Truth does not abide in you, then Life will not abide in you. Your lie may appear to be insignificant, inconsequential, but it carries immense negative consequences. Therefore, the Invisible World forgives many transgressions and errors, but not falsehood. Falsehood is the most difficult error to forgive because its consequences are the most severe and it carries within itself all other error. If you dwell in falsehood, you will be as one who is blind, mute, and deaf to the Truth.

With truthfulness, you always gain, and with falsehood, you always lose. At first, your loss may appear to be imperceptible, but falsehood has its destructive effect. For example, you tell a lie and later, when you return home, either you will break an expensive glass, or your wife or child will become ill.

The lies of a person cannot remain concealed: they will always be found out. Even the least lie will, over time, cause a person to go astray. The word "lie" contaminates: it is toxic. The use of this word should be avoided as much as possible. Instead, one can say that the "truth" has been stretched or that the "truth" has not been presented correctly. When you have been deceived, do not speak of it, lest you become contaminated.

The Laws of Thought

Once a question about thought arose. The Master said:

Through the internal radio, one can receive people's thoughts telepathically. These are ordinary thoughts. Human thoughts, in comparison with the Divine Ones, have longer wavelengths and lower frequencies of vibration. They cannot penetrate far away. The Divine Thoughts, in comparison with the human ones, have shorter wavelengths and higher frequencies. As a result of having powerful vibrations, Divine Thoughts can penetrate all other thoughts. No one and nothing can obstruct them.

Sometimes we see that someone's thought has stopped at two spans over his head and can go no farther; yet he says that he has prayed.

No one can oppose Divine Thought: it reaches its destination.

One needs to nourish Divine Thoughts: one needs to think the way God thinks.

To love means to think. Love contains within itself Divine Thought. The way you understand and feel love, this is not Love. Love contains that Divine Thought that resolves all difficulties and removes obstructions. Love that does not bring Divine Thought is not Love but ignorance; it is a lack of Love. So, if you have Divine Love, you have Divine Thought as well. Therefore, when I talk about perceiving Divine Love, I have in mind that Divine Thought that is also to be realized within us.

One of the Laws states: In order to improve your affairs, think because Divine Thought is the Reality that will produce a powerful influence. When you feel darkness within you and when you are sad, accept, then, Divine Thought. Why are you suffering? It is because you do not have Divine Thought. How long will you suffer? Until you accept it. All difficulties are resolved by this Thought.

If you love people, you possess Divine Thought. If you hate them, you do not. Everyone who does not think is a slave. But by "thinking," I have in mind "Divine Thought." Every person who thinks is a master. You say, "I would like to be good, to become knowledgeable, and so on." Begin to think and this will occur. With our thoughts, we can help in the uplifting of an entire nation and of humankind.

Thought moves at a high speed. In contrast, the movement of light is like the speed of a wagon driven by buffalo.

There is a Law: When there are strands that bind you, sever them from the moment they appear; do not wait for them to multiply and become ropes. This refers to a negative thought coming to you. Thinking that you will get sick is an example. Immediately replace this thought with the positive thought, "I will be healthy." When a thought such as, "You will get old" comes, immediately replace it with the thought, "I will rejuvenate." When the thought, "You are bad" comes, immediately replace it with the opposite thought, "I am good." When negative thoughts come to you, every one of them is like a strand. And when many such strands are added, they become a thick rope, which you cannot sever and which binds you. However, when you sever each strand, they cannot be twisted into a rope.

You are always a victim of someone else's thoughts when you lack knowledge. Sometimes you go out feeling happy, but you walk down a street where a person with negative thoughts has passed and you become ill-disposed.

One negative thought can paralyze someone; a positive one can liberate him. The negative thoughts and desires are like bombs. They will explode at some time or other. Stay far away from them.

If the water droplets fall continuously over a stone for many years, you will see what this water can do. Its quantity is a small one, but it will bore the stone through at the place where it has been falling. For the same reason, I say: The negative thoughts and desires, which have been falling over your mind and heart for thousands of years, have made a hole in them. These holes cause misfortunes for contemporary people. Every negative thought and desire has a negative consequence. The day will come when these negative thoughts and desires will bring us to such consequences that any further development will cease. They can bring you to a mental decline, to blindness, and so on. Just as you can perceive the smell of onion in a house, so can the sensitive person perceive the "smell" of negative thoughts and feelings in a house. If you think well of others, this is also good for you. If you think ill of others, it is likewise bad for you.

When I say that people need to think, I do not have in mind ordinary thought. One needs to be occupied with the sublime, the Divine Thoughts. Only these can save a person. Beautiful thoughts come from the Great Origin of Life.

Right Divine Thought indicates the presence of God. When we connect with God, then Divine Thought, Knowledge, and Light will come.

There is one Knowledge that it is not permitted to talk about. I understand this as Joy. Then the entire Universe opens up for you. This is something that cannot be defined. It is like music.

The Advanced Beings can heal with their powerful Thought from a great distance.

Knowing the power of thought, cultivate within yourself those powerful Divine Thoughts that elevate and envelop you. It is sufficient to have a vigilant consciousness in order to perceive the Divine Thought of the Advanced Beings. Work on your mind that you may become a conduit of Divine Thought.

The least Divine Thought can uplift you and place you on solid ground. Accept and guard the least Divine Thoughts within you as a mother protects her children. Guard them that you may enjoy greater Thoughts in the future. The least Thought matures, blossoms, and gives fruit. It makes people great. The seed is small, but from it grows a big tree. Within the Divine Thought, as small as it is, is hidden a miraculous power. The sun of human life has not yet risen, but people have guidelines, which lead them. These are the least Divine Thoughts, they open the path to our bright future.

The Great Divine Thought has preceded the Creation of the material world. The Thought is the power that moves things. When human thought becomes unchangeable, it can alter the surrounding environment. But if you think in one way for five years in a row and, in another way, for another five years, then you cannot achieve anything.

Sorrow is the first impulse for the emergence of a thought. Sorrow is the first stimulus toward thinking. It is the mother who says, "Get up!"

If you have one sacred idea, this will be received by thousands of people. You should express it and not worry about who will receive it and who will not. Thousands of people will hear and receive the idea that you have expressed. You have some thought; do not be concerned with whether or not it will be realized. Just say it, and the thought will become widespread.

Property

This morning we went with our beloved Master to the mineral spring (in the nearby village of Rudartsi). The path was winding down the mountain slope among the bushes and the young forest. When we came to the field near the path, we sat down to rest. The fields were ready for harvesting. The air was refreshed from the rain, and one could sense the ozone. Opening in front of us was a fine view of the vast valley, delineated into squares by fields and houses. Here and there, small villages could be distinguished by the smoke of their chimneys. One brother asked a question about private property.

The Master said:

Just as the field produces wheat, you take it and say that it belongs to you. You take possession of the field and say that it is yours. You see the stones and say that they are yours. If you need to pay taxes for the light and warmth you receive from the Sun, how could you pay? When people are not aware of God, then they claim that all bounties belong to them. When people turn to

God, they realize that everything existing in the world belongs to God. When they come to that realization, they become sons of God and inheritors of all His Wealth, inheritors of the Kingdom of God.

You have a house, so you say, "This is my house. I inherited it from my father" or "With this money, I built a house." The house is not yours; neither is the money yours. Are the stones for the house yours? You have taken them from the mountain. You say, "I bought them." You have bought them from the person who has appropriated them.

To you belongs only what God has given you. Only what you have been born with—the mind, heart, soul, and spirit that God has given you is yours. Be aware of the attachment to private property that can suffocate people. To be first in the world, to be the strongest and the richest, these are the ideas of private property.

There is an anecdote about a conversation between a field and its owner. When the owner bought the field, he warned it, "I will draw the reins and whether you want to or not, you will bear fruit for me." The field turned toward him and said, "I have sent off many like you; I will send you off as well."

Wealth is a common bounty. It is a result of the activities of all Advanced Beings. What farmer can say that the fruits are really his? Along with him, have worked oxen, horses, and hired laborers. Also, all the elements of Nature have assisted. Therefore, the wealth in the world is a result of the combined efforts of all beings. You cannot say that the wealth is yours alone.

It is not allowed that you build your happiness on the unhappiness of others.

What shall we expect from the New Life? That which sets people free from their attachment to the private property.

People ask how to improve the world. If you collect iron shavings in a bottle and shake the bottle, they produce noise. Yet, when they are melted together, they become a total mass, a whole and no longer make noise. When the New comes, people will come together, and then this attachment to private property will be outgrown.

The New Human Being

The Master once said:

What is the distinguishing feature of the new people? If you would like to know whether someone is a "new" or an "old" human being, observe what kind of thoughts and feelings that person is nourishing within. The "old" human being is feeding himself with negative thoughts and feelings, and the "new" with positive ones.

When I speak about the new people, I have in mind those of the Sun who live with Joy. They are cheerful, generous, and overcome their difficulties easily. They are heroes, people with open hearts. They use everything wisely. They enjoy everything. In both suffering and pleasure, the new people are filled with an inner joy. They know that both bad and good conditions are given in order for them to grow.

Guidelines for the Spiritual Student

The Master instructed us:

When you tread on a muddy or dusty road, become a bird and fly up to where there is no mud and dust. If you face some obstacle or contradiction in your mind, you need to elevate yourself to a higher realm. When you enter the realm of sublime Thought, you become free from all contradictions.

Do not bind yourself with temporary, transient things. If you bind yourself with them and begin to love them, then when you lose them, you will suffer.

If you do not want to be ruined by the collective ordinary thought of people, you need to connect with the forces of Living Nature and elevate your consciousness to God.

People treat their environment carelessly and without appreciation, but are attentive toward their material conditions. Parents provide the environment for their children, but no matter how good the parents are, the children are not attentive toward them. However, when there is a concern about the condition of some friend, the children will always accept that person with enthusiasm and expectation. The father spends thousands of leva each year for the son to study abroad, yet the son writes not even one letter of gratitude. However, if one of his friends buys him a ticket for the theater, he writes a letter to him immediately and thanks him for the pleasant evening they spent together. Why does the son behave in two different ways? It is because the father represents the environment, and the friend, the condition. If your friend starts to take care of you like a father—that is to say, changes from being the condition to the environment—then you would stop thanking him and being attentive toward him. Therefore, guard yourselves from making things ordinary. Let every bounty you receive be a new expression, a new revelation for you of the Sublime World, and not as something ordinary.

Do not interfere in other people's affairs—by this you take on half of their debt.

One Law states: The less faith you have, the more severe the Sublime World becomes toward you, and vice versa.

An artist knows that when he plays a role on stage, this is not real but imaginary. He gets rich or poor, he cries or laughs, but all this is only fictitious. Similarly in life, whether you are laughing or grieving, whether you are suffering or joyful, you need to understand that these are merely appearances: you are on stage.

The Beloved of the Human Soul

One morning we climbed the highest peak of the mountain with the Master, and from there, we could see the distant mountains in the early dawn sky. We recognized some peaks and greeted them as good friends. We felt close to them and were thankful for their presence. The valleys were covered by a mist, which hid the land. And here above, the summit shone in the clear sky, illuminated by the first rays of the Sun.

From out of this stillness, one brother asked, "Master, what does the human spirit seek and long for in its most sacred strivings?"

The Master answered:

It is God, the purpose of Life, that we seek. At present, everyone in the world is searching for something. What is it that they are searching for? God, the Great Cause of Life. Life originates from God. God dwells within every living being. You have a thought, God is within that thought.

There is something that people are searching for. They have only one aspiration. They search here, they search there. They search continuously—in one lifetime, in another lifetime—for their Ideal. People seek God. The Beloved One of the human soul is God. God—this is the intrinsic longing of the human soul.

When someone experiences suffering and adversity, this is a striving of the soul to expand and to see God. And when the soul sees Him, it will be ready for all forms of sacrifice.

The Master was leaning on a rock. He continued:

This rock upon which I now lean has waited a thousand years for this moment. Man waits for years as well for a Visitation from God.

What is it that a person searches for in this world? For God. Whether or not one is cognizant of this, that is another question. Whenever you desire to find God, you need to elevate your thoughts and feelings and attune your "radio receiver" in order to make contact with the Sublime World. Do you think that if the Image of God enters into your soul that it will not produce a great change within you?

When someone is searching for Love, in reality, one is searching for the Sacred Image of God, striving for God. All embark on the Quest for this Sacred Image.

You ask, "Why do people love one another?" The love between two people is an expression of that fundamental Love existing between God and the human soul. And yet, when the soul descends to Earth, it does not awaken immediately and cannot comprehend its primordial Love relationship. It will therefore express its love toward whomever. You are permitted to love anyone, but the consequences of such love will differ according to the object of your love. If you love a horse, your love will have a certain result. If you love a fruit tree, your love will have a different result. However, when you love God, the results of this Love will be completely different from your other expressions of love.

You need to employ all of your aspirations that you may see God. You tell someone, "I would like to eat." This means that you need to find God within your food. Thirty minutes spent with God is more valuable than a million years without Him.

God's Love for us is like the mist coming from the ocean, and our Love for God is like the river that must return to the ocean. If nothing comes from the ocean, the rivers will dry up. And conversely, every river shall go to the ocean to become saline. By the phrase, "become saline," I refer to that essential balance within the human being.

First, one needs to learn to drink from a pure wellspring. Those who become addicted to alcohol believe that they cannot live without wine. One can live without wine, but not without water. It is possible to live without human love, but not without Divine Love. You need to think about God as the most magnificent, the greatest Being in the Cosmos. And by continuously thinking about Him, He will eventually reveal Himself to you. The solution to this matter is to be found in Love. Faust presented a partial solution to this issue. Faust found fulfillment by working for the good of humankind. He never came to the Ideal of working for God. In the social context, one works for the good of society, for the good of humankind. Yet in the Divine, one works because of one's Love for God. Faust did not attain this level of comprehension.

Love for God is a Science for the Sublime Beings. This is the Great Path on which they have trodden. Those who love the Great One, the Great Creative Cause, and the Creation, when they go to the Invisible World, they will have access to all places.

I desire that all of you would fall in Love with God, and in such a way, that your houses will start to burn at all four corners and your hearts will be filled with Love toward Him.

Flowers, wellsprings, and celestial bodies, all of them know where your Beloved is. Love them and only then they shall show you where He dwells. They know Him: and so, begin to love them!

Love for God is the essential mystical experience that some will resolve in one way, others in another way.

Earthly existence is significant for one reason alone—coming to know God. The human soul abides in Him. Humans dwell in Divine Love, in the Love toward the Infinite One Who makes Himself manifest throughout the Universe. Do not believe that you can achieve the Great without God. Greatness is only achieved with Divine assistance. When you come to love God, your face will become illuminated. When we love God, we are in Paradise. When we begin to doubt Him, this is being in "hell." There you will find misery, darkness, and frustration. Suffering will pursue your every step.

At the moment, you are in Paradise. Make every effort to avoid error so that God will not ask you to leave. When you deny God, suffering will come. And yet, when you begin to have faith in Him, all suffering will vanish. It is possible to live without suffering. When? When you come to love God with all of your mind, heart, soul, and will—and in such a way, that you begin to work mindfully to transform suffering into joy. Otherwise, you will remain in a transient existence and will fail to attain what you desire. You will grow old prematurely. It is said, "I will not let you perish."[41] This is the experience of the one who loves God.

If you have Love for God, He will visit you and your life will improve. If you have been ill, you will recuperate. If you have experienced deprivation, everything will be supplied. You will live in abundance. Even if you were to pass through fire, you shall not burn. All doors will be opened for you.

Someone tells you, "I do not want to suffer any longer." Begin to love God and everything will come to you. Blindness and deafness will be no more, and all your affairs will be put in order in a wondrous way.

---

41. See also John 10:28, "And I give them eternal life, and they shall never perish; neither shall anyone snatch them out of My hand."

When Love abides in you, all will come to your aid. Where Love is, there the Mother is also. The opposite holds true: Where Love does not dwell, the Mother is absent.

A Law states: When you love God with all your mind, heart, soul, and will, you will then be in harmony with all of the Cosmos; and because of this, you will be able to draw upon the energy of all the Cosmos. This energy will renew and uplift you.

Those who love the Great One will be given everything they ask for. They will be surrounded by kind people and all will be good to them. If you are a farmer, the fruitfulness of your land will increase. You will receive all bounties. However, the one who does not have Love toward the Great One does not receive any bounties. That is to say, that person is not able to perceive them.

All people desire to be accepted and loved by others. As long as that is their desire, they will suffer. If you desire to be accepted and loved, you should first have Love for God.

Only the person who has Love for God has character, only that person is outstanding. I call this one who loves the Infinite, the true human being. It is this Love that makes that person a true human being. Then you will blossom and emit a sublime fragrance. Only then will you be that wellspring whose flow is never-ending. Only when you love the Infinite One will you enter into Freedom.

The Love for God is centered in the upper part of the head. This center is called "the thousand-petalled lotus." It has not yet blossomed. Until it does, you cannot comprehend your existence. Address your thoughts toward this center that it may blossom. If you do not have Love for God, you will remain bitter, angry, and always discontent; you will remain immersed in the coarse elements of life. With the Love for God, you will draw to yourself the Forces of the Universe. They will provide the conditions for your gifts to manifest.

Do people today love each other? Their love is illusory. That is to say, it is transitory. I speak about the majority of people. Their love is based upon their feelings, but they are not mature enough to have Love for God.

Love for God is a new idea. The idea began to permeate humankind from the time of the prophets, but it is still in its infancy. Love for God is not given without effort, and yet, it will be gradually attained.

It is necessary to build four bonds. The first bond is from God toward human beings. The second bond is from us toward God—that is to say, from the created toward the Creator. The third is from human being toward human being. The fourth Bond, and the most sublime, is from God toward God. What is the significance of the fourth Bond? It signifies being able to see God within myself and within you as well.

When you find God, you will find all people as well. We need to have Love for God that we may learn to also love other beings. When you attain Love for the Infinite One, you will then see the most beautiful countenance in whomever you look at, the likes of which you have never seen before. From within this person, there will be a manifestation of kindness and intelligence.

Love for God is the Harvest that we need to reap. This is the foundation for the New Culture. You cannot be genuinely fulfilled until you have Love for God. By this, I understand to mean, Love for the Whole of Creation and all living beings.

Coming to Know God

Sometimes one needs to come out of the dense aura of the big city and climb high, to submerge oneself in the pure world of the mountain. Only here can certain questions arise and be answered.

Ostritsa is a modest peak of the Mount Vitosha—solitary, pure, and hardly visible among the high-mountain meadows. The peak is surrounded by beautiful clearings filled with fresh grass, flowers, and the fragrance of junipers. Scattered among these are small groups of fir trees and silver birch. Often we came here with our beloved Master and sat among the rocks on the peak as we contemplated upon the peace of the mountain and talked.

On one occasion the Master said:

The thought of God should be foremost for all people. In order to come to know this, all need to have one Idea alone; and yet, when it comes to worldly things, each may think as he wishes.

At least once in your lifetime you should have this experience: to come to know God. In reality, God is the most known and the most unknown Being in the world. God is hidden within the bread you are eating. God is hidden within the water you are drinking. God is also hidden within the air and within the light.

We have a great task in front of us: to come to know God. When we come to know God, we will be illuminated with such a Light that we will be ready to offer true sacrifice.

If you think that in a few thousand years you will find and come to know God, you are deluded; even more so, if you think that you can find and come to know God in 10-20 years. The Angels, who are so intelligent, they do not yet know Him in full. The coming to know God is an eternal, continuous process. All will study, and will study eternally, as to how to come to know God in His Infinite Love, Wisdom, and Truth. Even the Divine Beings, when they come near to God, they feel like little children who do not know anything.

The beauty of Life is in the uncomprehended things. Which are the uncomprehended things? The great ones.

In order to come to know God, we need to sacrifice everything for Him. The one who comes to know God will begin with a new science, education, and culture, such as the world has not imagined. For a human being to come to know God not only one Eternity is necessary, but a few.

To be not interested in God means to not be interested in the lessons you are being taught—that is to say, to skip classes from the School of Life. Everyone who does not draw closer toward the Sublime in the world loses. And the one who loses subjects oneself to great sufferings.

The Law states: You cannot come to know God if you do not love Him.

Eradication of the Old

Material culture creates the forms and goods, but it remains fruitless and meaningless if people do not realize the Laws of the Eternal Life.
Once when a question about the New Culture arose, the Master said:

A new Wave is coming from out of the Cosmic Space, the Wave of Divine Love. It is also called "Wave of Fire." This Wave has powerful vibrations, which not every human being can endure. For this reason, it has been said that God is an all-consuming Fire. Those who are ready to withstand the vibrations of this Wave and receive this Wave will become luminous. Yet for those who cannot bear them, it will be a Fire that will either consume them or will cause them to pass through great suffering. This will prepare them to awaken and receive Love. For this reason, this Wave of Love, which is coming, is also called the Divine Fire. Everything old and impure will burn in it. After humankind passes through this Divine Fire, the Kingdom of God will come to Earth. I say: When the Fire of Love comes, some people will become luminous; but others will burn and pass through repentance.

Today you find yourselves in a great phase of Life. Not too much time will pass before you find yourselves passing through the Fire. This will be in your lifetime. This Wave of Fire will soon pass over the world and purify it. All human thoughts and desires will pass through this Fire and become purified in the most perfect way. The Great Life will enter you and you will become transformed. As the smith places the iron in the fire in order to refine it, so too, the Great Intelligent World will pass us through the Fire so that we can be purified and tempered.

Those Beings who descend from above, say, "We will turn the Earth on its head and will chase away evil from it." Evil will not attempt to come among you again.

The great destruction that occurs today is due to this great Life, which is coming now. If people do not accept Christ voluntarily, the modern culture will pass through Fire seven times, but in the end, it will be purified and renewed.

The Wave of Fire will pass through the minds of all people. You all will pass through this Divine Fire; you will free your souls and be liberated from bondage.

If people do not awaken and arise, all the "blankets" in which they are wrapped will burn. Everything that one has created will burn and turn into ashes and dust. What I am speaking of is the Coming of the Day of the Lord. I say now: We are in the Day of the Lord!

Only a half hour remains before the last train leaves. Woe to those who have not yet managed to settle their accounts. If Europe does not correct her past mistakes, great tribulations will come her way.

The Lord is coming and He has already set His Foot upon the Earth. I can easily prove that He has set His foot upon the Earth. How? The great suffering, which is constantly increasing, is the proof that the Lord is coming into this world. Do you know what His decision is? Everything impure is to burn. One has never before seen the dust that will be raised on Earth. You have never suspected what great cleansing is coming before the Great Day. Nothing will remain of the European nations and of the planning of the European diplomats. Love will destroy everything old. After that we will begin to build. This turbulence among societies, this unrest among those who are in distress, indicates that God permeates everything. All this is linked to the eradication of the karma of humankind, which has accumulated for thousands of years. Until all old concepts, thoughts, and feelings burn in the Fire of suffering, humans cannot enter into the New Life, which is due to come now.

It is because for thousands of years we have been under the influence of negative forces that these forces now turn against us. People have strayed from the right path, and all misfortunes are due to that. They have deviated from many things and for this reason have remained behind in their development. The Invisible World wants to help them so that they may develop properly. The Invisible World is sending workers with their hammers to work on people's homes. These misfortunes are called "the unfavorable conditions of life." With their imprudent way of life, people let evil loose, and as a result, tribulations come. What we today experience and feel hanging heavily over us is our own karma. This is a debt that is due to be paid. In Matthew, Chapter 24, the woman who was "taken" has paid her karma; she is free of any debt. On the other hand, the woman who was "left" has not yet eliminated her karma. And so, the present events indicate the paying off of an old debt, the eradication of karma. Acceleration in the eradication of the past error of humankind is taking place at present. Everything that has accumulated is being eradicated.

In autumn, all old leaves fall whether they want to or not. Only the buds that will produce new branches, leaves, and flowers in the coming spring remain on the trees. The beauty of life is in the changes. After a storm, the weather clears. The present events are like a storm: they will pass. Everything that occurs is for the better. We think that the present order is good, yet God is weary of the transgressions that people commit.

The karma of the European nations is already ripe and creates suffering for the whole of humankind. These tribulations indicate that people need to change their way of life and apply the Divine Teaching. The Jews did not accept the Teachings of Christ, and tribulations came upon them. The Christian nations did not apply Christ's Teaching and the present tribulations came. Troubled times are coming because people did not accept voluntarily and with an awakened consciousness the fulfillment of the Will of God. These troubled times have already come. Even greater disturbances, external as well as internal, will come in order for people to awaken and fulfill the Will of God, to serve God. This will be forced upon humankind.

Modern culture is in its departure. The New Culture is coming, and its application in life will begin. The Invisible World has decided to teach modern civilized people a lesson, which they will remember for a thousand years. The Scripture says, "Because of these things, the wrath of God is coming upon the sons of disobedience."[42] In other words, the Potter will break the imperfect pots.

On another occasion, the Master said:

---

42. See Colossians 3:6.

The whole Earth at present is undergoing a great change, a reconstruction. This will continue until its forces become balanced. The Earth will undergo disturbances. There exist ways to predict in which region of the planet the greatest turbulence will occur.

All of Europe is in turmoil. The entire world is in disarray. Be not afraid. In such times of trouble, people will come to know God. They will come to understand that He is the Great Omniscient Power that turns all things to good. You need to remain calm and peaceful and know that the times in which you live are most favorable.

All of Europe will pass through unimaginable trials. Modern Europeans have built a dam on the river that one day will collapse. Therefore, whoever is above the town should search for refuge in the mountains, and whoever is at the low level should run for higher ground. I speak symbolically.

People ask what will become of them in the future. Imagine that you live on the North Pole where everything is ice. Your homes are made of ice; nowhere can you see water. I say to you that you need to take some precautionary measures because the Earth will undergo great changes. The Sun will start to shine very hot. It will melt the ice, the homes will fall apart, and you will start to sink. You say, "What bad fortune has come to us." This is not bad fortune, the ice simply melts. I say the same to you now: If you do not correct your life, the same will happen to you. I do not say this to frighten you. It is the natural course of Life. The Great Wave, which comes now, breaks up the ice and turns it into water. This is the Great Omniscient Wave in the world that already draws near.

After these events, human egotism will vanish, and people will begin to live freely and as brothers. The time has come for all people to abandon the old way of life.

The God of whom I speak to you will shake the Earth. Only then you will come to understand whether or not I have been speaking the Truth. The Scripture says that God will shake the Earth and that every living creature will realize that Justice, Truth, Virtue, Love, and Wisdom exist. All people everywhere need to know that God is present in the world—and people will come to know this.

You say, "We are not prepared yet." When will you be ready? You say, "The time has not come yet." Who told you that the time has not come yet? If you do not follow the Divine, the Earth will begin to shake.

After the Earth shakes, after all your guns and cannons are destroyed, you will be asked, "Will you obey?" You will say, "Yes, we will obey." When you observe all these things, you will become wiser. The entire Earth will shake with such power that no trace will remain of the present culture. This will take place as based upon the great natural Laws. Not one nation in Europe will remain unpunished, the present order and all human falsehoods will vanish.

Christ has said, "The Sun will be darkened, and the Moon will not give its light; the stars will fall from Heaven."[43] Interpreted, this means that all false human religious beliefs will lose their meaning, all worldly power will be overshadowed and lose its hold. Therefore, the disciples should work to improve themselves. They should clothe themselves in armor and put on helmets in order to withstand this Wave of suffering and trials that humankind needs to endure. This armor is Love.

Many people are given the ability to learn only from their own mistakes. If one tries to speak to them, they will not comprehend. Such people will learn on the path of suffering. The turbulent flow, which represents the tribulations and conflicts of humankind, will abate by the end of the present century. Naturally, human souls who are more advanced will be freed from this flood sooner. The nations are healed through suffering. It is impossible to heal a nation without suffering. It is the only medicine.

What needs to be corrected will be corrected. What needs to be destroyed will be destroyed. Take advantage of the short time that remains. Now is the time to begin living the New Life. Evil has exhausted all the conditions for its existence. It can no longer succeed and it is retreating; only its dregs have remained. The Light will drive away all the darkness. Owing to the present

---

43. See also footnote 16.

tribulations, humankind will awaken. Unless the pure is sifted from the impure, human life will be meaningless.

After these events, the New will immediately gain control of the world. Good times will come. Now it is difficult. We all know that life is hard during winter and it is easier when spring comes. It is also easier to live in summer and fall. At present, we are coming to the end of the winter.

When the New comes, violence will no longer exist. Nothing will remain of modern weapons or of modern courts and prisons. The present order will be cast out. God is creating a New World. The old world is giving way to the New.

When people enter the New Life, they will converse with the Angels and with God. How will they speak with God? In silence. In silence you will look at the stars, the Moon, the Sun, and you will be filled with gladness. God is in all of them. You will be joyful for every little stone, plant, and animal. God lives within them. You will rejoice in the soft wind, the pure wellspring. Within them is God.

The New Epoch

The world was in darkness. Humankind was caught in the madness of destruction. One could not find a way out, nor could a light be seen. Anxiety filled the hearts of all; uncertainty was pervasive. In such moments, the Master possessed the ability to bring peace and to inspire faith. He revealed opportunities for a bright future, describing the image of renewed, reborn, and enlightened humankind. A question about the coming new epoch was asked.

The Master said:

Our Solar System will depart from heavier matter and enter into a less dense medium. Because of this, there will exist conditions for the manifestation of a higher consciousness for humankind. The Solar System departs from the so-called "13th sphere." At the same time, the Sun will enter the Age of Aquarius. Now is the end of the dark epoch, the *Kali Yuga*. Because the Earth is entering a new realm, all the old forms will change. New forms will destroy the old ones. People will not notice how they will grow and become new people. Old forms will fall away as do the leaves in autumn. In the place of the "old" people, new ones will come with new ideas.

The Earth, after making many millions of rotations, makes one exception from its usual rotation. This departure is occurring today.

New organs are forming in the human brain for the human beings of the future. Until they are formed, many things will remain unexplained. When a great artist begins to paint a painting, is it possible for the beauty of it to emerge immediately? No. On the first day, he will only dash colors on the canvas with a brush. Even if we do not like the painting, he would only smile. On the second day, you will see that the painting is in the same state. The artist will tell you, "Do not hurry with your judgment. When I finish the painting, then you can express your opinion." You hurry to express your opinion about Life now, but Life is not yet finished.

A sister asked, "Master, when will the time come when everything will become clear to us?"

We are now in this time. Today, the world comes to a specific stage, a stage of transformations that will become its new principles of organization. Today a new type of human being, a new generation of Love, is being formed.

God leaves to people the free will to arrange the small things, yet the big ones He arranges by Himself. The contemporary epoch is one of the birth of the human being of Love.

Every new epoch begins with a new rhythm. Today a new rhythm to Life comes. The Divine makes its way everywhere. The Wave, which is coming now, will elevate not only us, but all minerals, plants, and animals as well. Those who cannot be uplifted by this Wave will remain for the future. Remember: There will be no other Wave such as this because in Nature there is no repetition of phenomena. If you wait until the future, the conditions will be more difficult then.

A New Knowledge, a New Culture is coming into the world. I call it: the Culture of Divine Love, Wisdom, and Truth. It will teach people how to live.

The old life is suffering, but the new, joy. The roots are the old life, and the branches the new one. Today we are at the end of the deprivation of Love and at the beginning of Divine, unconditional Love.

Who awakens the human being? That one who is taking care of him. The mother awakens the child. This shows that she is taking care of her infant. God is the Watcher for humans, which shows that He is taking care of them.

Those who do not awaken during the modern epoch will be left for other times. We wonder what will happen to those people who are not able to accept the Divine. The issue is clear. I come to a fruit tree and collect the ripe fruit, and for the others, I will wait. When they ripen, I will pick them as well, and the bad fruit I will use as fertilizer. Afterward, they will become beautiful fruits as well. You ask, "Why is it so?" Because it is not possible to be otherwise.

It is said in the Scriptures, "Search for Me until I am close."[44] This means: use the favorable conditions until I am close to you. If people were to be surprised by what the future is bringing to them, this surprise would deprive them of the opportunity to make use of the Good that is coming. Therefore, in order to make use of the conditions of Life, one needs to possess the knowledge that brings peace into one's soul. Ignorance fills people with worry.

Today the New is coming into the world everywhere. What is the New? In what form it will manifest that can be understood only by a few? A new cycle is being formed. Those who can enter into it will find before themselves great opportunities. If you are not ready, then you will miss the favorable conditions. The Divine is coming into the world.

Today is a most dangerous time. You could fall asleep and remain on the outside. The Divine Train is very punctual! You may be late by only a second. Therefore, your

---

44. See also Jeremiah 29:13, "And you will seek Me and find Me, when you search for Me with all your heart."

consciousness, your heart, and your mind need to be vigilant. The one who has lived for thousands and millions of years on the Earth and has been through so much suffering—does that person want to miss this moment, to miss the Train and not receive the Divine? If God finds you vigilant when He comes to you, you will grow up like the seed; you will develop and will give fruit.

The day has two halves. One is when the Sun is rising, and the second is when the Sun is setting. Until noon, we have ascent; and in the afternoon, descent. The Law is the same with relation to this epoch. The current epoch is in descent and this cannot be stopped. The forces of darkness are leaving. The Good will come exactly at the determined time, just as the spring comes at its time. When spring comes, everything blossoms. The same will happen with the coming of the Divine.

An illuminated epoch is coming. The idea of brotherhood will come into realization. This Divine Spring will come gradually, not all at once. People will change without noticing. They simply will not notice how they will change. One day they will awaken, and they will find themselves in a new stage similar to the caterpillar, which enfolds into the cocoon, and, once inside, transforms itself into a butterfly that cannot feed on leaves any more. What is coming now can be called "Manifestation of the Divine Origin in the human being." The new generation that is coming will renew the world. This means that we are in the epoch when the caterpillars will transform into butterflies. Those caterpillars that did not become butterflies yet will ask how one can live in the air. When they become butterflies, then they will learn. As caterpillars, they cannot learn.

Today life is more active. Years ago infants could open their eyes not earlier than three weeks after birth. But today, they open their eyes the moment they are born. This exists everywhere, in every nation.

Humble people will put the world in order. Who are the humble? Once two people went to court. The son of one of them came and told his father, "Father, we do not need that for which you are in court. Let's forget and forgive." This son was considered unassertive, but he stopped the trial.

Daybreak

The Master said:

The Invisible World is organized very well. Now it is preparing something to put order into the world. One of the greatest experiments in the Universe is set before us. Advanced Beings are descending from the Invisible World. They come to transform the conditions of life. They will put order into the world. Do you know what Forces these Great Brothers have at their disposal! The Luminous Beings are coming and bringing the New Culture. After these events, spiritual knowledge will be applied on the physical plane. Those who work in the Divine Arena will be needed more than ever.

The Luminous Brothers have besought all of humankind and have given people an ultimatum. If people do not subject themselves to the Divine, they will move into action.

Through the Light, the Advanced Beings—the Forces of Light—fight with the forces of darkness. The Light is the most powerful weapon. The Forces of Light have already had the upper hand over the forces of darkness. Victory is on the side of the Good.

Today, we are engaged in great battles. When we finish traveling, we will reach the Promised Land. We will sit under the fig tree, and we will rest.

The reason for the failure of prior cultures was that the Astral World had not yet been ordered and cleansed.

The New Culture of the Astral World will be introduced to the Earth.

The most beautiful Life is coming now. Until now, you have had no brothers and sisters. Your brothers and sisters are coming now. Great Blessings are coming to the Earth after its adversity. Something good is coming into the world. It is better for hardship to come first and then the blessing than vice versa.

The contradictions will continue until we come into Love, which overcomes everything in the world.

The New Teaching does not need to make a stir in the world. We do not come to uproot: there are others who will come before us who will uproot and weed out. We will plant the seeds and cultivate them quietly and patiently until they mature.

You need to be happy that you live in one of the greatest epochs.

The following transformation will occur in the world. When the good people were in service to the bad ones, the bad ones were the masters. Now the opposite will occur: the bad people will serve the good ones. You want to eliminate the bad people. No. They will learn how to serve the good ones. Now the order is changing: the good will rule and the bad will be in servitude, just as the good were the servants until now. This means that the good will take the place of the bad in the leadership of the world.

The Intelligence of Nature

A strong wind was blowing the fog over the mountain. We had found a sheltered camp near a brook in the valley. Flames and smoke were curling up from a blazing fire. The surrounding thick bushes kept us sheltered. A blast of the wind would hit the fire from time to time, producing a shower of sparks. It was warm and comfortable around the fire. The kettles were boiling. The aromatic smoke from the dry junipers mixed with the scent of the tea and with the pungent fragrance of the fog. The big red kettle had been emptied a few times already.

We were seated among the dry bushes warming ourselves at the fire. Then a sister told the Master, "I cannot but feel that Intelligent, Advanced Beings exist behind all these activities of Nature."

The Master said:

Nature reflects the combined activity of Intelligent, Advanced Beings. You need to look at her as the sum total of Intelligent Forces. Behind the wind and behind the fog, other Forces exist that you need to study. Until you learn about the Intelligent Forces, which are active in Nature, you will always be in discord.

One of the tasks of people is to make contact with the Intelligent Forces. If we pick up a glowing ember with tongs and place it in the fireplace, the wood will be set on fire. The ember and the tongs do not know what I am thinking, yet behind them exists a conscious hand directing them. Behind every phenomenon, whatever it might be, is hidden an Intelligent Force that directs it. You visit a factory and observe how the machines are moving. Are their movements conscious? Who has set them into motion? The engineer. He regulates their movements. He has taken into consideration the order of the entire factory. The machines are moving at his directive.

By the same Law, the Sun also has a Technician who has set it into motion and determines its path. The Earth and the Moon have their paths of movement. Scientists are looking for the causes of this movement in the physical forces: they make calculations and create various theories. These scientists are correct, but they do not suspect that behind every physical force an Intelligent Force exists that directs phenomena.

Life manifests itself as one Universal Intelligence. From one end to the other end of Life, Intelligence exists. There exist Advanced Beings who work in Living Nature.

For me the rays of the Sun represent Higher Intelligence. A bud and a flower are windows through which I can see the one Reality, the one Sublime World: a World of Beings with great intelligence.

We see the material world as dead, but in reality, everything is alive. The pen is moving, but there is a conscious being who moves it. The pen does not know, but the consciousness of the hand that moves it knows.

There is a connection between the spiritual and the physical worlds. The physical world depends upon the spiritual. If you see the material world as being separate, you cannot comprehend anything. But if you look at it as the result of the Spiritual world, then you can comprehend it. When you realize that behind all physical phenomena Intelligent Forces are active, then these physical phenomena will exert another influence on you.

The geological changes are not the result of mechanical causes alone. Behind every change, Intelligent Forces are at work. The geologists are analyzing the data. If Intelligent Forces exist behind this data, that does not interest them. The Earth's crust has been folded many times and such folding occurs today. It will occur in the future as well. We observe such process of folding at the bottom of the Atlantic Ocean. Today there are places where the ocean floor is rising. According to what Law does this folding occur? How did the folding occur through which the Himalayas, the Alps, and the other mountain ranges were raised? The Intelligent Forces are the cause for this.

As for those who are not acting in accordance with natural Laws, Nature permits them to do whatever they wish, but also has them bear the consequences. Nature has a completely different relationship with those who live in accordance with her Laws, and she warns them when she is about to do something. It is said, "God has revealed His Mysteries to those who love Him."[45]

The New Teaching states that Nature is alive and intelligent. Many will smile at that statement and say, "We need to subdue Nature, to become her master." In this lies the adversity of people. They think that they can subdue Nature. This is impossible. The idea needs to be chased from your minds and from the minds of your children! It is not a question of subduing Nature, but of studying her, to come in contact with her Laws and to be in harmony with her. Many scientists attempt to overpower Nature, but, in reality, she is the master. Nature demands compensation for every attempt to subdue her.

This world war[46] teaches and educates people. Nature asks them, "How dare you invent these explosives? I will give you such a lesson that you will remember it for years." What have people done who have peeked into the secrets of Nature? They have invented explosives and airplanes in order to kill, to destroy each other. Is this the mastery of Nature? This is misuse of the Divine forces. Instead of using them for the development of humankind, people are using them for its destruction. One day, when people pass by Nature, they will not walk so

---

45. See also 1Corinthians 2:6–12.
46. Reference to World War II.

presumptuously and carelessly, but will become overcautious and will ask, "Please, is it allowed to pass through and only peek?"

Humans want to overpower Nature with their human will! In no sacred book has it been written that humans must subdue Nature. This misinterpretation creates a deviation in science, which has brought much adversity to humankind. There will never be a time in which humankind may subdue Nature. This is the error of worldly-minded people.

The Law of Divine Justice

The madness of the war was engulfing the nations. Over the Earth, oppression and violence roamed at large. Everything was in disarray, confusing and ominous. How would all of this be resolved? Many distressed faces were turned toward the Master. In the afternoon, a conversation about the international situation was initiated again.
The Master said:

The entire modern world is built upon a false foundation. Each nation is a part of a unified organism: humankind. Each develops specific virtues and abilities. Each nation represents an element in Nature, and for this reason has its own mission in the world. Each nation receives specific cosmic energies, transforms them, and passes them on to others. For this reason, each has had its place and significance throughout the entire existence of humankind. Each nation should give birth to an idea that will benefit humankind.

At present, people think that they are the only factors and that everything depends upon them. This is not true. A Divine factor exists, that people have overlooked. A Law states: Every act of statesmanship needs to have Divine approval. That is to say, it needs to recognize the Divine Law in the world. Each nation and every person should respect the Divine Justice in the world. In addition to this, Divine Justice requires that we respect each and every being, protecting those rights, which it has, and providing all of the conditions for its development. Do not damage the little flower! When you read a book, would you tear out its pages? All beings in Nature are like the letters on the pages of her Book. You should erase neither a single letter, nor a single word in the Book not to lose its meaning.

Every breach of Divine Justice brings its consequences. This is true for the individual life as well as for the collective life. Not a single secretary of state or statesman is exempt from this Law. Do you know what repercussions a statesman who has acted unjustly can expect? When he passes on, he will incarnate as an ox, and this ox will be taken for slaughter. As soon as this ox has been slaughtered, he will enter another ox, which will be slaughtered as well. And after that, he will enter a rabbit, which will also be killed. He will remember all of this very well. When he comes to Earth again as a human being, he will say, "Have you been an ox that has been slaughtered or a rabbit that has been shot?" After that, he will never violate the Law of Divine Justice.

This Law exists in Nature: Each nation that executes representatives of another nation and thus, deprives them of their bodies, must, after that, give them new ones. That is to say, the executed people will reincarnate into this nation. The Jews who were massacred by the Germans will reincarnate in Germany, and, in this way, the spirit of the German nation will be radically changed.

The nations need to be prepared for the application of Divine Laws. Intelligent statesmen are needed who will apply Divine Laws in the world instead of writing other laws.

All nations will become more prudent because the Law now comes from the opposite direction. Intelligent statesmen are needed in order that the many misfortunes, and great adversity that the nations suffer, can be avoided. And yet, because this is not happening, God now moves in the opposite direction. The nations are becoming intelligent and will not wait for their leaders to grow wiser.

If you follow the way of the New Teaching, you will discover the method for paying off your old debts. The power of the New Teaching lies in its ability to pay off all debts. If you accept the New Teaching, no debt will remain unpaid. By "old debts," I refer to karma. European nations suffer because of their karma. They live under its weight. When a nation listens to the ideas of the Brotherhood of Light, it prospers. If it does not, it is unable to prosper. This is true for Russia as well. If Russians listen attentively to the ideas of the Brotherhood of Light, they will prosper.

The trend now is toward the unity of all nations. All nations need to come together. In addition to this, the wellbeing of all nations—and not only that of the one—needs to be taken into consideration. A Law states: In every nation something good exists. When the nations unite, this good quality will flow through all the nations. The good qualities that the British, Germans, and Russians possess will flow into other nations, and a new vital current will be born. The bond among nations will give birth to the new human being, the new human character.

Nationalism will come to its end; hatred will not be fostered among nations. Nationalism will become obsolete. Some will say, "A great nation." This is not correct. Some nation desires to be great in order that it might rule over other nations. This idea belongs to the old culture. The purpose is not for one nation to be great, to be great in territory. Because all nations are represented in one organism, one great nation will look like an overly developed leg. One leg is well developed, while the other remains short. We will then have an abnormal organism. This will cause friction, suffering, and conflict.

Russia is the link between East and West. It is the mediator between Europe and Asia. This is one of its assignments. What we idealize in Russia is the Light that comes from the Forces of Love and Light. Bulgarians need to connect with Russia and with other nations as well. Every nation needs to serve God. This is the New in the world: this is the future for every nation. The nation that does not serve God will pay. The Bulgarian nation is not sent to work for the greatness of Bulgaria, but is sent to fulfill God's Will, to serve God. No longer will great Serbia exist, great Bulgaria, great Russia, great Germany, great England, and so on. No one great power will exist, and yet there will be nations that will serve God and obey God's Laws. Every nation that serves God will have God's blessing, will receive great abundance, and will become an advanced nation.

What does it mean to serve God? To serve God means the following:

To apply the Principles of Divine Justice.
To abstain from violence.
To have mutual cooperation among nations.
To serve, not dominate.

It is not the quantity that makes a nation great, but the quality. Every nation that does not wish to serve God will be deprived of its wealth and will disappear from the Earth.

The greatness of a nation lies in its service to God. A nation is then strong and no other power will be able to challenge it. It will always and under any circumstances be victorious. It will have inexhaustible bounties from God at its disposal.

The Advanced Beings who come from Above—the predecessors of humankind—will assist those nations who serve God well, but those who do not wish to serve will not be helped.

There will not be a single ruling nation. Those who think of being rulers are on the wrong side. At one time, large animals lived on Earth. But what happened to them? The Lord destroyed them. All the ones who want to dominate the Earth at present, He will do away with and send them off to another place. For this reason, it has been said in the Scriptures, "Blessed are the meek, for they shall inherit the Earth."[47]

Imagine that one hundred people owe you money. They will ruin your entire life. It is preferable that you forget about them and that you expect nothing back from them. Otherwise, if you should bring these one hundred people to court—one per month—how many months will you be arguing with them, how much trouble will you have? You would receive back one thousand leva and still, you would have to spend more.

A person comes to you and tells you, "I have nothing. I cannot pay." If he has nothing, leave him alone. The Turks have a saying, "Give not what you owe. Take not what you are to receive." This means: let there be an international reciprocal forgiveness of all debts.

---

47. See Matthew 5:5.

> One brother asked, "When will the New come to be made manifest on Earth?"
> The Master said:

By buffalo-wagon, one travels very slowly. It is faster by a horse-wagon, faster yet by car, with even greater speed by airplane, and faster yet with the speed of light. You are asking, "When will things improve?" If you travel by buffalo-wagon, the improvement will come very slowly. But if you move with the speed of light, in a very short while.

Regarding Intuition

> One sister related her experience regarding precognition. Other brothers and sisters told of similar experiences as well. Almost every human being has had such experiences.
> The Master explained:

In the past, you had precognition, but you have lost it. Now you should strive to attain the sensitivity that you had initially. Take a book, which you want to read, place it upon your forehead, direct your thoughts to the Sublime World, and ask with your mind whether or not to read it.

Intuition is an expression of the inner human being—what is hidden within. Its purpose is to correct the human objective mind.

There are methods that exist for the development of intuition. This is done through experiments and through exercises. One needs to work in order to develop it.

Anyone can develop his intuition and feel what will happen to him. Almost all nations have, to a certain extent, precognition. Not a single person exists who has not been warned about what will happen. We have an inner feeling that tells us what to do. When intuition is developed, a person knows what to do, what to study, what to say, and when. To have intuition means being able to know who needs what, and how to satisfy that person's needs. The proper conditions for intuition are given to people for free; they only need to make the effort to develop it. Someone with a well-developed intuition will have insight into the future. The one who is led by intuition has a pure heart on which the Divine Workings are written.

Make the following experiment: You are at home, and you want to know if your friend, who lives on the other end of the town, is at home. Instead of sending someone to check, remain calm and silent, direct your thoughts toward him, and listen attentively within. If you remain calm, without any wavering, you will know that your friend is at home. And if you check afterward, it will turn out that he has been, in fact, at home.

Someone knows that a change in his life will occur in 20 years. How does he know this? He feels that his conditions will worsen or improve in 20 years, and so it does.

Each one of you is capable of knowing the future. Anyone can read what is within. It is strange to have such a book within oneself and not be able to read it!

When you committed the first transgression, the Spirit turned away from you and there was no one to guide you.

Intuition is the illumination of ordinary consciousness by the Rays of Cosmic Consciousness.

The Culture of the Angels

It was one of those crystal clear days when the light reigns in space—the kind called by the Master "the diamond days of Nature." Every little stone, every blade of grass, was encircled with an aura of radiance. The light that illuminated the rocks made them appear to be ethereal, almost weightless in their radiance. It was one of Nature's holy days. We were high up on the mountain with our Master, high up in the luminous Universe, and he began to speak about the Angels:

The whole Cosmos, which God has created, is filled with Beings who are more cultivated than we are and much more organized. Beings of the Angelic Hierarchy exist on the Sun. They live in an ethereal world. Solid matter does not exist there in the same way as it does on Earth. Matter there is in an ethereal state.

There are also Advanced Beings who dwell on Sirius and on other celestial bodies as well. Compared to the Culture of Sirius, the culture of humankind is still in its swaddling clothes.

There are three kinds of solar systems. Some are related to the material world, while others represent the more sublime, spiritual element and belong to the Spiritual, Angelic world. After some time, when your spiritual sight will develop, you will be able to see all worlds. So far you can see, like the astronomers, only the material worlds. The third kind of Solar Systems is related to the Divine Worlds, which have been created from the most sublime Divine Element.

The human beings will eventually pass through all kinds of solar systems. Our Solar System is at the border of Cosmos. Someday, when your consciousness will evolve and ascend from this Solar System to one of more evolved culture than ours at present, your perception of things will be completely different.

By "Angels," we imply those Beings whose consciousness is so awakened that they shine like the Sun. If you were able to visit the Angels, you would see that in their world there exists a state of order unlike anything that exists on Earth. People have notions about the Angels, just as ants have notions about people. If you were to ask the ants where humans exist, they would say that humans are in another world. The ants have no knowledge of the human world. When an ant crawls over a person, it does not think, "This is a living being." Just as we can see the ants even though they do not see us, there are invisible Beings who exist and can see us although we do not see them. They work for the betterment of the world.

We think that humans are on the highest rung of the evolutionary ladder, but evolution is without end. Just as there are beings that exist below humans, there are Beings that exist above humans as well. These Beings evolved from the Universes of the past.

The Angels have a completely different scale of measurement. The more that the consciousness expands, the more the field of vision broadens. For them, only one thing is impossible: they cannot err.

The Angels have an evolved consciousness and they do not intermingle good with evil. The Angelic Universe is much larger than ours. We are children, they are adults. When Angels err, they are not accepted into Heaven for ten thousand years, whereas they are much more lenient toward human beings.

The Angels do not know human error. If they knew, they would be defiled. Even though the Angels have passed along another path, they are nevertheless interested in our world. For them, we are the objects of study, just as the plants are objects of study for us.

Some angels have passed through one mental epoch of humankind in which they stumbled and fell. When the angels were being tested, some of them remained luminous, while others darkened. Those who were conceited and prideful grew dark.

Angels take interest in the human beings. But they have no knowledge about the Divine in the humankind because we are moving on a different path of development, as opposed to the path they have passed along. The Angels are learning from human existence because there is something in it that is unknown to them. They have no knowledge of our experience, just as we have no knowledge of their experience. For this reason, we are interesting to them. Millions of years ago, they were the "humankind" of their world.

The Angel possesses knowledge that is applicable in all worlds: physical, spiritual, and Divine. What is the knowledge of an Angel? If you were to compile all of the knowledge of humankind, all that it has accumulated over thousands of years, an Angel knows all that and more.

For Angels to travel from one solar system to another, what kind of transportation do you think they would need? From the Sun to the closest star, an Angel will travel faster than the speed of light. The Sublime Beings who live on the Sun come down to our Earth. Beings from Venus, Mars, Mercury, and others come down as well. They have the means of transportation. The light that comes from some cosmic spaces takes 500 million years to get here. What a great distance!

However, for an Angel, this is just a stroll. Our scale of measurement is like that of a microbe. The Angels travel at a speed greater than light. For them, the speed of light is like that of a buffalo-wagon. If the speed of light is incomprehensible to human beings, then what about a speed much faster than that? Light travels at the greatest speed possible for the physical world, but the speeds about which we are speaking here belong to other, higher Worlds, to different dimensions.

Angels are Sublime Beings who send forth energy throughout the entire Solar System. The Earth is too small a field for the power of an Angel. An Angel moving at the speed of light would cross the entire Earth in a split-second, and yet they travel at even greater speeds.

Angels have bodies which are more resilient than ours. Angels can master their bodies in such a way that they can be either visible or invisible. When Angels look at human life, they do not see as people see. When an Angel visits you, you become inspired, but when common spirits come to you, you say, "We are stupid. We are ignorant. We are dull."

An Angel is a Being of Absolute Justice and Purity. Their clothing is classical in style. You need to live like an Angel in order to put on Angelic clothes. You need to think rightly to be able to dress in a Divine robe.

In the Sanskrit language, the word "Deva" means "Angel." The Angels are rich in Love and they work because of their Love. They intuit what God's Will is—that is to say, what God desires—and they fulfill it immediately.

A World exists where joy is real and suffering is make-believe. This is the World of the Angels, of the Luminous Beings. Happiness on Earth is not the happiness of the Spiritual world. In Heaven, they do not know your joys and sorrows, but know what bliss is. In the Angelic World you cannot speak a word that has a double meaning, nor can you say something negative. If you imply that something which is pure is impure, you will need to leave Paradise. On the Sun, if you want to speak an unkind word, your mouth will not open. If you want to speak a good word, then it will open readily.

Sainthood is one of the highest states of a human being on Earth, but the Angels stand higher than the saints.

There are different orders of Angels. There are Angels who are from the first, second, and third realms. They speak different languages. The lives of the Angels who live in the second realm are hidden from those who live in the first. And similarly, the lives of those who live in the third are hidden from those who live in the second. In the Angelic World, you can never pronounce a word if you do not like the object, that it indicates. For example, if you like apples, you will be able to pronounce the word "apple," but if you do not, you will not. You can never say, "I do not like you." It is because before you can speak the words, the one to whom you are directing the words will no longer be in front of you. Compared to the celestial Angelic language, the human language is like the sound of thunder.

If you go to the Invisible World, to the Luminous Beings, you will need to know their language, just as when someone comes to you, they will need to speak in your language. The Angels know all tongues. They will speak to you in that ancient Bulgarian language that has preserved its initial purity.

When Angels speak amongst themselves, people become joyful because in their speech, there is something new. Light emanates from their speech—it is something very beautiful. There is a saying, "When the Angels are eating, on the crumbs from their tables humans are feasting." That means that nothing is ever lost. In the same way, the ants are being fed by the crumbs that fall from the table at which people eat. Nothing ever goes to waste.

Angels are God's servants. There are Angels of Love, of Wisdom, of Gentleness, of Temperance, and so on. Each of the virtues is represented by specific Angels. The same is also true for all of the arts: music, poetry, and so on.

For the Beings of the Divine World, neither death nor reincarnation exists. The Divine Life is a Life of Perfection.

When we speak about the Sun and the stars, we should look at them as the result of the activity of the Advanced Beings who lived 25 million, 250 million, or 2,500 million years ago.

You say, "I am interested in the other World." It is impossible for you not to be interested because the aspirations of the human soul originate from the Higher Consciousness and Culture of the Advanced Beings from the other World.

Angels are Beings who have participated in the Creation of the world. All of the Divine powers pass through us. They are protecting us, helping us, and bringing us Divine blessings.

It is the Advanced Beings who work with and direct the life processes of the plants. There is a special class of Angels that works upon the plants. The whole plant kingdom is the accomplishment of the Angels. The consciousness within the plants is that of the Angels. For example, look how regularly the berries of the grape in a grape cluster are arranged, what perfect form it has. Through the apple, we connect with the Beings of the Sun. The apple is a radio that connects us with these Beings. The flowers are the children of the Angels. They are the paintings of the Angels—their art. Flowers should not be picked. And should you step on a flower, it is as if you are stepping on the thoughts and feelings of the Angels. We are very unruly children. We have a very high opinion of ourselves.

Angels work not only on the plants, but also on the whole of Nature. They work on all the natural kingdoms: mineral, animal, and so on. If I say that the Angels are among us, would you ask, "Where are they?" This very light by which we see today, this is of the Angels. They desire to influence our consciousness with their Light.

Angels are helping us. We have helped them when they have been in the evolutionary position of humankind and our bodies were as the animals. Now they are helping us. In the future, when the animals of the present reach the human level of development, we will be helping them.

At one time, when they were more like humans, the Angels resembled us in certain things, but in other things not at all. The lowest existence of the Angels is still higher than the most sublime existence of humans. This is the result of the intensity by which Angels live. The relationship between Angels and humans can be compared to the relationship between human life and that of the plants. In order for you to come in contact with one of them, the Angel must come down to Earth and prod you for a long time until your mind awakens and is put in motion. The Angel wants to tell you that you are in the presence of a highly evolved Being with whom you need to connect, that you may learn something.

In the Scriptures it is said, "Speak not an empty word in the presence of an Angel who is guiding you because this will destroy your work."[48] This means that if you do not respect the Angel who is guiding you, you will lose everything and will continuously feel discontent.

The Beings who have completed their development send their Love to us. We need to connect with them. Both Angels of our Sun and those of the other solar systems think of us. When you find yourself in darkness, when you are under attack by inferior beings, a Luminous Soul will come to you, will tell you something, and will bring you a new idea. These Luminous Souls will tell you, "We will be with you." These are the helpers, the guardian Angels of humankind. These Advanced Beings surround you, and because of them, your life can progress. You need to make every effort so that your heart and mind may become an altar in order that you may work with these Advanced Beings. You need to study not only the physical world, but also the spiritual. You need to be connected not only with the physical world, but the spiritual as well. You need to maintain contact with the Advanced Beings who are helping you along on your path. Many of our thoughts are the fruits of the thoughts of Sublime Beings. When a seed from one of these fruits lands in your mind, in your heart, or in your soul, it will organize its growth in and of itself. These are the Divine ideas that have come to grow within you. They are great treasures. Even if only one of these small, precious thoughts is accepted by you every day, within ten years, your life will have become drastically changed.

If you are in good spirits, this is an indication that Advanced Beings are sending their sublime thoughts to you. On

---

48. See also Exodus 23:20-21, "Behold, I send an Angel before you to keep you in the way and to bring you into the place which I have prepared. Beware of Him and obey His voice; do not provoke Him, for He will not pardon your transgressions; for My name is in Him."

the other hand, there are inferior beings as well, who are sending you their parasitic thoughts through which they attempt to prevent you from hearing clearly. Both kinds of beings are active. When people have a stale outlook on life, they have come into contact with beings who are on a lower level of development. When someone has new concepts, that person has connected with Beings who are on a higher level.

If you do not connect with the Luminous Beings, no future awaits you. If you nourish yourself in the proper way, you will come into contact with all pure and righteous souls. The Sublime Intelligent Beings from the Invisible World are sending their good thoughts to people, but should these thoughts not find good soil for their development, they will be deflected and will return to whence they have come from, or to their Source. This is the reason why, regardless of the great wealth, the great abundance of blessings, which God is sending to Earth, the majority of people are spiritually poor.

If, through the efforts that you are making, you are able to communicate with the Sublime Beings, you will be able to improve your destiny. This means that you need to have faith in God, to trust in God. Through higher reasoning, you can come into contact with the Angels—and through Love, with God. The beauty of Life lies in one's ability to live in harmony with the Advanced Beings. One needs to be in harmony with their thoughts. What greater music than to think as the Advanced Beings think.

The Angels who are teaching us are above us. Learn from them. Why should you learn from them? It is because they possess a greater understanding than you do. Follow the path of the Angels that you may correct your errors.

People today think that once they come to believe, the sciences and the arts are no longer needed. People are peculiar in their beliefs about God and in their attitudes about faith. Is it not God—the great God of Wisdom, the Great Cause—who has created all the worlds? Is it not God who has created the Angels? We need to come to know that there is another Science, another Music, another Poetry, another Art. There exist other Worlds as well, other forms of life, all a thousand times more beautiful than ours. There is much to learn.

You live in a world of intelligence, awareness. The Sublime Beings who participated in the Creation of the world are still working upon your consciousness and want you to learn, to come to understand things.

The real wealth of human beings is the good within them. As it is with the Good, so it is with Love, Wisdom, and Truth: they are inseparable. No one can say, "This Love, this Wisdom, this Knowledge is mine."

We have the ability to comprehend the thoughts of the Sublime Beings. Work upon yourselves that you may develop your receptivity, through which you may come into contact with more Advanced Beings.

The one who has experiences and personal encounters with the World beyond, should he become ill, he will be able to overcome his illness more easily. His Angels from the Invisible World will visit him, will take away his pain, suffering, and discouragement. The conscious, intelligent powers are very active in the world.

The benevolent Beings come from Above or from the right side; whereas the inferior beings, from below or from the left.

When you are passing through a trial, pray—the Luminous Beings will come to help you.

There is a Law that states: No act performed by a Sublime Being exists in which the loss is greater than the benefit.

If the heart of someone from the Earth is filled with sublime and noble feelings, it is sufficient for that person to think merely about an Angel, and the Angel will be there. Without these feelings in one's heart, no Angel will leave the Angelic World to help.

When I look at you, I can see what kind of relationship the more Advanced Beings have with you. This is because you are like a candle that has been illuminated. From the intensity of the light of your candle, of your mind, a determination can be made regarding the essence of your candle as well as the quality of the burning that is taking place within you, whether it be full or only partial. The Sublime Beings utilize this fire—that is to say, the energy of your mind—for their work. This means that when you endeavor to love, the Sublime Beings use this energy for their work.

There are Angels who are guiding the nations. The Angel is a very real Being, with both a body and a mind. Humans think, and the animals think, but what a difference between humans and animals!

Sometimes some of the Intelligent Advanced Beings reside in certain people for 10, 15, or even 20 years and act through them. This is more economical and saves time, compared to being born. In this sense, the genius is a collective being. One or more Advanced Beings have fallen in Love with him, have come to dwell within him, and manifested through him. Those people within whom an Angel comes to dwell, we call geniuses or saints. Within each great soul, a great spirit lives. A musician, in the true sense of the word, can only be that one within whom an Angel lives. All things in the world, which are sublime, are because of the Angels.

People's consciousness needs to be awakened that they may be able to connect with the consciousness of the Sublime Intelligent Beings and learn from them.

I believe not in enthusiasm, but rather in inspiration. Enthusiasm lasts for a day and a half, whereas inspiration endures forever. Whatever one seeks to do, one should have inspiration.

In the future, the Earth will be aglow, just as it was illuminated in earlier times. There is a saying in Bulgarian: To wherever it did flow, it will flow again. It is the Advanced Beings who order our lives. They are investing something new into your account. It is important for you that everything which they have imparted to you increases. It is important that you invest something in their account as well. How? Through your gratitude to them. Be thankful for your friends from Above who are helping you.

All the Sublime Beings gather around those who have sublime aspirations.

The Songs of the Master

The Master devoted exceptional attention to music. His songs accompanied everything that we were doing. We were always singing. The day started with music and ended with music. Each lecture of the Master began and ended with singing. For the Master, music was a condition as essential as the air. We all sang together, both in unison and as a chorus. At some special events, soloists would perform some of the songs of the Master.

The Master studied music constantly. He studied the effects and powers of expression of tones, scales, scale modulations, and rhythms. He pointed out their meaning to us as well as their significance in the Sublime Life. Through the language of music, he was able to interpret the Sublime Life for us.

We would all be filled with joy when he would bring his violin to class and would wonder what he would play for us that day. He would open up the big double case and take out his beautiful shining instrument, wrapped in soft velvet. He would clean it carefully with his handkerchief and then take out the bow. Each movement of the Master was beautiful, refined, and filled with attention. The Master's playing was gentle and soft, lacking in technical effects, yet displaying perfect technique, ease, purity, and expression. His music was awakening images and evoking deep feelings. Often he improvised at length melodies and variations that flowed freely, naturally, like a wellspring. Unfortunately, this musical treasure remained unrecorded.

In our presence, the Master would create a song from his text or he would start with a small motif—one or two measures only. And then in a simple way, a melody was created, a new song was born. At other times, prompted by the emotional state of a disciple, he would create a short melody in response to it, which had the wondrous power of transforming that state.

The Master usually gave us complete songs, perfect musical works to which nothing could be added or taken away. He presented the new songs in class or in the presence of a group of disciples from whom all the others would later learn them. The Master related to each new song with great love, as to a dear, long-awaited guest. This love was carried over to the disciples as well. Such is the Law.

The Master sang with inspiration. His voice was deep, had great insight, and was rich with inexhaustible possibilities. He could convey all nuances of feeling and thought. Standing upright with closed eyes, the Master accompanied his singing at all times with beautiful, expressive gestures. He was an entrancing performer.

The Master encouraged all of his disciples to play instruments and sing. There was hardly one who did not play an instrument or sing. The Master was surrounded by musicians. He worked constantly with them. During the last years, he appointed some of them to a regular work schedule. He passed down to them his last songs, those which he had kept to himself for

a long time, the sacred songs. He sang them or played them on his violin, showing the musicians how to perform the songs until they learned them well enough to write them down, and afterward, pass them on to the rest of the disciples. At the same time, he gave many concerts in which he presented songs that were rich in melody and modulation. These were examples of the new music. In some conversation he explained the Laws that were their foundation. Music was a favorite subject of our conversations with the Master.
The Master told us:

Our songs[49], the songs of the Brotherhood of Light, will not change even after thousands of years. For example, according to the song "The Bright Day" (*Svetal den*) or "The Sun Is Rising" (*Izgryava Slantseto*) there will always be a bright day and the Sun will always rise. The song "I Will Rejuvenate" (*Az shte se podmladya*) is not invented: its motif exists in Nature. The Beings in the Divine World live it.

One sister asked, "How are they living this motif?"
The Master answered:

While they are living, they are singing it.

Our songs exist in the World Above and are brought down to us from there. When we sing them, the Sublime Beings come to help us. Through our songs we go to them, and they come to us. Each of our songs is brought down from Above and corresponds to a song that exists in the Divine World.

Each of our songs is created according to the Plan of the Sublime Scales that comes from Above. And if we here—while singing or playing—are in accordance with the real essence of these heavenly Songs, which are brought from Above, then we will receive the blessing of the Divine World.

When one sings with purity, Love, and total harmony among the mind, heart, and will—all three turned toward the Divine—then at this very moment, we will connect with the Rhythm of the heavenly Songs from which ours are derived. Then we receive the Divine flow or blessing.

These Divine Songs are sung Above for Eternity; they resonate there forever. It is through them that the Universe is

---

49. The songs, mentioned in the lecture, are published in the book "Songs of the Master," 2006.

created and built. Mozart, Bach, Beethoven, and others have brought down to their compositions a small part of what is in Heaven.

In the future, the subjects for operas will be chosen from our songs as well as from some of the Paneurhythmy exercises. After that, the subjects for operas will be chosen from our life at the Seven Lakes of the Rila Mountains as well as from our life at Izgrev. Into these operas, our songs will be interwoven.

All of our songs are visionary and they carry within them fulfillment. All of the words in them have but a single meaning. We adorn these songs with images. The young beautiful woman who is spoken of in one of our songs is the sublime thought, the sublime idea, and the Divine in human beings. We will present the new idea to humankind through the images of the young woman and the young man.

It is not the past which is being spoken of in our songs, but the present.

Our songs are varied, in both the major and minor scales. Some of them start in the minor and finish in the major and others vice versa. The song "The Sun Is Rising" is in the major, while "Mahar Benu" starts in the minor and finishes in the major. The minor indicates the going out to achieve some gain, whereas the major is the returning with that gain, the returning from the battlefield. The song "In All of Life's Conditions Never Lose Your Peace" (*Pri vsichkite usloviya na zhivota ne gubi svoya mir*) is meant for solo singing and needs to be performed with ardor.

The same Law holds true for music as it does for precious stones. Some stones are formed under great pressure and high temperatures.

People who can value these songs are needed. Ignorant people will leave a precious stone, and say, "This is just a stone." In order that people may value music, they need to sing it themselves as well as listen to it when others are singing. This is not something to be studied only in theory.

From noon until sunset we have one disposition toward singing, and from sunrise until noon, another.

Someone sings the song "The Sun Is Rising," but does not sing it as it should be sung. When the Sun rises, the heart is quivering with anticipation. The Sun tries to give something to every blade of grass, to every little stone, and they all rejoice in it. And yet you sing this song in an ordinary way, without expressing all of this.

The song "March Forward for Glory to Fight for the King of Zion" (*Napred, napred za slava, v boy za tsarya Sionski*) I gave in 1888 in the village Hotantsa[50] before going abroad. There are still more songs I gave, but they have not yet been performed for large audiences. The song "The Prodigal Son" (*Bludniya sin*), I have played only a few times.

The Master remained silent for a while and then sang a new song:

"At the dawn of my life,
I awakened early
And met the rising Sun.
It brought me the joyful tidings
That I am loved by God."

Then the Master continued:

This song is very profound, sacred, and mystical, and therefore, it is not for a broad circle.

After that, the Master played another new song on his violin and said:

This song means the following: Everything in Life is possible when you know how to do it rightly. The song is a way by which one's life may be set right.

At present, we are the most musical community. Nowhere else can as many new songs as we have be found. We are a spiritual community that possesses a new music.

Some songs help the mind, others, the heart; and still others, the will.

---

50. Hotantsa is a village in Bulgaria where Peter Deunov was employed as a school teacher.

I had four music teachers in Bulgaria. The first was a lyricist, the second, a classicist; and the third I would call a Mozart type, one of joyful music. After that, came a classicist who was playing for me when I was taking classes from him.

It is necessary to form a small orchestra at Izgrev. We need to give a concert of the new music in Sofia.

An idea regarding the introduction of our songs into the schools arose. One brother mentioned that he is preparing a collection of our children's songs for publication.
The Master said:

One needs to understand how to teach our songs to the children and which methods to use. It is necessary to awaken in people the musical states that they may then create beautiful music. The method for teaching songs to the children is as follows: First, through preparation Nature needs to be brought to life for the children that they may begin to sing. How can a child sing about the river, the wellspring, the cherry tree, and so on, when all of these have not become alive for that child. They need to become living, real.

The Colors

Every living being, every little flower, every fruit tree bears certain forces of Nature. When you love and cultivate these forces, you will perceive what they are offering.
The Master used everything for practical instruction and learning. During our hikes and outings, he directed our attention to the plants, animals, rocks, and clouds revealing the idea instilled in them by Nature—in other words, the Divine, that at some point becomes manifested. The Master used the Divine in Nature as the most natural impulse in order to awaken it within us.
In springtime, when Nature awakens, we would go out with him to the countryside almost every day. Once, as he pointed to the sunlit world around, the Master said:

Colors are the greatest blessing. This is God's abundance, the gate through which all bounties come from the Invisible

World. The white hyacinth is a symbol of generosity. It has come to Earth to learn generosity, to manifest its generosity, to learn the ways of generosity, and to give. The carnation is a symbol of health. A person who desires to be healthy, resilient, and not be subject to any disease should grow carnations, no matter what color they are. The rose imparts tenderness. If you desire to possess tenderness, grow roses. Each flower imparts different virtues. The tulip teaches people the rules of giving or how to give. The person who desires strength needs to learn from purple, the violet color. It is a manifestation of strength. The color blue brings faith, yellow, wisdom. Green brings liveliness and health. Orange brings individuality; and red, vitality and agility.

You need to look at the sky, at its blue color, in order to develop faith. If nervous people gaze at the green grass, they will cease to be nervous. People who love the color yellow are extremely lively and agile. Those who like the color red are very active.

The Master pointed at the forget-me-nots growing in the grass around us, and said:

Develop your faith. Make use of all the blessings your faith is giving you. Observe the colors of the flowers and see what influence a particular color has upon you. Colors exist in the human aura as well. For those who can see, the color of hatred in the human aura manifests as darkness.

Nature heals through colors. Those who have the imagination and sensibility toward colors can rejuvenate themselves through them—and not only through the colors of the physical world, but also through those of the mental world. This occurs as follows: Concentrate and visualize a certain color—red, for example—in its purest form. Immerse yourself in it, imagining that a shower of red light is pouring over you and that you are suffused with it. Through the color red, you will receive vitality. You can do the same with the color yellow: it rejuvenates the thoughts, the mind. The color blue brings tranquility and peace. For example, if you are agitated, disheartened, or troubled, gaze upon the blue of the sky, and it will bring peace and tranquility to you. Through orange you will receive a positive self-confidence and self-reliance, through green, relaxation and growth, and through the violet, spiritual power and strength.

The seven colors exist in different worlds—in different octaves—and differ in their effect and meaning. In the physical world, they mean one thing, and in the other Worlds, something else. In its lowest octaves and nuances, the color red signifies a tendency to fight, while in the sublime, vitality. The color orange, in its lowest nuances, signifies individuation; in the sublime, individuality dedicated to the service of God and humankind. The color green, in its lowest nuances, signifies attachment to the material world. In the sublime, green signifies growth and development, meaning that people work on their perfection while they are helping their neighbors. The color yellow, in its lowest nuances, signifies intellect used for personal goals. The color violet, in its lowest nuances, signifies power used solely for one's own interest. In its sublime nuances, the color yellow signifies intelligence used in the service of humankind. The color violet signifies power used for the benefit of others.

Joy

Once the Master said:

Today, people have sorrow. When the Divine comes, Joy will come.

The meaning of your life and your true happiness depends upon the fundamental understanding of Love. Where there is Love, there is also Life. And where there is Life, there is also Joy. In a home where Love abides, all are joyful.

Those who do not perceive Love, Wisdom, and Truth will weep. It was said, "For I will turn their mourning to joy, will comfort them, and make them rejoice rather than sorrow." [51]

Love that does not bring Joy and Light is not true Love. Hell is the place where Love is missing. Where there is no Love,

---

51. See Jeremiah 31:13.

Wisdom, and Truth, there hell is. Where there is Love, Wisdom, and Truth, there Heaven is.

How could a home be not sorrowful if there is no Love in it? When Love comes, you will say, "All the suffering that may have come I will bear with Joy."

When you have Love, you are happy and have energy for work. When you lose Love, you fall into despair. When the mother loses her child, when the brother loses his sister, when someone loses his friend, they fall into despair.

When Love enters the human heart, the world takes on a different appearance. You will find everything pleasant, and you will work with Joy. When you love, the world opens up for you, and you see it as beautiful, as you have never seen it before. If you do not love, the world is dark and incomprehensible to you.

Acquaintance

The Master said:

People are sent into the world to become acquainted with one another. How many people do you know at present? Can you say that you know a certain person? You say today that you know him; tomorrow you will see that you do not know him. Today you say that someone is gifted; the next day you are doubtful about his gift. This means not knowing.

With the physical eyes, one sees only the shadow of things. Without Love there is no knowing, there is no seeing. Without Love, life has no meaning. Knowing comes from Love alone. Only if you love, can you come to know.

God knows us in accordance with the Law of Love. Do not think that He knows us only mechanically.

Which people do you know? Those who have done a good deed for you, who have helped you. When you do not like someone, you do not know him.

Come to love someone rightly and you will see that within his soul, mind, and heart something great is hidden. If you do not, then today you will be enchanted by someone and disappointed by him the next day. If you love someone, you will see within him many things, and the most wonderful ones.

The external, physical appearance of a person is not yet the true human being. Deep within the human being is hidden something very beautiful, which can become known only by the one who loves.

You will never be able to come to know a person as long as you see only his physical appearance. This explains why you do not like someone when others like him. You see only his appearance, whereas others know him from within and they see the Divine within. You say, "I find nothing special in this person." Why? It is because you do not love him. Ask those who love that person what they see in him.

The Path of Attainment

The Master said:

Enter a room and make a small experiment. Close the window, close the shutters, and remain in the dark. After that, open the window and close it again. Observe what the conditions are in the darkness as to what they are in the light. When the windows are open, this corresponds to the life with Love; and when they are closed, to that without Love. Without Love, things lose their power and significance. The angels who rejected Love lost a great deal of what they had and fell. At first they were powerful. But after that, an Angel appeared who bound them in chains and set them in the abyss. And so, they lost their power. I call the temptation of things "the slippery slope." You slide down because you have nothing to hold onto.

When someone loves, he needs to know that he will find himself in bondage to the most Intelligent and Sublime Beings. They watch and observe as to how he expresses his love. To love means to perform a sacred act—not in the face of one's peers, but in the face of the Sublime World. God's blessing depends upon how you perform this act. God extends His Hand to those who rightly express their love.

Love organizes the human spiritual body. Even matter is transformed through Love. With Love the human energies take on a different direction and begin to build the spiritual body in which the human being of the future will dwell. Through Love, those creative powers, which build, are called into action. For this reason, all good and saintly people experience such high vibrational states that ordinary people cannot imagine. They pass through great inner suffering in order that they may prepare for these vibrations.

Seemingly, Love is the least of all powers; but in reality, it is the greatest power in the world. Love is the lever of all things. Money and power serve Love. We are now coming to the end of the world of human laws and of money, and are entering into the realm of Love.

Love is nourishment for the soul, it is essential food by which people live. What is Love? It is that which continuously imparts Life to your souls.

If I should give someone money or do some small favor for him, if I invite him into my home, is this proof of my love for that person? No. Today you might give someone money, you might make him well received in your home, you might make great sacrifices for him, but tomorrow you do not wish to hear about him. And yet, in Divine Love, there is something great that is constantly building. It provides the necessary conditions for the development of the soul. The light and warmth of the Sun give to the plant the impulse to grow. In the same way, Love makes for the growth of the human soul. When the good conditions come, the flowers will come into being. This is not just because they have been planted—they had been planted already. Simply stated: Love provides the conditions for our abilities to manifest.

Love conquers death. People die because Divine Life has not been yet instilled in them. The one who abides in the Law of Love attains Life day by day. A Law states: For those who do not love, the Divine Life Force will not pass through them; and as a result, they will wither and lose their life.

To love someone signifies that he will grow and flourish from your love. You too will grow and flourish. Someone asks, "Why do I need to love?" So that you may grow and manifest yourself, so that your consciousness may awaken, and so that you may understand why you have come into this world.

Divine Love has nothing in common with ordinary human emotions and dispositions. It can be recognized by the following attributes. When Love touches the slow-witted person, it makes him intelligent and wise. When it touches the dead, he rises to life again. When touching the leper, he is healed. When touching the discouraged, all discouragement disappears.

All the knowledge of humankind, which has been accumulated from 8,000 years until now, cannot be compared to the least Manifestation of Divine Love. Therefore, so much more is there for you to learn.

In this Love, there is no despair, no disease, no darkness, and all conflict disappears. It settles all disputes and misunderstandings. If this should not happen thus for you, do not say that you abide in Love.

In the Law of Love, there is no contradiction. If you begin to do something with Love, it will surely be successful. The world may turn upside-down, but this work will be accomplished well.

To the one who ails, I say, "Accept Love. Think not about disease! Love is the power that can heal you." Love heals all disease. It increases the vibrations of the human organism and makes it capable of withstanding external influences as well as those of microbes.

When a person becomes demagnetized, he loses his life force and easily becomes ill. With every demagnetization, a fissure within the etheric double occurs from which a great amount of vital energy begins to leak. Once this fissure is sealed, the person becomes healthy again. From Love, energy emanates serving as a plaster that seals even the smallest of cracks in the nervous system.

A friend came by one day and asked me, "What can I do about my ailing sister? How can I cure her?" I said to him, "If your sister would apply Divine Love, she will be healed."

When you work with Love in healing a disease, you will notice certain improvements at the beginning that will be followed by a relapse. Then a greater improvement will come, this time followed by a smaller relapse. In this way, the conditions will alternate until a complete recovery takes place.

If someone is neurasthenic, it indicates that he has little Love. If he has pain in his stomach, chest, or has a headache, he has little Love. The one who has weak health, let him love!

Make some experiments in this field in order to see for yourself the truth of this Law. If you are suffering from rheumatism or have a fever or any other disease, manifest Divine Love and your health will improve in a short time. The sooner that you are healed the more rightly you have manifested Love.

If an ailing person even touches one who is visited by Divine Power, he will be healed.

Death is an indication that people have not yet resolved Life's issues: they have not yet found the right answers.

Someone says that he does not want to live. But you have not lived yet! Until now you have suffered; from now on, you will begin to live.

The Music of Nature

In nature, days filled with music exist. On such days you need to listen attentively, for even in the noises of the distant life there is music. To sing or to play music on such days comes as naturally as breathing.

Whenever we would gather around the Master, we would always sing his songs. It was a natural expression of the Universal Life. Even so, on special days such as these, when we attuned to certain scales of Nature, the songs sounded as new. The harmonies came naturally, and the melodies were infused with a special meaning, fullness and intensity. On a day such as this, we were gathered around our beloved Master, and question regarding the music of Nature was raised.

The Master said:

There exist Beings who sing as a chorus in the forest as they roam. There is a harmony within their music. This singing cannot be perceived with physical ears—it is an etheric singing.

And yet, this singing is real. The wind and the storm are musical, but the human ear does not possess the musical sensibility for perceiving this music.

Which is the most sublime of concerts? The sunrise.

In the storm, the thunder, the falling of the raindrops, I hear music. It is a great concert.

We will make an experiment with the sunlight. Let it speak to you: music is hidden within. No harmony of tones more sublime exists than what emanates from the vibrations of the rays of the Sun.

Each rustling of the leaves on a tree is a tone which is noise to the undeveloped ear. You go to concerts and listen to the music of Schumann, Mozart, Bach, and Beethoven. And yet, if the ear was more developed in modern people, we would prefer to listen to the music of the rustling leaves rather than that of the greatest musicians. Make contact with this other world of music.

Have you heard the music of the flowers when they bloom or the chorus of the ripening fruit trees? Have you listened to the music of the running waters? Have you heard the song of the summer breeze, which caresses the trees? You will say that all this is an illusion. No. And yet, one needs the ear in order to be able to hear these songs and merge with them. Everything in Nature is alive. In everything created by God, great meaning exists. Music and song exist in all things.

Every living thing produces sound. Imagine that the whole of Nature is one great orchestra. The cuckoo is the drummer: one, two, three beats and stops. Each animal in the orchestra emits its own sound. What a majestic orchestra the whole of Nature is.

The organs of the human body, according to the functions that they perform, are also defined as musical tones. For example, the heart represents the tone *do* (C); the respiratory system, the tone *re* (D); the liver, the tone *mi* (E); the kidney, *fa* (F); the spleen, *sol* (G); the gallbladder, *la* (A); and the digestive system, *ti* or *si* (B).

When the human respiratory system functions musically in all scales, we say that it is normally developed. With the least disturbance to the scale, its tone will be changed into another tone. This brings about discord in one of the organs. We call this discord "disease."

For this reason, that you may not become ill, you need to protect the integrity and frequency of vibration of your tones.

If you understand the key and the tones of your organism, you will be able to transform your states so that you may keep the functioning of your organism in perfect order. From the heart, the energy passes to the liver. This means that from the heart to the liver there is an open passage, but not from the liver to the heart. Understanding this, you should not let any negative feelings enter your heart for that might have a detrimental effect on your liver.

The one who knows and understands the music of his organism is able to heal any of his organs when he is ill. If any problem should exist in his respiratory system, he will sing or play music in which the tone *re* (D) repeats often. The gallbladder is treated with the tone *la* (A).

Each member of the human body can be compared to a musical instrument, and the body, as a whole, to an enormous orchestra, not one of only fifty or sixty players, but of thousands of instruments and thousands of beings who sing and play as a person conducts. You are great conductors of music.

The human being has billions of servants: these are the cells of the human body.

All organs of the human body emanate tones, radio waves that are musical.

The Angels are very musical. Today there are musical works written in notes, but there is no written music preserved from the past. Now one should search for it in the Archives of Angelic Music.

Can you perceive music that has three hundred thousand or five hundred thousand vibrations? This is the Angelic Music. Iron and gold will melt from such Music. This Music is able to heal the most incurable of diseases.

There is also that music whose vibrations destroy. What did the Jews do with their horns? While blowing them, they circled the walls of Jericho seven times, and the walls crumbled.[52]

---

52. See also Joshua 6.

If you would make use of such music, in seven days you could knock down the walls of your impediments and obstacles.

You say, "My heart is wounded." Sing and play! There is no better method than this.

Early in the morning, the Advanced Beings sing in Nature.

A sister shared her experience, "In 1928 while stopping by the fifth lake Mahabur,[53] I heard a chorus of Sublime Beings." Another sister had also heard the singing of these Beings at the fifth lake.
The Master said:

It was not that the Beings had gathered at the fifth lake, but that the singing had been broadcast on the radio and you heard it there. The privilege came about because this place at the fifth lake is sacred, and it is possible to perceive there the choral singing of these Beings, as if from a radio.

All of the great musicians have listened to the music of the Sublime World, and what they have heard, they have written down.

When such a chorus is audible, at the beginning, it will seem that the chorus is coming closer and closer. Then, gradually, it will seem to move further and further away.

A sister said that she was there, at Lake Mahabur, with a brother, but that he could not hear anything. Another sister spoke about a similar experience which she had at the Inner Bliznak.[54] "I was with a sister at the Inner Bliznak. The weather was perfectly calm, and it was close to sunset. There was no wind. I was standing there in contemplation. At some point, I perceived sounds as if they were coming from far away, like the sounds of water from waterfalls emanating music. I listened closely with attention and understood that this was not something that I was hearing with my physical ears. I understood that this was a more profound hearing. These sounds grew stronger and spread like a chorus with ascending voices—tenors, basses, sopranos. The sounds were majestic, fading away, and then becoming stronger. As they became stronger, one could perceive a glorifying song of praise for God like Alleluia, a song sung by thousands of voices that merged

---

53. *Mahabur* is the name given by the Master to Lake *Babreka* (The Kidney Lake), the fifth of the Seven Lakes of the Rila Mountains.
54. The Inner *Bliznak* is the southern part of the lake known as *The Twins*, the fourth of the Seven Lakes of the Rila Mountains.

together forming a mighty polyphonic voice. This continued for thirty minutes to one hour. If I had stayed, perhaps I could have listened longer, but it became dark and I left. I told the other sister to listen, but she could not perceive this music. On another occasion, on a bright moonlit night, I went purposely to the same place to re-experience the same, and again I heard the music."

The Master said:

The Angels need to open our musical centers so that we may hear the Songs, which are sung, and that we may hear the Music from Above. In the future, we will hear the Music of the Angels.

An even greater Music exists—the Divine music. When you hear this Music, you will forget everything. And when you return home, you will say, "All is finished with me. From now on, I will serve God." For the Angels, human singing is like that from a gramophone record. Earthly music is brought down from Above. It comes in aid for humankind: it comes from the Invisible World to help humankind.

Some composers and musicians will say that they have created something. In reality, nobody has created anything. One musician said to me, "Tell me about the new music." I answered, "I can tell you nothing about it because a dispute will arise among you musicians as to who has come up with it."

Choral, as well as instrumental music, is brought down from the Sublime World. Music comes from the sanctuary of the Temple. It has always been there, but now it is free to come out.

Beauty

The wheat in the fields was forming ears. The wheat was lush. The air was filled with a refreshing fragrance as after a storm. Large white clouds traveled across the sky. The Sun was shining over God's beautiful world. We made ourselves comfortable around the Master among the beautiful clearings in the fields. In conversation, someone raised a question about beauty.

The Master said:

Beauty is created according to internal Laws, yet people are searching for it in a superficial way. Three things create beauty in the features of the face: Love for Love—that is to say, that connection with Nature which forms the human mouth, Love for Wisdom that forms the human nose, and Love for Truth that forms the forehead, the eyes, and the gaze.

In the old life, the forms lacked beauty. Wherever the New Life begins, the forms are beautiful. In the Divine Life they come into perfect Beauty.

Ugliness is a result of negative thoughts, feelings, and desires from which one should rid oneself. These are passed on to him by his ancestors. They represent the material that one needs to process.

Beauty is a spiritual quality. When someone prays constantly, when he reads spiritual books and is occupied with beautiful works, his face receives particular lines and a special beauty.

Beauty is an expression of Truth. Only the one who is free can attain true Knowledge: the Knowledge of Nature. Only the one who is free can be beautiful.

Beauty is a manifestation of Cosmic Intelligence. It is one with Love and gives meaning to life.

Beauty is in the symmetry of the face, but also in its elasticity, flexibility, and liveliness.

God is a Source of Beauty.

Search for that Beauty which bears the Image of God within itself. There is something beautiful in Nature's forms. An invisible Hand is at work and it creates that combination of forms that we observe. The Image of God is expressed in Nature. Sometimes Nature appears more beautiful to us: the sky and the Sun appear to be lovelier, more radiant, and more beautiful. There are other times when Nature appears gloomy and stern to us. Does this change truly occur in Nature? No. When we do not live well, we cast a shadow and perceive the Image of God as gloomy.

Perfect Beauty is a human ideal. In the future, people will be beautiful.

Selflessness

This evening those who had cut the hay returned from the fields to the farmstead. They were sunburned, lively, and joyous. The majority of them were brothers and sisters giving a helping hand to the farmers. It took them several days until the hay could be harvested. After the evening meal a discussion arose in connection with the new forms of labor.
The Master said:

You need to impart the purest of thoughts to the production of food, clothing, and other goods. If you wish to build a home, hire those people who are not only building specialists, but are also of good character. While doing the work, not one bad word should be spoken, nor should a negative thought be permitted to enter one's mind. Otherwise, toxins will enter the house. Then it will become difficult for you to get rid of the negative influences.

In the future, those who prepare the bread should have sublime ideas, which they will instill into the bread. If the farmer applies this in his work, his fields will yield more and better fruits. If the wheat is cultivated with joy and love, the bread made of this wheat will be nutritious and those eating it will be inspired with new ideas.

If, in the future, we would like to introduce right education into the world, then in the building of the school, the best people should be called upon: the best builders for the building, the benches, the desks, as well as all the other implements for teaching. In saying "the best builders," I do not refer to the best builders in the trade only, but the best people as well. People will say, "The chairs, the desks—anybody can make these." Until now they have been made by anybody, and we see what kind of schooling we have. Every work that is performed without Love is torment. Discontentment creates bitterness.

Today's production is based upon human greed. What can you say about the shoes you are wearing on your feet? They are made from the hide of animals whose life was taken through violence. What kind of thoughts were introduced by the person who stripped the skin from the animals as well as the one who tanned them? Some have imparted their thoughts of discontentment from not having been paid well; whereas others want to increase their riches. What can beautiful shiny shoes contribute to your well-being? Only what is instilled in them, such as the negative thoughts and feelings of those who have produced them. Before too long a time has passed, these shoes will bring you some misfortune. The shoes may be shiny, but they bring misfortune to the one wearing them.

Rid yourselves of those shoes and clothing that have been produced from human discontent. You may say that this is superstition. Do not live in ignorance of what brings misfortune to people. One should put positive thoughts and feelings, and selfless desires in every work and deed. One's misery is caused by the discontent instilled in the shoes and the clothing one wears.

What good can a knife contribute when a murderous thought has been instilled in it? Whoever takes this knife into his hand will experience the desire to kill. In a short time a crime will be committed with this knife. The one who produces knives must impart to them his best thoughts. Then when you take such a knife into your hand, you will not experience any bad feeling or desire.

The knife that is used to commit a crime will be passed through fire: it will be made into a plow, a hoe, a hammer. It will pass through suffering. This is the only way that it will be purified and be set free of the criminal thoughts instilled in it.

I do not speak with the intention to persuade you, but I present those facts and Laws that are merciless. These are the Laws of the Intelligent Nature. Although you may reject them, they still exert their influence.

Torment, Labor, and Work

With regard to motivational causes, we can distinguish three kinds of activities. The first is torment. This means one is forced to work, and in so doing, descends. The second is labor. This means one works for pay, to emerge from the dense matter and ascend. The third is Work. This is activity out of choice, out of Love. Work—this is the true Culture.

Labor is a precursor to the New Culture. When one labors, one works for remuneration, for one's own reward; that is to say, for money.

The most sublime activity on Earth is the one that comes out of Love. An activity exists that stands above the ordinary. This is the activity motivated by Love. This is when you sacrifice yourself for the benefit of others because you are able to sacrifice yourself—as has Christ. But these are sublime matters that not everyone can understand in their fullness. The New, which is coming into the world, is to work out of Love.

Earlier I said that with regard to the motivation for activity, we have three kinds: torment, labor, and Work. For a clearer understanding, I will present the same idea in another way: there are mainly three motives for acting: law, money, and Love.

The first incentive is the law. When you work under the law, there is no freedom. When you work for money, you are more free. When you work out of Love, you have complete freedom. Until now we have served the law and we have served money. How is it that we cannot now serve Love?

You are drafted, and you are told, "You will fight for your homeland. You will do this job." There is no pay; there is nothing. This is by law.

The second incentive is that you will work for money. Someone asks you to come to work. You say, "I do not work for free." He offers you one hundred leva. You say, "I will not work." He offers two hundred leva. Again you say, "I will not work." He gives you two hundred and fifty leva; you accept and go to work.

After the incentives of the law and of money, we come to the third incentive: to work out of Love. When you work out of Love, you are also being paid, but in a different way. And so, a New Order comes now into the world: Love. It is the most powerful of all.

People need to make the transition from labor to Work. This is the sublime activity. This is the path toward Freedom.

Here is an example about Work: a musician visits a hospital and plays for the ill, but does not want a reward. He goes there because of a feeling of compassion. An artist exhibits his paintings in order to uplift the spirits of the ill. He does not seek a reward either.

Today we have labor, but not yet Work. Work will be the great task of the future generation.

The one who is in torment, let him move toward labor. The one who labors, let him move toward Work. Even the smallest service, the smallest work, done out of Love attains sublime value.

Love needs to be the first impulse in everything. There is a mythic tale. In ancient times, a king was strolling in his garden picking a basket full of cherries. A child caught up with him and asked, "Will you sell me some?" The king answered, "I do not sell." The child said, "Would you give me some?" "I will give to you," said the king. But this child was wise as well. When the king gave him the cherries, the child asked, "May I carry your basket for a while?" They walked together, the child carrying the basket. The king asked him, "May I pay you?" The child answered, "No."

When working for another, one expends Divine energy, which cannot be paid for. For this reason, he too should not be paid. Should he be given something, it will be a reward of Love, but not a payment.

Everything that is done without Love is a transgression. Everything that is taken without Love is theft. Everything that is done with Love is meaningful.

Work should be completely lacking in any material intent. We will then be free, independent. The new morality means absolute selflessness.

Work in which money plays a role is not Divine. Work in which money does not play a role is Divine. When you go to work for someone, you should tell him, "I will work for you for free." Finish the work and then leave.

Every nation has the need for new ideas, for a New Culture that will transform it, eliminating the prisons and the gallows.

Everyone will work without being paid. This will come in the future.

For how long will we be tormented? Until we begin to work out of Love. I will be the first to go into the field and work for five hours without any remuneration. Should we all do so, we would become an advanced nation. If all men and women would act like that, what would Bulgaria then become!

True Work is that in which Love participates.

People can be strange at times. When they become religious and spiritual, they abandon work, abandon service. No, from now on you should begin to work, and without money, at that.

True morality implies the following: everything that humans do will be dictated by Love. Where there is no Love, there is crime, deceit, and wickedness.

Why is the world not yet a world of harmony? We are now entering into harmony. The new humankind that is coming in the future is an emissary for the new Heaven, the new Earth, and the new order of things. In Heaven, the first article of the constitution states, "You will not work for money."

How much do you pay to the river that waters your garden? If the least river can serve without money, why cannot you do the same? One needs to understand this issue in its broadest sense. Do not expect money for your work. Do not expect gratitude or appreciation: this is the same as expecting payment. Instead you should work expecting nothing. When you are thanked for what you do, you have received your payment. And when you are not thanked, you will receive your blessing in the future. Whatever work you do, physical or spiritual, you should work with goodwill and love. The spiritual student is not permitted to remain idle.

In the new order, fruit will not be sold. You will give fruit with Love and will receive fruit with Love. Every work in which Love is the motivation is gratifying.

The human order brings adversity, whereas the Divine, Joy. Why is there adversity in the world? Because the human will predominates the Divine Will. Contradictions originate from the human order, whereas blessings, from the Divine. People have yet to explore the Divine Laws. At present, they study those laws that are not Divine.

When Love comes, you will sing and play music well. When Love is not present, there is no inspiration. When Love is not at work, things are at a standstill.

Pass by some place without Love one time and observe how the people act toward you. A second time pass by with Love and observe now how they now act. The world of Beauty is the world of Love. The Law of Love is the Law of Freedom. Only when you work with Love can you be free. Freedom is attainable when you serve God with Love. You often serve other beings who have done nothing for you. Why not then serve God, the One who has done everything for you, who has given everything to you?

We should all begin to serve out of our own volition. Then from torment and labor we will enter into Work. Torment and labor are karma, whereas Love is dharma.

One sister asked, "Which of these two Laws are we under?"

You are under dharma. When people come to live in the new understanding, they will be paid in advance. When the apple tree gives you its fruits, it is like saying to you, "Eat my fruits and plant my seeds."

In the New Life, Love will be the medium of exchange, not money. When you love someone, you have paid him in advance, and he will do something for you. At present, the medium of exchange is money. And so, the more you are paid, the better and faster you do the work, and vice versa.

Every work, as small as it may be, that is done in the name of Divine Love, Wisdom, and Truth attains great value.

At present, whatever work people may do, they always expect to be paid something. It is not bad for you to receive something for your work: it is a matter of course. And yet, when I say that you should work for free, I mean this: All work should be accomplished in accordance with the Law of Love, no matter if it is with or without payment. Every work that is done out of Love cannot be paid for.

A man hired several workers. The first one wanted 500 leva as a day's wage; the second one—400 leva; the third one—300 leva. The second to last worker wanted 10 leva. But the last worker said, "I do not want money. You can give me what you wish." In the evening, the employer gave everyone what they wanted, but he paid the last worker twice as much as the wage of 500 leva, which was asked by the first worker.

This spring you are working on several wellsprings in this yard. People in the world would be surprised that you work without pay and do so diligently and with joy. But the world does not know that those who work out of Love receive the greatest pay, the greatest reward. And yet they receive it in a mysterious way: they do not know what they will receive.

When you do a service for a beetle, you are serving God. The beetle prays to God, and when you are helping him, you are helping God. A plant is praying to God, asking for moisture. By watering it, you have done it a service. This good deed you have done is for God. The plants too will thank you, they feel things.

Nothing is more beautiful than the work for God. Such activity is neither torment nor labor. The present social order is one of torment. You serve only when you love. The rest is by force.

God has not created masters and servants, but human beings who should live in brotherhood. Masters and servants, this is a human idea. All people are brothers and sisters when they are in free and pure relationships.

There is a saying, "The strong ones will put the world in order." But how? The strong need to serve the weak. In the home, everyone serves the child because it is weak. In the new society, it will be the same: the strong will serve the weak.

Become servants to what? To Love, Wisdom, and Truth.

Political life that resorts predominantly to violence will be replaced by cooperation and service. Someone is asking if this is possible without money. We have made money our master, and so we say that it is impossible without money.

In the Divine World, no payment exists for any service. Everyone there works for free. The day will come when money will go out of circulation. You will ask, "How are people to live?" As in Heaven. Should you go to Heaven and offer money to someone, he will say, "Money is of no value here." He feels happy that he can give you something without money. And so, the Spiritual Life is the opposite of the earthly. The New Culture signifies the descending of the Spiritual Life to the Earth. Life of today is the result of wrongdoing. Above, in the Spiritual world there exists a Life of ideal order.

The social reforms, which we are undertaking, other Beings have had them already, and we are copying them. And yet, we think that the social order that we are arranging comes from us. What exists in the Spiritual world, exactly the same needs to be applied on Earth as well. Moses saw the model of the tabernacle as it was in the Divine World and made it exactly the same as had been shown to him.

Money is presently the motivational cause in the world because there is a lack of Love. It will not be so in the future.

After a concert, Paganini met a small girl who said to him, "I wanted very much to hear you, but not having the money for the ticket I could not. I am sorry." Paganini went to the girl's home and gave a concert only for her. For her, he played out of Love. Another example: in the town he saw a poor old man playing the violin on the street. His little money bowl was empty. Paganini took his violin and began to play. Many people gathered around and the little bowl filled with money. This is what it means to play out of Love.

Someone comes and asks you, "Do you want to work?" You will say, "We do not work for money. We will work for free."

I do not need money, but when I so desire, I can have some at my disposal. Someone will say, "Show me where the money is." But I say, "No. When you come to love God, you will have the keys to all cash-boxes."

Someone says, "Without money it is impossible." This is as true as when we say that a person who is ill cannot exist without a car. True. Yet the healthy one is able to do without a car. The ill cannot do without money, but the healthy one can.

The law and money are presently ahead of Love, but they must become Love's servant.

In raising a child until it is grown, a mother spends many sleepless nights, giving it much care and sacrifices. Who is paying her? Is she doing this for money? Here you can see that she becomes a servant to Love, by making sacrifices in the name of Love. Thus, we have an example of service without money: mothers serve without money.

The Divine Order is not for everyone. There are people who need money in order to live, and others who will live without money. Some travel by buffalo-wagon, whereas the one who flies in an airplane pays a higher price, but arrives sooner.

From my point of view, the world will come to right when people understand that they need to work selflessly: without money, and out of Love. Such an order will exist in the future. This will be the most sacred thing in the world.

The Slavs will need to set the example as to how money and personal interest should be replaced.

The Social Problem

People need to study the laws of their bodies and draw from there the entire order and laws for society. Then systematic order will exist in the world. The following three things need to be taken into consideration. Firstly, in order that the laws of the material world may be examined, we need to study the laws of the digestive system. Secondly, in order that the Laws of the Spiritual world may be examined, we need to study the laws of the respiratory system. And thirdly, in order that the Laws of the Divine World may be examined, we need to study the laws of the brain.

The stomach has millions of cells that, when working ideally, are specialized and in harmony. Even the smallest nutrient will pass throughout the body to feed it. If one should pay one *stotinka*[55] to each of these millions of cells, how much money would it cost? Or what if one pays 1 lev or 10 leva or even 100 leva to them? Does anyone have so much money? Are we able to pay for the work of these cells? We are not. And so, they work without being paid.

The same thing will be applied in the physical world as well when the Divine Order comes. All will work as one, as these millions of cells do so that the whole world may function in one harmonious order.

From the digestive system, everything is sent on to the respiratory system. From the latter, everything is sent to the brain and throughout the entire body.

In the future, all laws will be drawn from these three systems.

Every work, which you do, needs to be related to the physical, the Spiritual, and the Divine World. This work should not be purely physical, but at the same time spiritual and Divine.

The Master about Bulgaria

The Master traveled extensively throughout Bulgaria. He studied the Bulgarians for many years. Over a span of 11 years, he conducted research and took phrenological measurements.[56] *He studied the Bulgarians comprehen-sively. He was acquainted with their past and present, with their customs and character. He knew their positive sides as well as their negative. He understood the profound reasons wherefrom certain characteristics were acquired, under which conditions, and how they arose.*

Once the Master said:

The Bulgarian has three good characteristics. At first, the Thracian Bulgarians lived here: the ones who called themselves the "Blagaty people" or the "Blagary."[57] They were good. From

---

55. *Stotinka* corresponds to one hundredth of a *lev*—the basic unit of money in Bulgaria.
56. This refers to the period between 1901–1913 when the Master traveled around the country delivering lectures and performing phrenological studies.
57. *Blagati* and *Blagari* is translating as "good people."

them, the Bulgarians have received the inclination for the mystical, the spiritual. Later came the Slavs who occupied the Balkan Peninsula. From them, the Bulgarians have received the spirit of sacrifice—selflessness. Lastly came the Asparuh[58] Bulgarians. From them, they have received courage.

> *The Master understood the soul of this nation and the Divine instilled in it. He also understood the foreign elements that later infiltrated this nation. While studying the character of the Bulgarians, the Master searched for methods as to how to uplift it. He took many examples from the life of the Bulgarians—many images and types. He knew many anecdotes charactering the Bulgarians and cited them often in his lectures and conversations. Once, when we were in the mountain, a question about the Bulgarian nation was raised.*
> *The Master said:*

Until one comes to love a nation, one cannot know it. The Bulgarian government should offer a reward to the one who writes the best history on the origin of the Bulgarian nation.

You have been sent to Bulgaria. The ground here is uncultivated—raw soil with couch grass. One needs to dig half a meter in order to cultivate and seed it. If one wants to become tough and resilient, he can only learn that from the Bulgarians. He needs to live with them in order to learn steadfastness of the will.

What is the essence of the Bulgarian? He is the toughest element that exists. The Bulgarian is distinguished by his great toughness and tenacity. Every human being who comes to Earth should pass through the Bulgarians in order to attain toughness, to get the stamp for toughness. The best seed that grows is the Bulgarian. The *Bogomils* had come here to attain this quality, toughness so that they could better preach the Divine Teaching.

It is good for the Bulgarian to be tough, but to be reasonably tough; that is to say, not for the ordinary ideas. For them, he can yield. However, for the Divine, he should be prepared to make sacrifices and not be afraid—not even of death. A person who is afraid of death can achieve nothing. The

---

58. Asparuh is a seventh-century khan of the Dulo Dynasty who in 680 AD established Bulgaria as a state of the Alliance of Slavic tribes.

Bulgarian is very natural and just as well. In general, the Slav is conscientious.

The Bulgarian has many good qualities inherited from the past. For example, when he comes back from the vineyard, he carries a basket with grapes. From it he gives to the children and to everyone he meets. This basket is especially for passers-by. He does not touch the big basket that is for the house. When he picks from the vineyard or the orchard, he does not strip it completely. He leaves some fruit or grapes for the passers-by that they may pick some for themselves. That which is left is called the gleaning.

The Bulgarian has one distinctive quality: he dislikes to be given orders. Leave him alone; he will do much more for you. The Bulgarian is hospitable. When I want to visit some Bulgarian home, they ask me what to cook for me. I say, "Some beans and some onions." They wonder, "Do you not want chicken?" "No." They feast well and they ask repeatedly, "Why do you not eat this or that?" When they like you, they bring to the table the best that they have—the best watermelon, the best grapes.

When you go and speak to the people, the Bulgarian wants to know if you work for money or without money. They ask me, "Are you measuring the head for pay?" I say: without money. The Bulgarian believes a lot in the measuring of the head. He says, "This man is measuring; he is measuring the head, the hand." He is very curious, the Bulgarian.

I told one Bulgarian, "Your fortune depends on this horse of yours; do not beat him." He believes and begins to treat his horse or his oxen well, he becomes gentle with them.

In the Bulgarian, there is this feeling: he is always exaggerating. He can never speak of things as they are. He will exaggerate. This feeling is developed in him. Should a few people gather, he will say, "There was a crowd there. One could not count them."

The good side of the Bulgarian is his gratitude. When we went for an outing in the Rhodope Mountains, in the Tsigov Chark[59] in the area of the town Batak, the son put us up in the

---

59. Tsigov Char is a picturesque terrain in the Rhodope Mountains that is a contemporary resort.

sawmill. However, his father, a headstrong Bulgarian, did not even greet us. We were paying him, but he would not greet us. I said: Fine. One day while working with the saw, a wood-chip flew off and went into his eye, which then became swollen. The son came and said to us, "The eye of my father has become swollen. We must take him to Sofia." I responded, "There is no need to do that; I will help him." The father came to me and I told him, "If you go to Sofia, they will take your eye out. I can help you without your going to Sofia. You will see how fast I am able to heal you." I inverted his eyelid and took out my handkerchief. I then removed the splinter and daubed the place with ointment. I was very careful. I told him, "By tomorrow, your eye should be all right." The next day, this man was as soft as cotton. At our disposal, he put horses, bread, everything. And he told us, "We were behaving not properly." This man developed understanding. I inverted his eyelid, removed the splinter, and at once, he saw the good side. We built a fountain there.

The Bulgarian is known for his great destructive powers: he loves to destroy. When he goes through the woods with his ax, he clips here a tree, there a branch. If the Bulgarians could transform this destructive force into a creative one, they could become a great nation. The Bulgarian needs to come to an understanding of those dynamic forces that pass through him as a Bulgarian. The Bulgarians are a willful people. In them, the forehead, the nose, and the chin are equally developed. For this reason, they cannot be people of sentiments alone. The Bulgarian wants to express his love through action. He is good, intelligent. If the rulers would have only listened to the people, they would have made fewer mistakes.

Bulgarians can acclimate themselves to all places. In Bulgaria, they are tenacious, but going abroad, they become adaptable. This is a Slavic trait.

The Bulgarians have the most favorable conditions at present. The Invisible World is helping them. By their nature, they are pessimists. Within them, hope is poorly developed.

With regards to religion, one can find within the Bulgarian many false beliefs. They have not yet set themselves free of idolatry. The Bulgarians have many things in their lives that are not Divine, but human. They believe in amulets and do not work on Tuesday and Friday[60]. When a cat crosses their path, they think that they will not be successful.

The Bulgarian people are musical. One can find many people in Bulgaria with a good ear for music.

What is the hidden meaning of the word "Bulgarian"? Its origin is ancient. Its root is hidden in the remote past. By "Bulgarian," we understand this to mean someone who searches for his Teacher, then finds him and learns. This is the meaning of the word "Bulgarian" from the viewpoint of Divine Philosophy. This is to say: Bulgarians are those who search and find their Enlightened Teacher so that they may apply the Teaching and show their nations and fellowmen how to live.

Are you asking, "Am I a Bulgarian?" I say, "If you understand me, you are a Bulgarian; if you do not understand me, you are not a Bulgarian."

Two kinds of Bulgarians exist: those of the flesh and those of the spirit. Those of the flesh are many, whereas those of the spirit, few. The Bulgarians by flesh have no right to create a state; but thanks to the Bulgarians of spirit, they have received the right of statehood. A genuine Bulgarian is that one who possesses goodness, righteousness, beauty, and mindfulness. In other words, the genuine Bulgarian possesses goodness of heart, righteousness of mind, beauty of soul, and finally, awareness. The Bulgarians need to learn to rely on God alone.

What was the reason for the Bulgarians to have been under the dominance of the Ottoman Empire? This reason is hidden in the relationship of the Bulgarians to God as there was a breach in this relationship. All sufferings of the various nations come from impure thoughts, desires, and actions. The Bulgarians were under Turkish dominance for 500 years as a punishment for the *Bogomils'* persecution.

One brother requested, "Tell us something about the mission of the Bulgarians in the future."

---

60. In the past, farmers believed that working in the fields on a Tuesday or a Friday would bring bad luck.

When the time comes, they will see. It is so destined that Bulgaria will never be a big country. The Bulgarians need to be notable for something else, and not for their success in war. The rulers of Bulgaria have committed many crimes, in other lands, and in Bulgaria itself as well. These people had no wisdom. No violence, no murders and tortures should ever exist in Bulgaria. Some say, "It is impossible to be without them." This means: to kill, they can, but not to kill, they cannot! The Bulgarians need to understand that it is possible to be without violence. Does the Bulgarian nation have a future having in mind the way it lives now. Can murders bring happiness to Bulgaria? All need to come to know that an Eternal Law exists that judges all people equally.

Our diplomats are not reasonable. I call a diplomat "perfect" when he has courage, mindfulness, correct behavior, and selflessness. In Bulgaria, four diplomats need to unite— Stambolov, Stoilov, Stoyanovich, and Karavelov[61]—in order to form one diplomat.

One brother asked, "Are there any people of this kind existing in Bulgaria today?"

There are some, but they cannot be found. Let them be searched for—the same way as a farmer would search for grain in the barn to seed the field. If they are searched for, they will be found.

What is it that a Bulgarian can be proud of? That there is nobility within him. What has he contributed to the world? The Bulgarians did something for the world through the *Bogomils*.

---

61. Stefan Stambolov (1854–1895) was a Bulgarian revolutionary and politician who fought for the liberation of Bulgaria from the Ottoman Empire and served as the prime minister of Bulgaria from 1887–1894.

Konstantin Stoilov (1853–1901) was deputy to the Bulgarian National Assembly, leader of the Conservative Party and prime minister.

Ivan Stoyanovich (1862–1947) was a statesman and journalist who was one of the organizers of the Union of Eastern Rumelia with the Bulgarian Principality in 1885. Served as a deputy to the National Assembly and minister plenipotentiary in Budapest.

Petko Karavelov (1843–1903) was a statesman and leader of the Liberal Party until 1886 in the New Kingdom of Bulgaria.

What the Bulgarians have brought forth is the Principle of Freedom.

> *One brother asked, "Master, why was Bulgaria previously chosen as a center for the Bogomil movement, and now again, the movement of the Great Brotherhood of Light comes from Bulgaria?"*

It is because Bulgaria has many mountains. A mighty Divine current comes down from the Rila massif. Those who are close to this massif will naturally have good conditions for uplifting because they are under a beneficial influence.

The Bulgarians have existed in pre-historic times. A child's name can be changed three-four times, is not that so? However, the name does not change the person.

The Conscious Powers of Nature—the Brotherhood of Light—have been preparing the Bulgarians for 5,400 years for the present times. Now they are helping Bulgaria.

It is because Bulgaria is in its golden century that none can cause her harm. There is none who can take away the good and the beneficial conditions in which she finds herself. This has kept the Bulgarians safe during the present events. If these events had taken place in a different epoch, it would have been difficult for the Bulgarians to cope with them. Be thankful that God's Mercy has not abandoned you. The conditions for Bulgaria are very favorable at present. Ninety percent of the conditions are conducive so that Bulgaria could come out from this war unharmed. Only ten percent are unfavorable. The Invisible World is helping the Bulgarians to cope with the present situation. From Above comes the help for the Bulgarians.

Until now the Bulgarians have served the powers of darkness, but now they will serve the Powers of Light. Bulgaria today is like a holy land. People have brought me quinces weighing 1,000 grams each, and pears weighing 700 grams each.

The only place where the sky has changed is in Bulgaria. In the last 20–30 years, it has become like that of Italy.

The soul of the Bulgarian is like a well-fertilized field upon which all seeds grow regardless of what is sown there. It depends upon the gardener as to which kind of seeds he will plant.

If the Bulgarians want to broaden their horizon, they will need to apply the Divine Teaching. The Bulgarians are of interest to me insofar as they fulfill the Will of God, that they serve God. If they were not being helped, the Bulgarians could not save themselves. They are in such trouble that only the Divine can redeem them. All which is wise in the Bulgarians needs to be brought out.

The Bulgarians need to visit the wellsprings. The wellsprings will not come to them of their own accord. You yourselves should search for the wellspring from where the water flows.

One brother asked, "Should we understand by these words that the Bulgarians need to search for the New that has been given through the Brotherhood of Light, which is now in Bulgaria?"

I especially turn my attention to the Bulgarians to warn them that a great thrashing is awaiting them. The Whip has been prepared—not a human, but a Divine One. This Whip will be used on the backs of the Bulgarians for as long as it is needed, until their minds grow, until they submit to the Will of God and say, "We will put our minds and hearts in harmony with the great Divine Will."

If Bulgaria accepts the New Teaching, she will be given everything that is needed. If she does not accept it, nothing will be given to her. Christ preached to the Jews two thousand years ago, but they did not accept that Teaching. As one can see, two thousand years have passed and they still continue to wander the world without a homeland.[62] Do the Bulgarians think that if they do not accept the New Teaching a better future awaits them? If the Bulgarian nation does not accept the New Teaching, something terrible is in store for her. I will not say what, but you need to be warned: you will see what will come. And yet, should you accept it, you will become one of the "first nations."

---

62. In the lecture "The Divided Kingdom" held in 1918, Beinsa Douno said that Jews will be placed again in the old land, but their kingdom will be small. Israel was established in 1948.

In Russia, Tolstoy told the people to turn to God, but they did not obey. He was God's messenger, but his voice remained like a voice in a desert. After that, Russia suffered badly. Do you think that if you do not listen to me, Bulgaria will not suffer? It is my wish that the Bulgarians would be the first ones to set an example. It is important that the Bulgarian nation becomes spiritually enlightened and assumes with dignity its place among the other nations. If all accept the New Teaching, their paths will be set straight. Their families and schools will improve, and then it will be pleasant to pass through Bulgaria from one end to the other. You will be as if in the garden of Eden. You will walk, and you will rejoice that you serve God. Wherever you pass, the trees and the flowers will smile at you, the fruits will offer themselves to you. Young women and men will meet you with joy and cheer. All of them will be well-dressed and adorned.

Now I myself search for those people in Bulgaria who are of the true Culture within which I can implant something new. Among the Bulgarians, I have found sufficiently intelligent people. Bulgaria is full of young women and men who will unite for a great work. The most favorable conditions are in store for the Bulgarians. Turn to God, to His great Kingdom!

As Bulgarians, it is expected of you to be heroic. The English people excel with their honesty, the Germans, with diligence, the Slavs, with self-sacrifice. For you Bulgarians, as well, I desire that you would have self-sacrifice as your emblem. Only then will you understand the meaning of Life.

I bring favorable conditions to the Bulgarians. If I did not intercede for them with the Great, the Sublime Intelligent World, they would have become completely lost. The Invisible World wants to save them now. The present epoch has a great importance for Bulgaria. If Bulgaria does not now accept the Ideas that I offer—if she misses the favorable conditions, which are given to her—then they will disregard her, and she will not have the same conditions for uplifting for at least two thousand years at best. Under the worst conditions it will only be after fifteen thousand years, at the least.

In a short while, 4,444 Bulgarians will enter into the Sacred Fire of Love. Do you know how Bulgaria will look when they enter? After that, a Door will open, and others will enter—after them, still more. The Bulgarians who enter through this Door will gain something special. Whoever sees them will say, "This is what the true Bulgarians look like."

I tell the Bulgarians: If you listen to God, your fields will yield 10 times more than they do now. The vineyards will bear so much fruit that it will not be possible to pick it all.

It is my wish that the new human being will come to be born among the Bulgarians. This is possible because the Bulgarians have a good heart.

In Bulgaria there are many people with clairvoyance.

Originally the Jews had a republic, but later they wished to build a kingdom. They wanted a king. But the Bulgarians will act in the opposite manner. They have always had a kingdom and kings; now they will have a republic.

Rejuvenation

During conversation the Master said:

Even as an adult and an elderly person, one should preserve the child within oneself. It represents that purity which is necessary for one's health. Whatever knowledge you may acquire, try not to lose the childlike nature of your character. In comparison to the Great Divine Knowledge, your knowledge is still in its swaddling clothes.

The form of the adult is like the suit of a diver. People should abandon the diving suit. We have become adults because we are wearing the mask of our grand- and great-grand parents.

The first condition for rejuvenation is to have a connection with God. It has been said, "But those who wait on the Lord shall renew their strength."[63] This is the meaning of eternal rejuven-ation. Should a person want to rejuvenate, he

---

63. See Isaiah 40:31.

needs to have for his Love an object that does not age. The one who contemplates upon God rejuvenates.

Many have begun to age because of the lack of Love, because they do not think and feel correctly. Nothing else is left for them, but to wait for their death. However, this is not Life. This is premature death. They have aged because of the lack of Love.

I have come to rejuvenate you. Love makes life worth living and rejuvenates us. Wrongdoing brings premature old age.

Can I rejuvenate an empty, wrinkled bagpipe? When I blow air into the bagpipe, it becomes inflated. The bagpipe is rejuvenated through the air. What is air for the bagpipe, the same is thought for the human being. One can rejuvenate through one's thoughts. The sublime thought of a person creates around him a favorable atmosphere, which makes it possible for him to perceive the sublime and the beautiful in the Living Nature.

People age in an unnatural way. You desire wealth, might, power, glory, and so on, and so you age. Put away these desires, unload them from your back, and you will rejuvenate.

Selfless Service

In a conversation during a morning walk, the Master said:

Joy is full of wealth. And yet, it needs to transform itself into compassion. With joy, you take something; whereas, with compassion, you give something of yourself.

The one who is not acquainted yet with sacrifice does not understand Love.

The following Law is true regarding sacrifice: Those who sacrifice themselves remain eternally alive and growing.

Love implies two qualities: selflessness and higher intelligence.

The person of Divine Love has the greatest power and knowledge.

One Law states: Either you shall renounce yourself or you will be forced to renounce yourself. Either you will sacrifice yourself or you will be forced to make sacrifices.

Serving stands higher than learning because the one who serves has knowledge, whereas the one who learns is just now attaining knowledge.

When you receive a blessing, deposit it in the Divine Bank. If you carry it with you, you will be robbed. The astral world is filled with thieves who steal.

Do not think that when someone is good, that this has been achieved in one lifetime only. Not so. For millions of years he has been worked upon in order that he may become good and that he may cultivate within himself charity, service, humility, and other virtues. Do not think that if someone sees a compassionate person and has the desire to become like him, that this can happen all at once. Very little is achievable in one lifetime.

Many of you tell me, "I do not know what to do. Things do not go well with me." If I were in your place, I would find two beautiful earthen jugs. I would then go out where people take strolls and would treat them to water. And as you befriend these people, things will begin to work well for you.

We need to begin with the small things in the world. The one who waters a flower is able to turn to God. He has a good heart. He is a person with noble character and he is on the right course.

From my point of view, love for others should be expressed in the same way as the wellsprings, which flow in nature. When you go to a mountain area, observe how the wellsprings flow. Love for others should, like the wellspring, flow in the form of a long uninterrupted current. Wherever it runs onto a dry hard place, the water will soften it.

To love others signifies working for them. Love implies working for others.

The Little Brothers

The Master studied the plants and the animals with great love. For him, they were the living book of Nature. Sometimes he told us his remarkable and unusual ideas about them:

People cannot imagine a more intelligent world than this. This is because the Sublime Beings have participated in its Creation.

What is the difference between the walnut as a fruit and the walnut as a tree? The tree has manifested itself, whereas the walnut has not yet revealed its endowments. Such is the condition of the animals. They have not yet manifested themselves, unlike humans.

One brother asked, "What can be said about the factors of evolution?"

Some accept mainly the external factors: natural selection, the struggle for existence, and so on.

Another brother said, "According to the spiritualists, internal evolutionary factors exist as well."
The Master said:

The contradiction originates in the following: Some look only at the external manifestation of Nature, whereas others, only at the internal. When we look at both the external and internal manifestations, we will come to the correct understanding. The selection itself, which exists in Nature, is guided by the Intelligent Powers. The Intelligent Powers guide the direction of evolution. The biomechanical approach wants to explain the phenomena in a mechanical way, saying that only the external conditions, the external factors, have acted in the evolutionary process. However, Divine Science states that this process is guided by the Intelligent Powers of Nature so that internal factors exist as well.

Consciousness exists in all of the kingdoms of Nature. In the realm of the minerals, we have the lowest degree of the subconscious. When you crack a stone into pieces, within its subconscious, it experiences a certain pleasure. For the stone, this is its path for liberation.

We think that animals lack intelligence. Why are the birds of paradise so beautiful? The birds have learned the art of coloring their clothes in a natural way. They have knowledge. The butterfly also has skills. Whenever the wind blows, or it rains, the butterfly lands beneath a leaf to protect its wings from the rain or wind.

There exists an interconnection—an interaction—between humans and plants. When I enter a yard, by the look of the apple trees, I can discern about the inhabitants of this home. If the people have some shortcomings, the trees will have them as well.

If you are sensitive, you can verify the sorrow of plants in many ways. You are in good disposition, and yet in passing by a sad plant your disposition changes at once. The cause comes not from you, but from the plant or the flower that you have passed by. Look closely at it, and you will notice that it suffers from something: it may be dry, thirsty for water, or there may be another impediment in its way. Water it and your fair disposition will return.

I have said that the sorrow of the flowers is in their fragrance. However, this is in an earthly language. In reality, their fragrance is the most beautiful language of the flowers. This is how they speak.

I sit around a beehive and notice that more bees fly out, but fewer come back. This indicates that there will be a weather change, even though at the moment, the weather is good, [and the bees are in a hurry to collect and store food]. I count how many bees fly in and how many fly out within a ten-minute period and make my conclusions. The bees are good meteorologists.

The cat is an excellent barometer. When the stove is kindled and the cat turns her back to it, this means that the weather will worsen. Cold weather is coming, even though, at the moment, it is beautiful. Even by its distance from the stove, one can discern the degree of the cooling that is coming.

The spiders have also knowledge of the weather. When the weather is going to be good, the spider positions itself in the center of the web. And when it changes for the worse, he hides himself away someplace.

I have experimented with plants as well as with animals.

There are some very stubborn spiders. I look at a spider in the room that has caught a fly. I say to him "Let the fly go." The spider replies, "I have been waiting for such a long time to catch this fly, so I do not want to let it go." And so, I read the spider's thoughts. I say to him, "Let the fly go; otherwise you will fly out of the room." Some spiders, when they perceive my thought, agree. Yet others are stubborn and say, "You are not God. Who are you?" I say to them, "I am a spider like you, but much bigger."

In the town of Veliko Turnovo,[64] I made an experiment with wasps. I placed a flat cake on the wasp's nest and moved away about ten steps. They found me and began circling around me. I went and unblocked their entryway. After a while, I blocked the hole again and moved away. Again they found me. Again I unblocked the hole.

Once I met a snake on the road and said to it, "Move away from here. If other people see you, they will kill you." The snake moved away.

One time I was walking through a mountainous place where there were *Karakachani*.[65] Their whole herd dashed at me. The shepherd was afraid that the herd would follow me. I had to reassure him. I said to him, "Your sheep are very smart. They are of a good breed." The sheep told me, "How much longer are we to suffer? How much longer are they going to take away our lambs, our hides? How long are we to endure all this?" I said something to them. After that, the sheep calmed down and continued to graze meekly.

One brother asked, "What did you tell them?"
The Master was silent for a while. After that, he continued:

---

64. Veliko Turnovo: This town in the Balkan Mountains was the capital of ancient Bulgaria. During the period of 1909–1925, the annual meetings of the Master's disciples were held there.
65. *Karakachani* is a nomadic clan of the Rhodope Mountains who are known for raising Karakul sheep.

The animals perceive human thought. You can make experiments. One winter day, in the vicinity of the town of Varna, I saw a big flock, hundreds of ducks coming. I sent to them the thought to fly far out to sea, and they went. After half an hour, I said to them, "There is something good to eat on the shore. Come." And they came to the shore.

All minerals, plants, and animals are schools through which the human spirit has passed and learned. These schools we call worms, birds, mammals, and so on.

Every human being is a sacred book in which God has written many things. Do you know the history of this book? Do you remember the time when you passed through the mineral kingdom? Upon the minerals is written the names of the Evolved Beings, the Seraphim, and Cherubim. Do you remember the time when you passed through the animal kingdom? Another group's life from the Hierarchy of Angels is written there.

The New, Sixth Generation—One of Love[66]

The Master lifted the corners of the curtain and, for an instant, revealed the future that is descending from Above. For the ordinary person, this was like a fairy tale from "One Thousand and One Nights." Nevertheless, this was the real Life toward which humankind is headed.

The Master said:

Each new epoch is a creative Act of God. Modern times cannot be compared to the future that is coming. Now a nucleus of people from all nations is forming in the world. English, French, German, Russian, American, Japanese, Chinese, Bulgarian, Turk, Serb, and so on are forming a new generation, a nation with a new understanding, which is different from the

---

66. The Master explained that so far there have been five stages in human civilization. According to him, at the next stage, the new, "sixth, generation," which he called also the "people of Love," will emerge from all nations. For more information see the "Explanatory Notes."

present. Who unites these spirits? The Great Divine Law attracts them that they may come to know one another and work together. I ask: Could the Bulgarians be a contingent of such people? Yes, they can. If the Bulgarians do not send their representatives there, they will be its servants. Those nations that send their representatives to this nucleus will have their names inscribed upon this great kingdom. Those who do not, will see their names erased. The Scriptures stated thousands of years ago, "Those nations that do not serve God have no future."[67]

A glorious moment is coming for which you need to prepare. Be glad for your future and what is awaiting you.

Everywhere, in all nations, there are people present of the new epoch. You can encounter representatives of that group as an intelligent child, as a young person with a noble character, or as an elderly person.

One sister asked, "Are we going to see them?"
The Master replied:

You have seen them. It is said in the Scriptures, "All nations will come together and the Name of God will be glorified."[68] From the 12 tribes of Israel, one understands that humankind will be united. The 12 tribes are the 12 symbols of the zodiac, the 12 qualities of humankind.

People have small ideas. The Bulgarians wish for a great Bulgaria, the Serbs for a great Serbia. All wish to be great. In the Kingdom of God, all nations will be united. By the "Kingdom of God," one should understand the people of Love. They will live as brothers. All nations will be represented in one unity.

Those who do not understand the prophecies are worried about the future. Read Chapter 60 from Isaiah. This chapter is about the coming of the new epoch. In Jude 1:14–15, it is written, "Behold, the Lord comes with ten thousands of His saints, to execute judgment on all, to convict all who are ungodly among

---

67. See also Isaiah 60:12, "For the nation and kingdom which will not serve you shall perish, and those nations shall be utterly ruined."
68. See also Revelation 21:12, "Also she had a great and high wall with twelve gates, and twelve angels at the gates, and names written on them, which are the names of the twelve tribes of the children of Israel."

them of all their ungodly deeds." This is about an epoch whose beginning is now. Until now, the Good has being cultivated in the greenhouse. And yet, when the Kingdom of God comes, all flowers will leave the greenhouse; natural growing conditions will exist for them.

From the Invisible World, Advanced Beings, people of the sublime Love or the so-called forerunners of humankind, are coming. These are Workers who are coming from Above. When they find souls ready to work, they will incarnate in them and act through them.

New ideas are coming into this world. They will clash with the old ones. Why? It is because the old refuses to give up its realm. The new will reform the world radically. The old systems will be replaced with new ones. Those who accept these new ideas will be transformed. Their face will become illuminated and will take on a new expression. We are in a transitional epoch. We will all pass into the new epoch and will live in a new way. The old forms have become obsolete. The old life has no more material for work. The time has come for all people to raise their consciousness a step upward and give way to the Divine Power.

The Human Being of the New Epoch

Each distinct ethnic group of people throughout our civilization is characterized by certain qualities. Black people are notable for their imagination and strong feelings; the native peoples of the Americas—for their ability to apply geometry and mathematics. Asians are notable for their objective mind, and Caucasians—for their rationality: ever since they have been on Earth, they have been measuring and exploring things with precision.

The new human being expected to develop in the future has all the good qualities of the preceding stages. In this regard, it represents the essential synthesis of the human virtues.

While living on Earth one passes through all preceding stages of human development. As cautious as one might be, one nevertheless passes through these preceding stages and, if people are wise, they learn from this process.

The new epoch is one of Justice and of the Kingdom of God. This epoch is already coming, and then the Kingdom of God, on a small scale, will be established on Earth.

A brother asked, "Master, is not justice inferior when compared to the Kingdom of God? Because, according to the human law of justice, whoever works less earns less. Whereas, according to the higher spiritual Law, everyone must receive in compliance with their needs."
The Master replied:

The Kingdom of God—it is the same as Justice. I have in mind the Divine Justice.

The culture of the mind creates the external forms. The new, sixth, generation will impart content to these forms.

Each epoch has its own contribution. The one that follows, the epoch of Love, will offer the most. It will be represented by sublime, luminous souls. It will bring the New Culture to Earth. The ideas of the new, sixth, epoch are like the air: they already permeate all.

The Slavs will give an impulse to the new epoch. After the events happening now, the people of Love will become active in life. It will begin to take leadership. Many more representatives of the new epoch will be present on Earth than at the moment. They will give a new direction to the culture. The Slavic people will serve as the base for the engraftment of the new, sixth, generation—one of Love.

One brother asked, "Is there a possibility that representatives of the new epoch will appear in Bulgaria?"
The Master answered:

Yes, the conditions exist. For several thousand years, Bulgaria has been worked upon for this purpose.

The people of the new epoch will give order to the world. It will take up leadership in its hands. The Divine within man puts to sleep the base, the animal nature, within him. For thousands of years, the Divine has been lulling it to sleep in a manner similar to lulling a snake to sleep. The people of Love will be in charge and the rest will execute their orders. The learned ones, who will come, will put order and structure into the world. These are the people of the future.

The awakened people from all nations will form the new, sixth, generation of Love.

Slowly but surely you are advancing toward the new epoch. It is in store for you to meet with the luminous souls who love you. Do not waiver and do not doubt!

In the new epoch, each and every one will be aware that others have the same rights and privileges as he does.

It is said in the Scriptures, "If you are not born again . . . "[69] These words imply the new, sixth, epoch. The rebirth discussed in Christianity refers to the entering into the new, sixth, epoch—and repentance, conversion, and so on, are the preparation for it. Those "born again" are already of the sixth generation. Within it death will exist no more. When the time comes to depart, one will dematerialize, will become invisible. Cemeteries will no longer exist. They will exist only for the rest of the people, but not for the people of Love.

At present, four epochs exist simultaneously. This will be the case with the sixth generation too. We are only paving the way for Love, for the sixth epoch. The people of Love will be different. The mention of "the first resurrection"[70] in the Scriptures is meant for them. The Manifestation of Love in humankind is the first resurrection.

The sixth epoch brings positive beauty. The people of Love will have very proportional features: they will be beautiful. They will be inspired by the high ideal within themselves, which will make them beautiful. They will be a much more beautiful people than you have seen until now.

---

69. See also John 3:3, "Jesus answered and said to him, 'Most assuredly, I say to you, unless one is born again, he cannot see the Kingdom of God.'"
70. See Revelation 20:5, "But the rest of the dead did not live again until the thousand years were finished. This *is* the first resurrection."

The facial angle of the European is 80 degrees; in the dog it is 35 degrees. In the human being of the new, sixth, generation, it will be 90 degrees.

Rarely have I seen really beautiful people.

The brows of the people of the new epoch will be straighter. They will be curved very little, indicating that they are part of a very large Circle. The color of these people will be radiant like someone illuminated by the Sun. Light will emanate from their faces as if they were radiating. At night there will be no need for lamps. Wherever these people go, there will be light because human beings will radiate light. Their eyes will see at a distance; they will see also in the dark. When you look at a person from a distance, you do not know who he is. Yet, a member of the new, sixth, generation will see the details from far away.

We need to acquire that quality of light—selflessness—and that quality of water—suppleness. What the light has accomplished in illuminating space, you should do as well. And what the water has done in purifying things, you should do as well.

The human beings of the new epoch are already created—they exist. They have been here for thousands of years, but are kept under guard, they are hidden. They are not shown to everyone. Nature exists as a closed book. The one who knows how to open it can read from it. Many look at this closed book only from without, only at its cover.

With the coming of the new epoch, humankind will enter Paradise and will depart from error.

In the future, one will remember his past incarnations. It will be pleasing for him to remember them, but he will feel that he has departed from his old state—like the butterfly that previously had been a caterpillar.

The human being of the new epoch will be musical. When he visits people who are not well, just by singing or playing an instrument to them, the ill regain their health.

The Slavic Nation

After the air raids, we went with the Master to the mountain for a few days. There it was isolated and uninhabited. Down in the valley, the city of Sofia lay destroyed, burned down, and deserted. It was very windy, cold, and damp. Heavy clouds were moving above the mountain peaks. From time to time, the Sun was seen between the clouds. The Sun peeked through, and blessed warm rays came upon us. One could feel the freshness and vitality of the pristine life. Every color, every breath, every movement, every form was filled with this life. The mountain was a shrine. Man has lost his ability to talk to God. But even now, man can find again the lost Paradise.

We were seated around the Master on the soft fleecy rug of grass and were talking. The clouds withdrew, and the Sun shone over the meadows. A question about the Slavic nation arose.

The Master said:

The western nations have reached the height of their development. They have blossomed and have come to fruition. The Slavic people will blossom from now on and give fruit.

It is wrong to think that the Slavic nations need to dominate, to command other nations. The opposite is true; they will be the sphere in which the positive features of other nations will manifest.

The Slavic people will bring something new. They come now to create the New Culture. In a sense, they are now the spiritual Israel.

It is interesting to compare Russia and Palestine. The Caspian Sea in the Slavic region is a closed sea. There is an analogy between this sea and the Dead Sea in Palestine. The Volga flows into the Caspian Sea, and the Jordan River—into the Dead Sea. The Volga is the counterpart of the Jordan River. The Volga is a big river, and the Jordan, a small one. The Dead Sea is 25 meters under sea level, and the Caspian Sea is also under sea level. The difference is that there is no life in the Dead Sea whereas the Caspian Sea is full of life. The rivers from the Slavic region flow into the Arctic Ocean, the Black Sea, the Mediterranean Sea, and other seas. In Palestine, no river flows into an open sea. Therefore, the Slavs carry the Jewish culture to some extent, but there is also a difference.

The back of the head in the Slavs is developed. This means that they possess strong family ties and the capacity for a settled life.

The Slavs need to overcome a remaining influence from preceding stages in human civilization manifested as extreme materialism.

In general, western people have a developed intellect. In the Latin people, the feelings and heart are developed. The Slavic people now carry the power of the soul—Love. They are the people of Love for humankind. They carry the Culture of Brotherhood.

Among all the Slavic nations, Bulgaria represents the will. Therefore, it is like a central point in which the two forces—mind and love—need to become balanced.

God wants the Slavs to fulfill a mission. Through the Slavs, a sense of the new, of generosity, needs to be introduced. Generosity is a Slavic quality; no other people are as generous as the Slavs.

One of the great characteristics of the Slavic nations is self-sacrifice. In the Slavs, the spirit of sacrifice is working. Therefore, the future is in the Slavic nations. The New Culture will be born out of the Slavs. A beautiful quality of the Slavic nations is altruism. This is the Divine Cause within them. Until now, such a density of people as the Slavs, ready for the New Culture, has not existed.

The Slavic nations are the bearers of the Divine Idea. In the Slavic consciousness, there is something sublime: the Love for God.

God is passing the Slavs through Fire. There are no other people in the world who have gone through such suffering as the Slavs. God says, "From you, something good must come." It is determined that the Slavs, as one great family, need to fulfill God's Will. In this lies the greatness of their mission.

By the end of the 20th century, many Advanced Beings—the Brothers of Love and ancestors of humankind—will incarnate among the Slavic nations. They will bring a great spiritual uplifting. Yet they are not only the vanguards: they are the main forces.

The changes that are happening now in Russia are due to the actions of these Advanced Beings. These Beings who are now coming into the Slavic nations are bringing the Slavs unification and are working for their mission.

Scattered throughout different places in Russia, there are people who are working for the Divine Science. These are the Initiates, the Divine Messengers. In Russia, new forms of life for the future are developing. Russia is the creative field for these forms.

It is interesting that America and Russia are connected in the north. This means that they will come to an understanding through the Truth, that is to say: by being free.

England and Russia can have agreement in the name of Divine Justice.

The Slavic nations are a living tree onto which England, Germany, America, and France will be grafted. They are the four teachers of the Slavic nations. And the new, sixth, generation will be the fruit of this grafted tree. This fruit will combine all the positive features of these nations.

In the Russians, the nose is childlike, but it is blessed. It is written, "Assuredly, I say to you, unless you are converted and become as little children, you will by no means enter the Kingdom of Heaven."[71]

The Slavic people have already passed through their period of terrible frost and are now rising. Russia and the Slavic nations are now out of the cold black zone, out of the dark age. The Slavic nations now have the potential to take their place in the world.

Bulgarians are the pioneers among the Slavs.

The Latin people have given the forms, and the Slavic people will give the content.

We call the Slavs the "sunny people." Some call them coarse. The coarseness comes from the Sun because within the Sun's energy, there is abundant light and warmth. From this energy the animals and the plants are alive.

---

71. See footnote 12.

The Asian, the Eastern nations, have great confidence in the Slavic nations. The Slavs will introduce into these nations what they need: the Divine Order.

The Slavs will be united; they will be the bridge between Europe and Asia. All Slavic people need to unite into one. After the unification of the Slavs, the whole world will unite. The future people of Love will unite all.

The Slavs will introduce a spiritual element into the world—that we may become as brothers. Their mission is the unification of all nations.

The New Order

A New Order is coming into the world. When you return to the Earth after several thousand years, you will verify what I am telling you now. The houses will not be constructed as they are now, but will be built several kilometers away from one another. The animals will be given rest from the people. To the artists, musicians, and other people of the arts the best conditions for work will exist. This will be accomplished by the new, sixth generation.

The inner wealth, the knowledge that a person possesses, will be available to all. Now you are provided with air, light, and water. One day the bread also will be given to you like the air, the water, and the light. In the new epoch, people will have bread in abundance. Everyone will have a home, a garden, and fruit trees. When you pass through a place that is new to you, you will be asked from all sides to come in for a visit.

In the New Order, everything old will disappear, and all things will be completely new. The fruits—pears, apples, plums, and so on—will change; they will be different. At the present time, the lemon tree blossoms and its fruit ripens throughout the whole year. In the future, this will be the same with the apples.

The culture will be smokeless. Everything will be done by electricity.

What we desire exists. There are Beings who have this—they live this. The Angels live in such a Culture, the kind in which we will live after thousands of years. After thousands of years, we will live in the Angelic Culture. Everything in the world is real. Everything exists already, but it descends from above. The Angelic Culture descends to the human culture, and the human culture descends to that of the animals, and so on. Thus, a culture descends from above.

Someone may say, "When we are perfect, what will we do?" We will then begin to truly live.

The Path of the Strong Ones

The great Divine Life surrounds and penetrates us from all sides. The Master knew how, with simple words, to remind us of this Life, and to reveal its presence. Only when one has the Divine as an example, can he choose the right direction in life. Then he correctly solves his assignments; otherwise, he walks in darkness and always encounters obstacles in his path.

The Master explained:

When someone offends you, he gives you an unpolished diamond. You will polish it. When someone insults you, how will you forgive him? It is sufficient to remember God in order to forgive him. The human being needs to study for thousands of years until he learns how to forgive. The one who is insulting you is testing your love. If it is strong, you will remain calm. When someone does you wrong, you should forgive. This is the Law of Mercy.

Another Law says: If you forgive, you will gain your freedom; otherwise the chains of karma will bind you. When someone does some mischief to you, and you wish him some harm, you create karma that you will need to pay off. Unless you reconcile with people, you cannot enter the Kingdom of God. In this world and in the World beyond, you will be tormented by him whom you do not love. He will be the servant who will torment you. You say, "I am ready to give everything to be released of this burden." No, you will be released from him only when you begin to love that person.

You should forgive people because all souls come from God. If you do not forgive, you will break your connection with God and with God's blessing, which is coming from Him to you.

You say, "I would like to go to God." Do you know how to go there? Where He is, the heat is a few million degrees. How could you endure this? It would be enough to look at Him for only one moment for you to melt. Before you go to God, meet with the one who has insulted you and say, "Thank you for the nice words you have said to me. I will never forget you." Offer your hand and forget the whole offense. If you decide to go to God and tell Him how you have been insulted, nothing will remain of you.

When you quarrel with someone, you lose the light of your faith, your hope darkens. When you quarrel with all people, the luminous forces within you stop functioning, and you remain in darkness. You say, "What do I need to do?" Reconcile with people. When malice comes and does you wrong, do not resist it, replace it with good. But if instead you start a fight with evil, you will always be beaten.

There is no weapon in the world that can withstand the Power of Love. Do not oppose evil with evil, but with the Power of Love. One sister was in disharmony with another. I said to her, "Read and contemplate on page 101 of the book 'The Royal Path of the Soul' (*Tsarskiyat pat na dushata*).[72] On this page, it is written that one should pierce his enemy with the sword of Love."

To love your enemy, this is heroism. How will you love him? Imagine that someone does the greatest wrong to you. One day God takes all his wealth and makes him the poorest person. As a beggar, he comes to your home to ask for alms. If you receive him well, if you give him food and drink and do not say any word about the wrongdoing he has done to you, then you love your enemy. Let's say that you have spoken badly about

---

72. The Royal Path of the Soul is a collection of talks given by Beinsa Douno during the summer of 1935 at the Seven Lakes of the Rila Mountains. Published in 1935, Sofia.

some people. How will you correct this offense? You should do some favor for them. Only those who are strong can forgive. This Teaching is not for the weak and faint-hearted but for the strong ones.

To love those who love you, this is natural. The mother loves her child, and the child loves her. To love your enemy, only a few can achieve this.

A powerful Joy is the one that absorbs sorrow; strong Love is the one that absorbs hatred. If your love cannot dissolve hatred, what kind of love is it? If the good in you cannot dissolve the malice, what good is it?

A wise man is the one who can replace hatred with Love. If your mother-in-law is not of good character, try to educate and teach her. Be her professor. She has been given to you as an assignment. You will teach her. You will put her in a fire of thirty-five million degrees to melt without being burned. After she passes through the fire, from having been your enemy, she will become your friend. This means that a powerful fire is necessary for all. You complain about your husband; put him in this fire to melt and be purified.

To love your enemy is not a sign of weakness; through the Power of Love, the enemy will become disheartened and will surrender. When someone treats you in an unfriendly way, you should treat him well. Then his state will be transformed: the good in him will conquer the negative, and he will change. If someone receives you coldly, pray for that person when you leave. He will then realize, "I gave a cold reception to this person, but I should better change my attitude. Next time I will give him a cordial welcome."

The Scripture says, "When someone's path is pleasing to God, He reconciles him with his enemies."[73] When someone is offended in your presence, tell the offended one, "Do not be angry with him. The faults of other people are our faults as well."

---

73. See also Luke 6:35–36, "But love your enemies, do good, and lend, hoping for nothing in return; and your reward will be great, and you will be sons of the Most High. For He is kind to the unthankful and evil. Therefore be merciful, just as your Father also is merciful."

Everyone who reconciles without Love commits a crime. If someone owes you 10,000 leva, think, "Could I, in the Name of Love, forgive this person's debt and forget about it?" If you would like to forgive him, take the promissory note and put it into the fire to burn. Do this experiment without hesitation.

Some people would like to enter the Kingdom of God without experiments. This is impossible. You will pass through the Fire and will burn all your promissory notes—that is to say, all misunderstandings, all grievances and insults—and you will emerge from the Fire purified.

The New Agriculture

The small farm was harvesting the fruits of its labor. The threshing-floor was readied in front of the house. All of the brothers and sisters were participating in this. After the harvest was winnowed and sorted, the wheat berries were stored in the granary.

After the last threshing, we gathered around the Master in the yard, and he told us:

Without harmony, nothing can be accomplished. Why does deprivation exist in so many nations? It is because harmony is lacking. Hatred, oppression, and envy are three of the many things that cause deprivation and disease.

One virtue exists that is capable of uplifting the Bulgarian people. I could give you a method for cultivation that would make the Earth bountiful and produce more wheat than it ever has before. But for this, a noble heart and a mind that is enlightened, and not wicked, are required. People need to be good and honest.

If I cultivate one decare[74] of land according to the new method and someone else cultivates 10 decares according to the old methods, I will have a harvest that is as large, if not larger, for those with the 10 decares.

---

74. Decare is a a metric unit of area equal to 10 ares or 0.2471 acre.

Methods for saving time and energy exist which you are able to make use of in special cases. However, these methods are not yet known to you. Because they are still unknown, you will say, "It is God's Will." This is not correct. You have digressed from your natural path of development, and the consequences of your errors are that your existence has become so difficult that you cannot rest.

What is the new method? Love. I have given some of the brothers specific suggestions as to how they might work by the new method, and they have obtained wonderful results.

One sister commented, "A brother asked you if there was a way to increase the harvest and if it were possible to support his family with 10 decares of land. You gave him the methods, and he was able to provide for his family with his 10 decares."

The Master continued:

Some will say, "These methods cannot be implemented, you speak of an ideal." Not so. One can test these methods even now. The new method is already in use. It can be implemented even today.

One significant economic question arises: Should all the hills around the villages be reforested with fruit trees so that no place remains bare? Plant fruit trees: pear, apple, plum, walnut, and so on. In addition to this, line each side of every road not with just decorative trees, but with fruit trees. Then in a short while, Bulgaria will become a paradise, with an abundance of fruit. Bulgaria will then have sufficient food because fruit provides all of the significant nutrients.

This is the direction we should work upon with determination. The desire to plant everywhere fruit threes suitable to the specific climate and soil needs to permeate the entire Bulgarian nation. We should also consider what kinds of fruit trees grow best at which elevation above sea level.

A Letter from the Master

The letter from the Master, which follows, was addressed to all brothers and sisters. We do not know exactly when it was written: it only has become known to us now. This letter is for all spiritual students in all times:

The Universal Teacher—the One who called forth a new existence from out of the old—said, "Therefore you shall be perfect, just as your Father in Heaven is perfect."[75] In which ways should one be perfect? In Love, Life, Justice, Wisdom, and Truth. Truth is the way in which Love manifests in life. Can this Truth be verified in practice? Do you know the dimensions of this all-encompassing Love of the God of all gods—of the Master of all masters and the Teacher of all teachers—who has pronounced 70 times 7 that we need to forgive the brother, the friend, and the spiritual student who turns to ask for forgiveness?

In the same way that Love has been your companion in the past, it continues to be with you now as well. Is it possible for Love to change and become different? No.

Woe to the wealthy who are not rich! Woe to the impoverished who are not poor! The Law of the Great Brotherhood of Light and of the Great Divine School is to be rich in the Divine and to be poor in worldliness.

Love without an External Stimulus

At the end of the summer, we went with the Master to the Mount Vitosha where we spent a few days. We made ourselves comfortable in the small mountain hostel under the peak Ostritsa. In the early morning, we climbed the peak where we greeted the Sun, offered our morning prayer, and did exercises. A new day was beginning, a day unexpressed until now and unique as the Word of the Eternal.

On the mountain, the Master was finishing his work. Down in the valley the war was devastating the world with fire, but here peace and light had not left the Earth. While humankind was recklessly breaking its relations

---

75. See footnote 6.

with God's Intelligent World, the Master preserved the sacred link that can save humankind: the relationship with God.

As he talked to us, gathered on the mountain around him, he spoke to humankind—the contemporary one and the one of the future. His deep and penetrating vision perceived the tragedy of contemporary people and his hand showed the path of salvation. For that purpose, he came to the Earth in these times.

The World of Love is the true, the real, and the great World. The Master came for it. He was living in it. He was speaking about it in the earthly language of a small nation. Love was already approaching the Earth. The Master revealed its Laws to us, its richness and power, its unity and universality. The Master could foresee the future—the Great Conscious Life, the Life of Love, toward which humankind approaches according to the ordinances of the Eternal Divine Law.

The Master said:

If you want to free yourself from the old, accept Love. In order to keep Love within yourself, guard the sacred rule: Love without expecting to be loved. In this respect, be like God: He loves without expecting to be loved.

There is nothing greater for the human soul than the aspiration to love every living being of God's Creation. Love, as the Sun loves. When the Sun rises, it sends forth light to all living beings—ugly and beautiful, small and great.

The true human being never regrets that he has loved. He loves without being concerned if he is loved or not. This is Love without an external stimulus. Do not think that when you love someone, he is indebted to you.

You say, "Nobody loves me." This is not your concern. Do not expect people to love you. Your first thing is to love people; if people love you, this is their own concern. You do not have the right to have an oar in every man's boat.

Divine Love always gives and never thinks of receiving. Love is like a wellspring that flows continuously.

One of the rules of Love states: Guard the freedom of others as you guard your own. Someone impedes the freedom of others and limits them. Why? It is because he is outside of Love.

You tell someone, "You do not love me." Leave him alone and do not interfere with his love. He is free to love you or not. The only thing that no one can take away from you is what you manifest by yourself. Nevertheless, you come to the opposite conclusion and say, "The others must love me." You say, "I love someone but that person does not love me." Why are you concerned with whether that person loves you? You cannot demand that others love you. This is not your right. If you love someone, nobody can interfere with your love. This is God who is manifesting through you. Nobody has the right to interfere with God's Affairs. Do not call upon God to account for how much He has given to whom.

If you were in harmony with the Great Law of Love, you would not worry if others love you or not. If you are not in harmony with this Law, even when you are loved you will still live with inner anxiety.

It has been said, "Do not judge."[76] You judge people for not having the love toward you that you desire.

The one who has Divine Love gives without expectation. You should enjoy the Love you have within yourself and do not look for it in the external. Love is as such: you give without thinking about it, and you do not ask to be honored or rewarded for this.

You possess a true moral when you do not change your attitude toward a friend who has fallen out of love with you. You need to know that man is a collective being and is therefore not always responsible for his actions and feelings. Human actions are both collective and individual.

Do not demand that people love you because Love is the freest act in Nature. It manifests without restraint.

As long as a teacher wants his students to love him, he appears foolish to them because he wants something for himself. But when he loves his students and wishes them well, they will begin to love him.

Someone says, "I want people to love me." If you have made such a choice, you will meet great contradictions in your life. If you demand to be loved, you will suffer.

You say, "I love no one anymore because no one loves me." In this case, you are a merchant.

---

76. See also Luke 6:37, "Judge not, and you shall not be judged. Condemn not, and you shall not be condemned. Forgive, and you will be forgiven."

You meet someone and ask him if he loves you. If he loves you, there are reasons; if he does not love you, there are also reasons. Thus, when he loves you, be happy; and when he does not love you, still be happy. Do you know how difficult that is?

Measures within Nature

For eleven years, the Master had conducted a phrenological study of the Bulgarian people. He spoke little of the results of his research. Once when we were hiking in the mountain, one of the brothers asked the Master about the measures and the correlations with the human body and about his study of the Bulgarian people.
The Master explained:

Phrenological studies present a difficulty as there are people with low vibrations. When the head of such individuals is measured, those who make the measurements should take the time to purify themselves afterward.

Some years ago, I went to a high school and asked the teachers to bring me 10, 15, or 20 students. I told the teachers, "You may choose the students and I will tell you what each student will become and what their capabilities are." Regarding one student, I told them, "This student is not inclined toward mathematics; he received a low score of two."[77] Regarding another student, I said that he received a three; and regarding still another, a four; and another, a six. The teachers asked me, "How did you know these things?"

After that, I measured the heads of the teachers and their wives. I told one of the teachers who doubted the measurements, "You are in need of convincing. I will tell you what will happen to you in one month." What I told him came to pass.

---

77. Grades in the Bulgarian school system: two, three, four, five, and six. Two is the lowest score; six is the highest.

After staying for three or four days, I traveled to another place. I met a man who was ill. I measured his head and told him what he needed to do.

I made measurements of the Bulgarian people in order to determine their characteristics as expressed in the physical plane: whether or not a future exists for them and what they will become. I was interested in knowing what God had imparted to the Bulgarian people. I was looking for those precious things that God had instilled in them. A method exists for determining a person's character: When you meet someone who has bad thoughts, these negative thoughts will influence you and you will begin to be like that person. Conversely, when you meet a person having good thoughts, you will likewise begin to be like this one.

People will live according to the way in which their human bodies are structured. The entire history of humankind is contained within the cranial bones. In the future, history will be learned by the study of people's crania. When the upper part of the head is wide, the conscience is well developed. If the head is narrow in the front and in the back, the conscience is not well developed. When the upper part of the head is wide, this person would do well to be a cashier.

Light emanates from those centers of the brain that are developed. For instance: if the center of conscience is well-developed, a pleasant white light will emanate from there. If spirituality is developed—that is to say, the Love for God—then from the center of this feeling, which is situated in the upper part of the head, light emanates.

The heads of criminals are very wide around the ears. The right cranial proportions are breached. The head of the wolf is wide around the ears. Sheep do not have such a head: they are peaceful.

If I were to give my data to people—the whole truth regarding the determination of character, and they were to attempt to read a person's existence from the head, face, hands, and so on—then they would only look for the negative characteristics in one another.

For me, a person is like the seed of a beautiful apple. When it is sown, it will give fruit. Each person is interesting in his own way.

A portrait of a politician was shown to the Master. He said:

Here, the distance from the ear to the bone of the nose is short, and from the ear to the back part of the head is too large. This shows that he is a materialist and that he is only now beginning to work in the field of science.

The intelligence and capabilities of a person can be determined by the measurements of the forehead, nose, and chin. The correspondence between the width and height of the chin gives measurements through which human intelligence can be discerned. If the forehead is high and narrow, intelligence is limited. If the chin is low and wide, such a person has breadth but not depth.

The chin is the realm of the soul. The chin is small because the soul is far away. The nose and the cheekbones express the life of the heart, and the forehead expresses the world of the mind. A person's will is expressed through the chin. If the chin has a cleft, if the chin is dipped between its point and the mouth, this indicates loyalty, friendship, and devotion. If the strength of a person starts to diminish, the chin will diminish as well, and the thumb will become shorter.

Only those who are intelligent, honest, and good can transform their body: that is to say, improve their forehead, nose, and chin. The least improvement in the emotions is capable of improving your nose. The least improvement in the will can mold the chin, and the right thoughts will bring improvement to the forehead.

The lower part of the forehead represents the objective world, whereas the upper part, the subjective.

The forehead is divided into three parts: the lower part is the world of information, the middle is the world of laws, and the upper is the world of cause and effect. The lower part of the forehead perceives the facts; the middle catalogs them; and the upper organizes and properly disseminates them.

All of the sciences of measurement: phrenology, physiognomy, and others as well have been distorted. Everything has been used for the material affairs alone. At present, only the defects of people are being studied. We need to begin to deal with the real Science. It is necessary to determine the norms for the nose, the mouth, the eyebrows, and so on. If they correspond to the norms, then they have the right normal structure. The entire body should have the right proportions.

The length of the nose shows intelligence, the width, the intensity of emotions. A wide nose shows warmth, and a long nose, lightness. This is known by only a few artists.

The wider the nostrils are the more active is the person. The largest width of a nose is four cm. Such people will be distinguished by a tremendous emotional activity. Whatever the work they begin, they will finish.

The upper lip is active, and the low, passive. The lips need to be equally wide. Should the upper lip be wider, a person will give more and receive less and vice versa. People whose lips are thick are slow moving. If the lips are particularly thin, this too is not good. If you have a child whose lips are thick, you need to know how to educate him or her in such a way as to influence their energy. If someone's emotions are over-active, that person's lips will thicken.

The life of an individual can be determined from observing the ears. As a person develops, the ears will move further back and the distance between the nose and ears will increase.

Those who are not inclined to mathematics will not possess receptivity and their center for mathematics will be poorly developed. In some, the memory capacity is poorly developed. The center for the memory is in the middle of the forehead. Few people have a well-developed memory capacity.

Should someone have thin eyebrows, this softens the person's character, but weakens his will. If the eyebrows are very thick, then the willpower is strong: that person is very observant, but at the same time, coarse. Judiciousness exists in those who are observant. People with thin eyebrows have much sensitivity and intuition but less judiciousness. The eyebrows of an honest person have a definitive number of hairs. Those who are not honest are missing a certain number of hairs. The specific number of the hairs for the eyebrows is determined by the Invisible World.

Those whose hair is long are magnetic: they possess much energy. And conversely, people with hair loss are not magnetic: they have a tendency to be hot-tempered. The hair is a conductor of good feelings. The reason for hair loss does not come out of a single lifetime but over many generations. The hair of an intelligent person is soft and fine. When the hair is coarse this indicates that this person has lived in a coarse and undermining environment. When the hair is soft, this indicates that the person has lived in an environment that is favorable to his development.

The hair of the eyebrows relates to the Laws of the Divine and the Angelic Worlds. The hair of the head relates to the Whole of Creation. Each hair represents a great natural Law. Hairs operate as antennae.

In the future, the human face will be more beautiful. Modern people have an ideal in mind, but it is difficult to find a perfect image for the human face at the present. Some people have rectangular faces. People such as these are very active. An elongated face expresses a creative nature. Emotions are predominant in those with a rounded face. When the face is very wide with big cheekbones, these people are very conservative. The cheekbones of many people today are abnormal. It is necessary to take into account the proportions as well, that is to say, what the relationship is between the nose, the ears, the entire face, and so on.

A person's character is determined not so much by the lines of the face, which are static, as it is by those lines that are dynamic.

The curved lines, which are present in the ideal human being, approximate straight lines because they have a large radius. People who have many curved lines study things objectively, from up close. One who is bent on destruction will have a face that is densely covered with hair. That person will also have a receding chin. Their nose will be shorter than most; their forehead and their ears will be smaller. These are indications of degradation. Every negative thought and every negative emotion are imprinted in the face; it will gradually become coarse and distorted until it completely loses all human expression. This happens not only with individuals but with entire societies and nations.

Do not attempt to ruin a beautiful Divine Thought!

The nose, the ears, the eyes, and so on are alive. We should not treat them roughly or harshly, but gently and delicately. What God has created is magnificent.

The upper part of the hand, the part covered with hair, represents the masculine principle. The lower, the smooth part, represents the feminine principle. Lines cover the upper segment of each finger, underneath the skin. These are concentric in some fingers, in others, spiral-like. In the latter, the influence is more beneficial.

When we shake hands, we place the thumb over the other's hand. This indicates that we are telling the person with whom we shake hands to walk in harmony with the Divine Life.

You have feet, but you do not know how to walk. Do you understand the significance of the way you walk? A person can determine how you will act throughout the day just by the way you walk out the door.

A sister asked, "Are there certain indications by which a bad person can be distinguished from a good one?
The Master replied:

Yes. There are people who emit certain unpleasant emana-tions. The ideal human being should possess male and female characteristics. When curved lines predominate in the face, the face is feminine. When straight lines predominate, the face is masculine. In the ideal human being, there is a balanced combination of curved and straight lines. When you complete your studies of all the sciences in the human and Angelic worlds, you may then enroll in the First Grade of the Divine School. Some think that they know much. And yet, how much is it that they actually know?

Ideas about Music

The Master told us:

Anyone who aspires to sing should have a luminous mind and a flexible will. Music exists that is suffused with light and warmth: it is known as the "music of the emotions." In reality this is not music of the emotions but the Music of Love. However, the real Music of Love has not yet been given to humankind. Contemporary music is not the Music of Love: it is the music of the emotions.

There is music that travels with a buffalo-wagon; another, with a horse-wagon. And then there is the Music that travels on its own. I like this Music best.

Music and poetry need to work together, hand in hand, and philosophy to follow. Music will provide the vanguard, poetry will provide the form, and philosophy will provide the impulse for them. When one sings or plays an instrument, one should impart form, substance, and inspiration to the music—which is to say, meaning.

Music appears in three worlds: the ideal, the real, and the physical. In the ideal World, music is without discord; in the real world, only one discord exists; and in the physical world, fifty.

Every tone has a specific wave with its amplitude. The waves of the tone "*fa*" [F] have a circular form. They overlap and close.

Every tone can be beautiful when it is suffused with light, warmth, and power. The mind receives the light of the tones; the heart receives the warmth; and the soul, the power. Some music carries predominantly light; other kinds of music, warmth; still others, power. Some people are inspired by the beauty of a tone; others by the warmth; and still others by the power it carries. These are the three fundamental qualities of music. When the combinations and permutations are added, these become seven.

In the old music, the aim was toward softness. And yet, music that becomes too soft loses its power, and such music becomes effusively sentimental. If, however, the harmony dominates, then the music will sound harsh.

There are more than three hundred octaves. For example, the tone "*do*" [C] is repeated more than 3,000 times. The highest octaves only exist in the Sublime Worlds; the human ear cannot hear them yet.

The new epoch of Love that is coming will give a new impulse to music. Consider a person who is inclined to do something wrong. And yet, by listening to this new music, this inclination is relinquished. Music awakens the Divine within people, and they will heed its call.

It is not the intensity of the sound that gives significance to music, but beauty and softness. Within the beauty and softness of music, great power exists. Those who sing loudly will attract inferior beings to themselves. However, those who sing softly and gently will attract beings who are more sublime.

The Gospel of Music is Love.

A violinist who has given many concerts may have experienced material success. And yet, the most important concert of his life will be the one that can dissolve someone's despair or can awaken in those who listen to his music the desire to become good and noble, to love their fellowmen, and to have love for God.

Music awakens the center for reason in man, the aspiration toward the beautiful and sublime in the world, develops the center of rhythm, and so on.

If a musician would work more from the mind, then when you listen to his music every candle within you would be kindled. Should his music come from the heart, then you would feel warmth within. Should it come from the will, then the power of his music would give you the impulse to progress.

Within every tone, three "angels" can be heard: one of the will, one of the heart, and one of the mind.

The soprano brings light from above; the bass brings warmth from below. Should you perform as a bass, then the emotions will participate more. The tenor brings the power of the will, and the alto, the adornment. The bass is included to provide the foundation. The soprano brings beauty. The soprano, more than anyone else, represents Divine Beauty; all the others are arranged around it for adornment.

The playfulness of modern music is needed to bring about health. Health is the result of Divine Harmony in Nature.

Tempo in music may be understood by the following: adagio is like a ripe grain of wheat—its movement is slow; allegro may be compared to the movement of the horses when they flail the wheat.

If you pluck one and the same tone on the violin—first with one finger, then with a second, and finally, a third, there will be a difference. The tones will not be the same.

Musicians experience different levels to their inspiration. The mind of a musician, and the solar plexus, as well, should participate in the creative process. At times, the mind alone participates; at other times, only the solar plexus. In the latter case, clarity is lacking.

In order for the voice to be transmitted afar, it must first be transmitted to the etheric, and then into the atmosphere.

Should a violinist desire to play well, he needs to instill his spirit into the instrument. He should interpret the music as he plays, that he may make his music understandable to his audience. And for this reason, the violinist needs to think when he plays.

Musicians receive guidance from Above.

All musicians feel disturbed when they perform. They are impeded by the idea that they might not be well-received. Musicians should be given total freedom of expression when they perform so that they may develop a rapport with the audience. What will help a person sing well during performance? One should love one's audience. Musicians should be able to feel in their hearts the soul of the people.

A fundamental rhythm exists, a rhythm that is common to all of humankind. And yet, particular nuances for each culture exist within this rhythm.

In some of the songs today, the lyrics do not correspond to the melody. For example, one verse might be in ascension; whereas the melody might be in descension, and vice versa. It is better when right correspondence exists between the lyrics and the melody. Whenever a gifted musician plays, the Divine within the music is spread throughout the Earth for the good of all.

When the Angels play their Music, the trees blossom. The entire plant kingdom is created through Music.

Wherever flowers are in bloom, if you have a perceptive ear, you will hear music. Wherever the Angels sing or play, the trees grow. The buds of their branches blossom with leaves unfurled and give forth fruit. Music becomes a physical manifestation: the fruit is the end result of the Angelic Music.

Should a violinist or singer perform for the fruit trees or the wheat in the fields, the fruit trees would mature as would the stalks of wheat and more fruit and grain would be given forth. One can conduct experiments in this direction. In order to tell if someone is a good musician, we will ask that person to play, and then observe whether or not the flowers blossom.

Music, when combined with movement, is able to transform a person's state with ease.

When one speaks, it should be musically, not in a monotone. I understand this to mean that when a person speaks aloud, this should sound like music.

Whenever a musician plays, thousands of Beings from the Invisible World participate. The musician of genius is a product of collective effort. Those who play or sing with Love connect with the musical Beings who surround and inspire them.

To sing without inspiration is mechanical. When, however, you sing or play out of inspiration, you connect with musicians from the Spiritual world. Then your work will progress. When you do not feel inspired—this is because you are not connected with these musicians, and your work will not progress.

When a prominent musician comes into the world, the inclination for music increases.

The stage fright, which comes over great musicians before a concert, is a sign that musical Beings of genius from the Invisible World are participating. This can be compared to the wealthy man who guards his jewels for fear that they might be taken away from him.

The music of Paganini is a breath of fresh air—joyful. He had lived under limiting conditions, and yet he composed joyful, refreshing music through which he set himself free. Thus, we feel something innocent and childlike in his music. The art of replication was strongly developed in him.

Beethoven, as well, struggled to achieve freedom of expression—to free his spirit. Therefore, the themes of struggle and freedom are found throughout his music. Through his music, Beethoven tells us, "The music that has set me free, will set you free as well." The Invisible World needed to put Beethoven under adverse conditions that he might compose and seek the Truth; otherwise, he might not have composed what he gave to humankind. There are places in his music which demonstrate that he had come to know the Love of God and had received insight into the World of Great Reality.

Mozart is a Venus type. His music is joyous.

The music of Chopin gives expression to the great trials through which the Polish people are going to pass.

One sister inquired: "Master, how is music best applied in education?

Education should first begin with music, it will provide the impulse for sublime ideas and sublime desires. People today need to make use of music as an educational tool. Children should learn songs primarily about nature and, first of all, about the fruit trees: cherry, apple, pear, and so on.

The Good

During the morning walk, the Master said:

Those who do good works are connected with the Sublime Beings.

If someone does good works, but says, "I did this because I am a good person," that is incorrect. Instead, that person should think within, "God did the good through me." You should do good for God and not for those things that people might say about you. You should do good without expecting anything in return for yourself.

We are good only because the Divine that dwells within us is good.

When you do good, you should not do it as a personal favor, out of partiality, but with the understanding that you do it for the whole, for God. Rid yourselves of all partiality.

Someone tells me that he does not know how to behave properly. So, when not being well-received, he says, "They should not be acting in such a way toward me." I tell him, "Act in the manner in which you would like others to act toward you, and you will be well-received."

Evil operates in the fractional, whereas Good, in the soul. As expressed in other words: evil was born out of our separation from God. God has enervated evil from the moment of its conception. Evil is barren; it does not give any fruit.

When the Wrath of God is mentioned, in reality, this refers to the following: In his separation, man has put up a wall between himself and God, and therefore he is not able to receive God's blessing. In his error, man has created a dark cloud, an obstruction between himself and God.

The good that you do is like sowing a field. Sow that you may reap. When you take the wheat grain out from the granary, scatter it over the field. It will not be forgotten. It will produce and will fill your granary once again. In this world, God does not allow the least good to go unblessed.

You cannot bring anything with you from this world to the World beyond except for the good you have done. The good that you have done will return to you. Remember: in helping others, you also help yourself.

If you have been to the wellspring and give a cup of water to one person, and then to a second one, and to a third, and so on, you should not speak of what you have done, but are content that you have shared these bounties.

Some will ask, "Where will this lead us?" If you water a fruit tree, it will give fruit, will it not? This is the Divine Order, and within this Order, the whole of Life is arranged. That is to say, there is nothing for you to arrange. You only need to fulfill God's Will.

One brother asked, "How can one do good selflessly, without expectation of reward or blessing?

When you do good selflessly without expectation of reward, the reward will come nonetheless.

After any good you do, the Divine World will increase your credit. Those Above who love you are helping you because you are moving in the right direction.

Strive to walk on the Path of Mindfulness, the Path of the Good, of Love so that you may have the support of the Enlightened Beings. For the least good one does, one receives the support of these Beings.

What is the difference between good and evil? With the good, one always gains; whereas with evil, one always loses. You have done some good for someone—this is as if you had deposited capital in the bank. You have said a good word—the same. You have said a bad word—for this you will pay a fine in accordance with the Law.

When you do good, you become more free. With every error, you limit yourself. Originally, you had been free. Originally, all people had been free; but when they erred, they limited themselves. Now they need to do good in order to free themselves.

Whenever good is done for you, you need to pay interest for this good, regardless that it has been done for free. Once a great artist was teaching a poor girl, who was gifted, and he often played for her as well. The girl told him, "Let me be the one to carry your violin." And so, we need to carry the violin that produces the sublime tones to which we listen.

The Good is only born out of suffering. From out of the suffering of this world, the Great Divine Good is born. Why does suffering exist? That the Good may be born.

Each day you should do at least one small good deed. A system exists that determines how much good you need to do each day and how many people you need to help. Should you not fulfill its requirements, empty spaces will appear in your life. As spiritual students, the least effort is required in order for you to do good. It might take you a minute, or only a second, but your future will depend on this. Should you fail to spend not even one moment each day to do some good out of Love, this will demonstrate that you are not able to apply the Law of Love.

Conduct an experiment in the field of Love beginning with the least, the smallest amount of good. And first try to do this for one whom you do not love.

To save an ant that is drowning, this is an act of heroism. Why? Because you are fulfilling God's Will. God takes care of even the smallest of beings. Do for some person what no one has ever done for him.

Co-Workers with God

The days came for the meeting of all the brothers and sisters. Despite the difficult conditions, people arrived from all over the country. The house was filled with people. Many of the guests accommodated themselves in the garden.

It was a time of great suffering and trials. People were killing each other according to plan—methodically, "scientifically." The uncertainty of life was overwhelming everyone. Only here in this brotherly environment could joy shine, peace reign, and creative activities exist. Here one could relax and feel that he was in a refuge.

In reality, it was Love that was creating the miracle. But it was necessary for us to possess Knowledge of its Laws, rules, and methods of their application. All this Knowledge was given by the Master in his lectures and talks.

Early in the morning we came together for our prayers, and after that, the Master gave a lecture. Throughout the entire day, he accepted guests and conversed with them. From time to time, he went out under the big walnut tree and then, with all of us gathered around him, a conversation began:

First the mother serves her children, and when they grow up, the children need to help their mother. When someone wants to plow the field, does he wait for the field to come to him? No, he goes out to it. When someone wants to take water from the wellspring, does he wait for the wellspring to come to him? No, he goes to the wellspring. This means that we should not wait for

God to do everything for us, but that we as well need to work. The human being can live in one way alone: by serving God. We want to serve God because we have received everything from Him. We have had His Trust, and He has given all of us His blessing throughout the centuries. And if we do not want to serve Him, where is our righteousness? When I say that we need to fulfill God's Will, I am implying that we are employed to serve others as cashiers in the Divine Bank because all that we have is from God.

We have come to the Earth to see what God has created, to connect with Him and to do something for Him. A verse from the Scriptures states, "We are co-workers with God."[78] When you work for God, you participate in His Work. Then all of the strivings of the human soul will be fulfilled. However, do not desire to attain everything at once. Do not desire for all the flowers to bloom at the same time.

The meaning of life is in serving God, the Great Creative Source. This is your task. This is the most sublime goal! Those who serve God need to be the best, the most knowledgeable, the strongest. They will pass through all trials so that they may be tested as to their readiness for service. One needs to be interested in all living things, in every manifestation of God.

Man's worth lies in his service to God. God gives power and knowledge to those who love Him and are ready to do everything for Him. How many people are ready to pass through the Great Divine Fire?

Service to God should not come by law or force but freely and without any personal interest. One should not serve God for pay or for praise.

When God gives you work, give up every pleasure. After you finish it, relax. Christ's words "to renounce yourself"[79] imply that you should hold in your mind one Image alone: the Image of God.

---

78. See also 1 Corinthians 3:9, "For we are God's fellow workers; you are God's field, you are God's building."
79. See also Luke 9:23, "Then He said to them all, 'If anyone desires to come after me, let him deny himself, and take up his cross daily, and follow Me.'"

Until you stop seeking your fame in the world, you will have a culture like the modern one. The one who seeks the fame will be a slave to conditions. But the one who seeks the glory of God will be free.

In what is the joy of the wellspring hidden? In that whosoever comes to it, it quenches his thirst. Whether or not you praise the wellspring, this does not interest it. It is happy when you drink of it.

When man came to Earth, he promised to realize God's Ideas and fulfill God's Will. When he fulfills his promise, man will be like the wellspring that gives crystal pure water; he will be like the flower that blooms, the tree covered with ripe, delicious fruit.

What is service? Whatever you do, perform it for God. This means service to God. The one who serves, who sacrifices himself, will have the first fruits.

To manifest Love, this is service to God.

The Service to God

To serve God means to apply His Laws. When people speak of the Divine Laws, but apply their own, their life will not improve.

Sometimes at night you may hear a Voice telling you, "On such and such a street and number lives someone who is in a difficult and desperate situation. Go and help that person!" And so you go there and find out that everything is as the Voice has said.

A good thought—an idea enters your mind. Yield to it. This is serving God. Do not put it off! You put it off for a year and then you want to complete everything in one day. If you do a little of the work each day, then the work will progress.

One brother said, "I have noticed that if one puts off a task that the conditions in the future will become more difficult."
The Master continued:

There is a voice within you telling you, "Leave this for now: put it off." It wants you to put off your work in order to steal your blessing. When someone insults you, a voice will tell you, "Why endure this insult? Why do you not retaliate?"

God does not expect big things from you. He seeks the small things. You are sitting and do not know how to occupy yourself. You hear a Voice telling you, "Go into the next room." In this room, a fly is buzzing, caught in a spider's web, and it prays to God to free it. Free the fly. Fulfill God's Will, and God will be pleased with you.

When things are not clear to you, the Advanced Beings will help you. And as soon as you begin to understand them, you will begin to help less advanced beings, and they, too, will begin to understand.

When you visit someone, do not begin preaching. First you should begin to love him. Find those who are seeking God and speak to them instead. The one who dances *horo*,[80] leave that one to dance.

Until now people have thought and worked for themselves; and for this reason, they have come to an impasse. If you do not fulfill God's Will rightly, you will break your connection with God. When someone departs from God, then heartache, worry, disease, and sorrow appear.

A prominent and erudite ecclesiastic once came to Ioan Kronstadtski[81] and told him, "I have heard that you have strayed from the true Christian Teaching. I prohibit you from preaching." Ioan Kronstadtski answered and said, "Well and good." Two days passed, and the ecclesiastic lost his speech. He wrote a note to Ioan saying, "Speak whatever you wish and also pray for me." Ioan said a prayer and the ecclesiastic regained his speech.

By a "weak person" I imply someone who is not yet awake. Strong is the one who walks along God's path. When one

---

80. *Horo* is a traditional Bulgarian folk dance where the participants join hands to form a circle.
81. Ioan Kronstadtski (John Wonderworker of Kronstadt, 1829–1908) is a Russian Orthodox priest known for his compassion, eloquence, and gift of healing.

strays from it, one becomes weak. Similarly, those lofty beings that strayed from the Divine path, fell and became weak.

We see in the Book of Revelation how the Angel comes down from Heaven and chains the fallen spirit for a thousand years. I ask: What kind of Power is this which is so great? The fallen one did not comprehend where the real Power laid. The true Power is in those actions that comply with the Divine Will and in service to God. When you do something for God, you gain energy and power. God is just. When we serve that Master who is just, we will become just.

A Law states: When a person does something that is pleasing to God, he will feel joy; and when he errs even in the least way, he will feel sorrow. When you feel sorrow, this indicates that you have done something wrong. Feeling joy indicates that you have done something good. When you begin to live rightly, Peace and Light will come to dwell in you. But when you begin to do wrong, darkness will set in. If you do not fulfill God's Will as you should, you will encounter a lion along your path, and it will devour you. If a person is feeling indisposed, and he begins to serve God, his indisposition will vanish. If you desire to keep your thoughts and feelings sweet, you need to serve God.

If all people would serve God, they all would be happy. Those who serve God have everything. They have all the favorable conditions for their work, as does the woman who has wool in her house and can make out of it anything that she wishes. That is to say, she is not deprived of the good conditions. The one who does not fulfill God's Will will become both rich and poor. But the one who does will be neither rich nor poor.

If you feel within yourself that you have gained something, then you have fulfilled God's Will, and the blessings will come on time. Otherwise, they will be delayed. Every person who serves God is successful and protected. The one who does not seek to serve God and the Good is lost. When one does not serve God, the Great Omniscient Cause, one's life will become meaningless, and in the end, that person will be unhappy.

When we have God's blessing, all Sublime Intelligent Beings will help us, and our affairs will be arranged. Let each and every one serve God in his own way and all things will be set right. When we do not use our mind, heart, and will for the service of God, we can attain nothing.

Someone is saying, "When I settle my affairs, then I will serve God." Those who are not working for the fulfillment of God's Affairs will never settle their own. If you desire your affairs to work out well, first work for God. In this case, you will be investing your capital in the Divine Bank.

When people give nothing to God, He sends to them burglars to whom He says, "Because these people are rich and do not give anything voluntarily, let them give it to you." And so they enter a rich person's home, rob it, and leave. After they leave, the rich person says, "These burglars took a lot of things, but thank God that they left me alive."

We need to understand that all that we have is God's and not ours alone. Ownership cannot exist in the world, for private property does not exist.

In that moment when you embrace the idea to live for God, it eradicates all error.

Through disease, you pay for your debts. The moment in which you instill the desire to serve God within yourself, He pays them off for you. In this way alone is one able to be free and healthy. God is the wealthy One. As long as you work in the name of God, everything will work well for you. How can be this explained? The following Law exists: When you work for God, you become receptive to those forces that all the Cosmos emits; otherwise, you will not be receptive.

Human beings fall into temptation when they are not fulfilling God's Will. But when they are fulfilling it, no temptation can come to them: then they have a cash-box filled with gold, and nothing can tempt them. Wherever one may find oneself—even in Paradise—if one is not fulfilling God's Will, temptation will come.

Once you have chosen to serve God, do not be concerned with what might happen to you. Everything can happen to you, but in the end, such a miracle will occur for you as you have never seen.

We will improve the world only when we serve God.

The Sky

The Master looked up to the starry sky above us and said:

Learning about the sky develops the mind, the consciousness, the ego-consciousness, the sub-consciousness, and the Higher consciousness. When I say that you should study the sky and the stars, I have in mind your connection with the Intelligent Forces that operate through them. This elevates and uplifts us.

From the Sun comes an electromagnetic current that envelops the Earth and turns it like a transmission drive. The Earth's axis has moved several times. When the plants came into being, the North Pole had been down and the South Pole had been up. When the animals came into being, the Earth's axis had been horizontal—that is to say, in a position perpendicular to the present one.

Our Solar System orbits around the central Sun of our Universe. One solar year is equal to many millions of earth years—the time in which the Solar System completes one full revolution. On the other hand, our whole Universe, with its hundreds of millions of stars, moves as a whole toward another place in the cosmic space, and after a time, another Universe, another stellar formation, will come in its place.

The Laws of Human Development

Morning walks were taken regularly in the small community. The Master usually went with a small group of friends in the early hours of the morning. To the east, dawn showed its beautiful color. The high clouds were covered in gold and purple from the sunrise, and the last stars were fading in the west. The light in the pale sky changed as if the pages of a giant book were being turned.

The Master liked very much the solemn morning silence: the moments of blessing before the Earth awakens. In these hours the air was the purest: fresh and cool from its contact with the Universe. The Master, who never missed the hours that belong to the Great Life, did not miss the first rays of the rising Sun. During one of those morning walks, in a conversation, the Master said:

You come to Earth to go to school for a special program assigned to you. It is determined for almost every day what needs to be studied. You are sent here for school and for an excursion.

Do you know from where you have come? You have been unhappy, and in order to be consoled, you have been sent on a trip with a free ticket. You are tourists. You should thank God for this excursion. When you return home, you will always bring something. While you travel, you should keep notes. Upon your return, you will tell your friends what you have seen.

You cannot accomplish all your desires in one incarnation. Therefore, you will come to Earth many times until you fulfill them and attain perfection.

Someone comes to Earth in order to atone for his misdeeds, another, to become perfected. Another one comes to help others. For these three things you come to Earth. When you are sent to reform, this is not by your free will: you come by Law. When you are sent as a student to learn, to improve, you are a little bit more free. And when you have come to help, you are even more free.

There are certain things about which one cannot talk and needs to keep silent. Someone asks, "Could you tell me about my past?" I answer, "No. Because if I speak, the relationships among you from the past will come to light." There are many bad memories from past incarnations and if someone remembers them, they will hinder that person.

You have passed through different nations in order to come to perfection. Every nation is a laboratory of the Invisible World.

You have passed through different schools as well. You have filled all levels of social status, both of a master and of a servant.

What is old age? It is an affliction of the human flesh. For the human spirit, there is no old age. The spirit knows how to work and how to conserve its energy.

When you liberate yourself from your karma, you will come to Earth of your own free will.

One sister asked how to free herself of her karma.

This is how: Do not desire to take possession of the one whom you love.

Nature allows you to do what you want, but after that, she will teach you a good lesson. Let's say that someone is at the bottom of an inverted cone. Within this cone, a fruit tree grows upward. If one should want to throw a stone to shake down some fruit, the stone will fall upon that person's head. This example explains the following Law: Everything that a person does, good or bad, returns to him.

Someone commits a crime. Intelligent Nature gives him a good lesson: she makes him pass through suffering. As time goes by, he forgets. When he comes to Earth a second time, he again commits crimes. This suffering sometimes needs to be repeated ten times in order for him to learn his lessons well.

Correct a fault immediately: do not let interest accrue. At the beginning, it is easier to correct. This is the Divine way. The more someone delays, the more difficult it becomes to correct. The least transgression is a seed. Someone says, "This is nothing." Yet the consequences are great. The small seed grows into a big tree. Small faults create great misfortunes. A safety match is small, but it can destroy an entire city.

When an angel makes a mistake in the Celestial World that angel can no longer live there. When you get angry with someone in the Celestial World, you cannot stay there any more.

The Great Intelligent World determines the destiny of a person, not in a fatalistic way, but according to his thoughts, feelings, and deeds. When he changes them, then God will also change His Judgment of him, and the person's destiny will change. There are statistics about this. For example, you are a merchant. A poor person comes to you asking you to help him. You tell him, "Go and work." But after that, a recession comes.

You lose thirty–forty thousand leva. The farmer violates Divine Laws and a draught or flood comes and takes everything away. The farmer will remember this for a long time. You hesitate to do someone a favor. An illness comes and you will pay.

According to karmic Law, the Russian aristocracy went from the highest status to the lowest. This happened in one lifetime and not, as in other cases, in some other reincarnation.

As long as you live without Love, you will continue to pass through birth and reincarnation. When Love comes, the reincarnation cycle ends. Love eradicates all karma.

Today most people's karma is eradicated through suffering. In order to manage your karma easily, keep in mind the following: do not speak badly about each other. If someone is quick-tempered and cannot avoid talking badly about others, at least the others should be careful not to feel hurt. To the first I say, "Refrain from speaking badly about your fellowmen." To those about whom ill was spoken, I say, "Do not feel hurt." Both those who offend and those who take offense do not resolve their problems properly. Karma then comes to resolve them. Karma is strict and implacable. If you are waiting for karma to resolve your tasks, you will attain nothing.

Another way by which you can resolve your tasks is through Love. For the person who chooses this path, the following verse applies, "And God will wipe away every tear from their eyes."[82] This we call the eradication of old karma. All people are entangled in it. Relinquish it!

One day God will erase all human error. Karma will be erased and will remain only as a movie. You will then see what you have been in the past, what you have been doing. The past will be erased as karma, but will remain as a film. We need to leave the realm of karma. There is no solution to the issues in it. It is a deviation from the Divine path.

Dharma is all those conditions that are favorable for development. Dharma is a Blessing. Blessing is not given by

---

82. See Revelation 21:4, "And God will wipe away every tear from their eyes; there shall be no more death, nor sorrow, nor crying. There shall be no more pain, for the former things have passed away."

chance, but to those who are ready to benefit from all that is given to them. It is spoken to those who can understand and gain.

Two types of martyrs exist: those who die in order to be released from their karma, and those who sacrifice themselves for their fellowmen.

Gratitude

Our modest luncheon under the walnut tree in the yard finished with a short blessing and a few songs. The Master looked around at us, smiled, and said:

Everything, which has been given to us, I have been paying for in an invisible way. When I receive a *banitsa*[83], I look at it to see what it is made of. It is made of flour, and so I connect with the one who planted and reaped the wheat. I bless this person's labor and continue. I find the sheep from whose milk the cheese was made and I thank it as well. I find the cow that gave the milk for the butter and thank it as well. Lastly I thank the person who made the *banitsa*.

When we are thankful, we maintain and protect our inner connection with God. All our desires will then be fulfilled.

What is the difference between the worldly life and the spiritual? When someone eats and is not thankful, he does not realize that everything is provided by God—he is in the worldly life. Yet when he eats and gives thanks to God, he is in the spiritual life. This is true for all other blessings as well.

When God takes part in your work, you are in the spiritual life. As soon as God does not participate in your affairs, this is the worldly life.

Be thankful to God even when you meet with difficulties in your life. You should always be content. This is only one moment—it could be only a second or a minute. Be content in

---

83. *Banitsa* is a traditional Bulgarian pastry prepared by layering a mixture of whisked eggs and crumbled feta cheese in between filo dough sheets brushed with melted butter and then baking it.

this moment. You are sorrowful because of some difficulty or burden. This might stay only for a minute and then will go away.

Contentment and gratitude do not imply resignation. If you are ill, make an effort to alleviate your illness; yet be content and thankful in every moment of it. When one receives something, one should always thank God. In this way, he will be giving something of himself as well.

When you receive and you do not give thanks, you will not benefit from the bounties of Life.

Let's say, you love someone. Be thankful to God for manifesting Himself in your beloved. Love does not belong to the person you love. Be thankful to Love. Gratitude is expressed by sharing part of what you have received with others.

One sister asked, "Master, how can I give thanks for the attentive way in which you received me in our conversation yesterday?"
The Master replied:

By showing the same attention to others.

The one who goes to a cherry tree and eats of its fruit without giving thanks to God, has no understanding of life. Human beings suffer because of this ingratitude.

Someone is discontent, and yet God has given him many talents which he has not developed, however. Lack of gratitude hinders this person's development. When someone is not satisfied with what he has, he will descend to a lower level and start to manifest some animal qualities.

You have a small joy. Be glad and give thanks for it. Do not wish for a greater one. Imagine that you have a tattered hat, worn shoes, and worn clothes. Someone comes and brings you a pair of shoes. Thank God for the shoes, and the other things will come as well. If you do not give thanks, the shoes will also disappear. To the one who is thankful for the least virtue, the other virtues will come as well. When you travel and you are satisfied with the weather, even if it is not so good, it will improve.

We require great things in order to express our gratitude. Be satisfied with the small things. The one who is satisfied with the least will attain the greatest. The one who is satisfied with the least blessing will see it grow and give abundant fruit.

We wish for things to happen our way. This is the "original sin." God has created the world, and we should desire for things to occur in accordance with His Will.

A great Book exists that contains all Knowledge. It will be given to you when you obey the following rule: When you rise in the morning, first give thanks to God for the life He has given you, for the mercy with which He has showered you, and for the sublime thoughts and feelings that He has sent to you.

The Three Stages of the New Culture

We greeted the rising of the Sun on the mountain. It was still dark in the valley below, but here it was already light. The air was pure and fresh, like water from a wellspring. We offered our morning prayer, performed our exercises, and then sat down on the grass around our beloved Teacher. The warmth of the Sun penetrated us like a blessing from the Eternal One. We were silent for a long time, listening to the still, small Voice.

The Master told us:

Love is the Path for all who abide in God. Wisdom is the Path for all to whom God makes Himself Manifest. Truth is the Path for all who are learning to serve God.

Each day of human existence should be the one in which: Love is made Manifest; Wisdom is made Manifest; and Truth is teaching us how to serve God.

Let Love be fulfilled in you, as a measure, to bear Life. Let Wisdom be fulfilled in you, as a measure, to bear Light. Let Truth be fulfilled in you, as a measure, to teach you how to fulfill God's Will.

Freedom ensues from Truth. Man is free, but he should not misuse his freedom. We are set free by the Divine that dwells within us.

Love resolves all contradictions. Without Love, man cannot make sense of this existence. Wisdom overcomes the contradictions of the mind. Truth overcomes the contradictions of human will.

Love builds harmony in the world. Wisdom is the highest Peak. It resolves the contradictions between good and evil: it puts them both to work. Truth is the greatest leader: it directs all of the Cosmos.

Divine Wisdom is the most difficult to learn. Even the adepts, the angels, and the gods have fallen when they encountered the trials of Wisdom.

Love is the greatest Force in the world; and yet, Wisdom and Truth are required that Love may be applied.

EPILOGUE

In the last days of the year 1944, a man arrived at the brotherhood's settlement, called Izgrev. He was running. He was in haste.

"Tell the Master that I wish to speak with him."

For his entire life, this man had been wavering between the spiritual life and the worldly life, and now he had made his choice.

"Please, tell the Master that I would like to speak with him."

A disciple informed the Master saying, "A man wishes to speak with you, Master."

For a long while the Master remained silent and then softly spoke, "Tell this man that the concert is over."

Again he said quietly, "The concert has already passed."

Biographical Information about the Master Beinsa Douno—Dates and Events

1864: Petar Konstantinov Danov (also Peter Deunov) was born on the 11th of July (29th of June by the Julian calendar—Saint Peter's day) in the village of Hadurcha (present day Nikolaevka), near the Black Sea in the district of Varna. He was the third child in the family of the Orthodox priest Konstantin Danovski and Dobra Georgieva.

1872: Peter Deunov entered the Elementary school in Nikolaevka.

1879-1884: He attended the all-male school in Varna, but did not graduate because of prolonged illness.

1887: Peter Deunov graduated from the American Theological School in Svishtov.

1887–1888: He was a teacher in the village of Hotantsa, Ruse district.

August 1888: Peter Deunov left for the United States and enrolled at Drew Theological Methodist Seminary in Madison, New Jersey.

May 19, 1892: He completed a preparatory course in Theology (except Greek) at Drew Theological Methodist Seminary, Madison, New Jersey.

1892–1893: Peter Deunov enrolled in the School of Theology in Boston University as a special full time student. He graduated on June 7, 1893 with the graduation thesis "The Migration of the Teutonic Tribes and their Conversion to Christianity."

1893–June 6, 1894: He attended only for one year courses in Medicine at Boston University.

1895: Peter Deunov returned to Bulgaria, but refused to become a Methodist preacher or an Orthodox priest in Varna.

1896: He published the book "Science and Education" in which he analyzed the human path in the world drama and the coming of the New Culture.

1897: On March 7, at the age of 33, in the village of Tetovo, Ruse district, Peter Deunov had a mystical experience that divulged his spiritual mission together with his spiritual name— Beinsa Douno. The same year he published his mystic booklet *Hio-Eli-Meli-Mesail.* This year was the turning point in his life, the beginning of his work as a spiritual Teacher.

1898: The Master gave the talk "An Appeal to My People— Bulgarian Sons of the Slavonic Family" before the members of the Charitable Society "Mother" in Varna as a message for social and spiritual self-determination.

1899: Peter Deunov wrote "The Ten Testimonials of the Lord" and "God's Promise."

1900: The Master summoned his first three disciples: Penyo Kirov, Todor Stoimenov, and Georgi Mirkovich, M.D., to a meeting in Varna in July. It was the First Gathering of the Brotherhood of Light, which he called "meeting of the Chain."

1900–1942: Annual gatherings were held, usually in August, at different places: Varna and Burgas (1900–1908), Veliko Tarnovo (1909–1925), Sofia (1926–1941), the Rila Mountains, and Mount Vitosha.

1901–1912: The Master traveled across Bulgaria to hold lectures and performed phrenological research studies of the Bulgarian character.

1906: He settled in Sofia, at 66 Opalchenska Street, where he began to deliver the Teaching he brought in the form of talks.

1912: Beinsa Douno worked on the Bible in the village of Arbanasi, near Veliko Tarnovo and completed "The Testament of the Color Rays of Light," which was published in September the same year.

1914: He began to give regular Sunday lectures to the general public in Sofia. These lectures were recorded in shorthand by his stenographer disciples. Later, they were decoded, edited, and published in the series of lectures "Power and Life," which presented the fundamental principles of the New Teaching.

1917–1932: Beinsa Douno held a Special spiritual course for married women in Sofia.

1917–1918: During the First World War he was interned in Varna under the pretext that his talks were weakening the spirit of the soldiers at the front. The followers of the Teaching he shared increased after the war and reached approximately forty thousand people in the late 1930s.

February 24, 1922: A School of the Universal Brotherhood of Light was opened in Sofia with two classes for spiritual students: the General Esoteric Class, and the Special (Youth) Esoteric Class. The Master delivered his lectures before the two classes twice a week in the course of 22 years until December 1944.

1927: A settlement called Izgrev (Sunrise) was established near Sofia (today a residential area of the city) as an intentional spiritual center for Beinsa Douno's followers. The Master settled permanently there, where he lectured on various subjects in a hall specially built for this purpose.

1929: The first summer camp was carried out at the Seven Lakes in the Rila Mountains. The gatherings at the Rila Mountains and the Spiritual School there became a tradition for the followers from Bulgaria and abroad. Nowadays they take place every year in August with thousands of participants.

September 21, 1930: The Master began a new series of the Teaching called the Sunday Morning lectures, which continued up to April 1944.

1934: He presented *Paneurhythmy* (The Cosmic Rhythm of Life)—a series of 28 exercises containing music, lyrics, and movements. Later on, he added two more parts: "The Rays of the Sun" and "The Pentagram." The *Paneurhythmy* was finally completed in 1942.

1944: Beinsa Douno, with a group of followers spent the hardest months during the Second World War (January 14, 1944–October 19, 1944)[84] in the village of Marchaevo, near Sofia, in the house of Temelko Stefanov Gyorev. This house is preserved and functioning now as a museum.

December 20, 1944: The Master delivered his lecture "The Last Word" to the General Esoteric Class.

December 27, 1944: The Master ended his earthly path in Sofia. By the ordinance of a special permission he was laid to rest in the Izgrev quarter. This sacred place is now turned into a beautiful garden open daily to the public.

The Master Beinsa Douno has left an invaluable spiritual heritage contained in his numerous talks and lectures, prayers, formulas, and songs, physical and breathing exercises, spiritual methods and practices for personal and group work, for self-improvement and conscious living.

---

84. In some other sources January 11, 1944 was mentioned as the date, when the Master departed to Marchaevo.

APPENDIX

The Spiritual Teacher Beinsa Douno (Peter Deunov) in Marchaevo
By Hristo Madzharov[85]

Past events gradually disappear from people's memory, overshadowed by daily survival needs and covered by the dust of time. Thus only a few still remember or know that events of biblical importance and worldwide impact took place during the stormy days of 1944 in the small village of Marchaevo, which is huddled at the western side of Mount Vitosha.

At that time the world was overwhelmed by WWII, which took the lives of more than 50 million people. On December 13, 1941, the Bulgarian government was forced by Germany to declare a token war on the United States and Great Britain and was immediately punished for this provocation. The Master Beinsa Douno predicted that Sofia, the capital of Bulgaria, would become like a chunk of Emmentaler cheese perforated with holes. And this came true as 1,784 bombers dumped their deadly load over the city day and night. Bombs fell in the vicinity of the spiritual center Izgrev as well, but did not explode. The Master's explanation was that he had covered the place with a protective white mantel. The bombing was heaviest on January 10, 1944. As at that time the Master was staying (as often lately) at the house of his disciple Boris Nikolov, situated in the vicinity of Simeonovo,[86] they both went to the Izgrev community the next day and found out that everyone had left. After an hour spent in prayer, the Master said, "The conditions for people to maintain their communion with God no longer exist in this place. Let us

---

85. Hristo Madzharov is a Bulgarian academician at the International Academy for Bulgarian Studies, Innovations, and Culture. He is a renowned lecturer and writer of esoteric science with many international recognitions. He is the author of: "Cosmic Plan 5,500 years ago," "New Age," "Bulgarian Mysteries," :The New Culture in the Age of Aquarius," "Melchizedek—the Path to Faith," "Bulgarian Mysteries," "The Return of the Bogomils," "Love and Evolution," and "Mysteries in the Dawn of Aquarius."
86. Simeonovo is a village on the outskirts of Mount Vitosha.

leave." This phrase brought an immediate change to the course of events. After an hour one of his disciples, Simeon Kostov, ran up to the Master, out of breath, "Master, come to Marchaevo! My house is at your disposal!" After another half an hour Slavcho Pechenikov (a publisher known also as Svetoslav Slavyanski) came too and offered the car that was in his possession at that moment.

Peter Deunov set the departure for early in the morning on January 14, Friday. But the car they were traveling with was delayed because the bombers overshadowed Sofia again. The streets were full of panicked running people and that is why the car was moving very slowly. Then the Master went deep in concentration, leaving his body. As a result, the bombers left the city and dumped their bombs over the mountain terrain of Stara Planina.[87] In the afternoon the Master Beinsa Douno, accompanied by hundreds of his disciples, arrived at the outskirts of Marchaevo. But he directed his steps not to the house of Simeon Kostov, which is in the center of the village, but to that of another disciple, Temelko Stefanov Gyorev.

When I first visited brother Temelko, I saw a man with a petrous face reflecting his profession of a stone cutter and strong willpower. Yet, at the same time it expressed enormous gentleness—attained as a result of the beneficial influence of the Master.

I kept coming to his home and listened again and again to his stories about the Master, learning new details every time. These talks revealed to me the profound life of an honest man who had completely transformed himself under the guidance of the great spiritual Teacher. I am going to share some of Temelko's experiences during the stay of Peter Deunov in Marchaevo. The deeds of the Master need special attention:

"My daughter Kossena warned me, 'Father, empty your room as the Master is coming to stay there.' 'Do not repeat this,'

---

87. Stara Planina (the Balkan Mountains) is a mountain range in the eastern part of the Balkan Peninsula. The Balkan range runs 560 km from the border of Bulgaria and Eastern Serbia eastward through the Central Bulgaria to the Black Sea. This mountain has an enormous role both in the historical and modern development of the Bulgarian nation and people.

I scolded her. 'We do not deserve the honor to welcome such a great Teacher.' 'I am telling you, father, vacate the room,' she insisted. A week later Kossena told me, 'The Master is putting together his luggage. Everything is ready; he is coming! And when he arrives, you will be obliged to make his room ready for him.'

"And still I did not listen to her. At noon, my second son, a soldier in leave then, came and said, 'Congratulations, father, you are expecting special guests!' 'What guests?' I wondered. 'Your Teacher and almost sixty people coming with him.' I was shocked and felt sorry that I did not listen to my daughter as her prediction came true.

"After the greeting the Master went directly to the living room and sat on a chair. Evidently he knew that his room was not ready yet. I tossed everything from the room through the window and my wife began to clean. We overheard someone telling him that there was a room waiting for him somewhere else, but he did not accept. When we finished, he came in, even before our invitation. And the Master stayed ten months with us. In this house he held lectures and received many guests."

The arrival of Beinsa Douno in Marchaevo was marked by an important event—the electrification of the village. The disciples took an active part in this event when it happened. And when the first electric lamps lit up, the Master mentioned that now it would be more proper for the village to be called "Svetlyaevo." This means: in the light. The first day after the Master's arrival he led the disciples to a clearing, which was later covered with pine trees. Nowadays there is a tall forest there.

In Temelko's backyard Peter Deunov combined a few small wellsprings into a big one and named it "The Wellspring of Good." A platform of colored stones was made around the wellspring. Three granite steps led to it, symbolizing Love, Wisdom, and Truth—the three Principles guiding the human soul toward the Great Wellspring of Life. At this Wellspring the Master guided the events in the world using sacred formulas and movements.

He suggested to build up another wellspring at the eastern side of the backyard and called it "The Wellspring of Wisdom."

The numerous visitors coming to see the Master were walking the beautiful path along that wellspring. They washed their faces and drank from its crystal-clear waters, refreshing themselves both physically and spiritually. Because of its magical healing effect, this wellspring is known as "The Wellspring of Health."

Many beautiful flowers bloomed around both wellsprings, and people could smell their aroma from a distance. The drinking water in the village was not tasty at all; and when the villagers heard about the nice, tasteful water of the "magical wellspring," they began coming to get water from there.

Four kilometers west of the village was a big source of mineral water. By then it was used only for laundry. However, after the Master pointed out its healing properties, people from neighboring villages began to use its water for drinking. Years later, after an extensive drilling around the source, the debit of the mineral water was dramatically increased and two big swimming pools were built. Thus the place was transformed into a relaxing and healing spa center.

Metodi Konstantinov, a disciple of the Master, who was also evacuated in Marchaevo, went every day to Sofia, where he worked. Returning from work in the evening, he ran in to see the Master and spent long hours sharing the latest news he acquired thanks to his previous work at the Ministry of Information and asking many questions. Some of these talks were recorded in shorthand by Boyan Boev, the so-called "secretary" and are included as a part of this book. It was Metodi who told me that many Bulgarian political leaders and foreigners were coming to visit Peter Deunov in Marchaevo in order to learn more about what is going to happen to Bulgaria and the world, and what their destiny will be.

After arriving in Marchaevo, the Master asked that two flowers be planted, one white and the other red. Two pots were to be used. He explained that the white flower represented peace, and the red one, war. When asked whether the war would destroy the world or whether peace would reign, the Master pointed at the flower-pots. The sisters watered them regularly, but gradually the red flower withered and died.

Where the Master Beinsa Douno stayed, Life and Beauty blossomed. Human culture seemed to follow in his steps.

The Master Beinsa Douno at Izgrev (archives *Byalo Bratstvo*)

Lecture in the mountains (archives *Byalo Bratstvo*)

Marchaevo, August 1944 (archives *Byalo Bratstvo*)

Marchaevo, waiting for the lunch: Boyan Boev, Beinsa Douno, and Ivan Zhekov, M.D. (archives *Byalo Bratstvo*)

Vesela Nestorova and Vlado Nikolov in front of the "Wellspring of Good" in Marchaevo (Reprinted by permission of the publisher from *Izgrevat na Byaloto Bratstvo pee i sviri, uchi i zhivee* [The Sunrise of the Brotherhood of Light Sings and Plays, Studies and Lives], v. 24, Zhiten Klass, Sofia, 2008)

Beinsa Douno with a group of his followers at the mineral water spring in the village of Rudartsi (Reprinted by permission of the publisher from *Izgrevat na Byaloto Bratstvo pee i sviri, uchi i zhivee* [The Sunrise of the Brotherhood of Light Sings and Plays, Studies and Lives], v. 23, Zhiten Klass, Sofia, 2005-2006)

The village of Marchaevo in the spring

Temelko's home in Marchaevo, now a museum of
the Master Beinsa Douno

Marchaevo, 1990:
Temelko Stefanov (1896–1990) in his home

The Master's room in the museum

Rila Mountains: Paneurhythmy at the 5th Lake (Mahabur) of the Rila's Seven Lakes

Summer Spiritual School at the Rila Mountains: the camp at the 2nd Lake (Elbur) and meeting the sunrise at the Mount of Prayer

The Master's resting place at Izgrev, Sofia

Beinsa Douno

The Wellspring of Good

The Last Words of the Master

ISBN 978-151-434-875-8

Compilation and translation by Antoaneta Krushevska
Editor: Sean Vernon
Cover and graphic design by Steve Eagle
Cover art by Veneta Docheva

Evera Books Publishers
P.O.Box 3275,
Walnut Creek, CA 94598
USA

www.everabooks.com

Printed in Great Britain
by Amazon